Applied Psycholinguistics:
An Introduction to the Psychology of Language Learning and Teaching

The principles of language learning and teaching are presented for language teachers, especially teachers of second languages. The authors synthesize and explain the main issues connected with the application of linguistics, psycholinguistics, and research methodology to classroom practice and inform teachers and educators about the kinds of psychologically based techniques that can be derived from a consideration of current research on language.

Applied Psycholinguistics examines principal linguistic theories, recent research into first-language development, second-language learning, psychometric methodology, and other important topics in a way that makes the technical literature accessible and relates it to pedagogical practice. An 'integrated' methodology, developed and used with success by the authors, will prove especially valuable to teachers attempting to make informed choices about appropriate teaching strategies.

The extensive, up-to-date bibliography and glossary of technical terms make the book an important reference tool for classroom teachers. Language teachers in teacher-training institutions and in departments of linguistics, applied linguistics, psychology, and educational psychology, and especially all who are involved in courses on methodology, will find this volume particularly practical.

RENZO TITONE, an internationally recognized expert on the psychology of language teaching and learning, is editor of *Rassegna Italiana di Linguistica Applicata* and professor in the Faculty of Education, University of Rome.

MARCEL DANESI, author of numerous studies on second-language learning and teaching, is professor of methodology and Italian in the Faculty of Education, University of Toronto.

RENZO TITONE
MARCEL DANESI

Applied
Psycholinguistics:
An Introduction to
the Psychology of
Language Learning
and Teaching

UNIVERSITY OF TORONTO PRESS
Toronto Buffalo London

© University of Toronto Press 1985
Toronto Buffalo London
Printed in Canada

ISBN 0-8020-2526-9

Canadian Cataloguing in Publication Data

Titone, Renzo
   Applied psycholinguistics

   Bibliography: p.
   Includes index.
   ISBN 0-8020-2526-9

   1. Language and languages – Study and teaching –
Psychological aspects. 2. Language acquisition.
3. Psycholinguistics. I. Danesi, Marcel 1946–
II. Title.

P53.7.T57 1984   407   C84-099225-4

Contents

PREFACE ix

ACKNOWLEDGMENTS xi

1 THE SCIENTIFIC STUDY OF LANGUAGE 3
1.0 **Introduction** 3
1.1 **Language** 3
1.1.1 Language as Pattern 4
1.1.2 Language as an Open-Ended System 5
1.1.3 Language Design and Scientific Linguistics 6
1.2 **Linguistic Structuralism** 8
1.2.1 Paradigm and Syntagm: Two Basic Structural Concepts 8
1.2.2 Structural Phonology 9
1.2.3 Structural Morphology 13
1.2.4 Structural Syntax 15
1.2.5 Structural Semantics 17
1.2.6 The Structural Model of Language Design 18
1.3 **Linguistic Transformationalism** 19
1.3.1 Deep and Surface Structure: A Fundamental Dichotomy 20
1.3.2 The Base Component 21
1.3.3 The Transformational Component 23
1.3.4 The Phonological Component 25
1.3.5 Some Recent Developments 27
1.4 **Language and Communication** 28
1.4.1 The Sociology of Verbal Communication 29
1.4.2 The Psychology of Verbal Communication 31

1.5 **Linguistics and Language Teaching** 33
1.5.1 Applied Linguistics and Applied Psycholinguistics 34
1.6 **A Pedagogical Summary** 35
1.7 **Signposts** 35
1.8 **Suggestions for Further Reading** 36

2   THE LANGUAGE-LEARNING PROCESS 37
2.0 **Introduction** 37
2.1 **Verbal Behavior** 37
2.1.1 A Representational Model of Verbal Behavior 37
2.1.2 An Informational Model of Verbal Behavior 39
2.1.3 Linguistic Relativity 41
2.2 **Neurological and Psychological Components of Language Learning** 42
2.2.1 Language and the Brain 43
2.2.2 Language and Perception 46
2.2.3 Language, Memory, and Cognition 49
2.2.4 Language and Personality 50
2.3 **Theories of Language Learning** 52
2.3.1 Behavioristic Theories 52
2.3.2 Cognitive Theories 57
2.3.3 Humanistic Theories 59
2.4 **A Pedagogical Summary** 61
2.5 **Signposts** 62
2.6 **Suggestions for Further Reading** 63

3   FIRST-LANGUAGE ACQUISITION 64
3.0 **Introduction** 64
3.1 **Patterns of First-Language Acquisition** 64
3.1.1 Phonological Development 65
3.1.2 Grammatical Development 67
3.1.3 Lexical and Semantic Development 72
3.2 **Factors Influencing Language Development** 75
3.3 **Theories of First-Language Acquisition** 77
3.3.1 Behavioristic Theories 77
3.3.2 Cognitive Theories 79
3.4 **A Pedagogical Summary** 81
3.5 **Signposts** 81
3.6 **Suggestions for Further Reading** 82

4 SECOND-LANGUAGE LEARNING 83
4.0 **Introduction** 83
4.1 **Neurological and Psychological Aspects of Second-Language Learning** 84
4.1.1 Neurological Aspects 84
4.1.2 Psychological Aspects 86
4.2 **Psychopedagogical Aspects of Second-Language Learning** 90
4.2.1 The Learning of Structure and Function 90
4.2.2 Errors in Second-Language Learning 93
4.2.3 Translation and Second-Language Learning 98
4.3 **Bilingualism and Multilingualism** 100
4.4 **A Pedagogical Summary** 104
4.5 **Signposts** 105
4.6 **Suggestions for Further Reading** 105

5 THE LANGUAGE-TEACHING PROCESS 107
5.0 **Introduction** 107
5.1 **Language-Teaching Methods** 108
5.1.1 Inductive Methods 108
5.1.2 Deductive Methods 110
5.1.3 Functional Approaches 112
5.1.4 Affective-Based Methods 115
5.2 **Language Teaching and Applied Psycholinguistics** 118
5.3 **Language-Teaching Models** 123
5.4 **A Pedagogical Summary** 124
5.5 **Signposts** 126
5.6 **Suggestions for Further Reading** 126

6 MEASUREMENT, TESTING, AND RESEARCH 127
6.0 **Introduction** 127
6.1 **Some Elementary Statistical Concepts** 127
6.1.1 The Presentation and Organization of Data 128
6.1.2 Central Tendency and Dispersion 133
6.1.3 Statistical Significance and Inference 141
6.1.4 Correlation 148
6.2 **Testing** 154
6.2.1 Reliability and Validity 154
6.2.2 Types of Tests 155
6.3 **Research** 161
6.3.1 Controlled Experiments 162
6.3.2 Experimental Design 164

6.4 **A Pedagogical Summary** 165
6.5 **Signposts** 166
6.6 **Suggestions for Further Reading** 166

7 A GLOSSODYNAMIC MODEL OF LANGUAGE LEARNING AND LANGUAGE TEACHING 167
7.0 **Introduction** 167
7.1 **The Glossodynamic Model of Language Learning** 168
7.2 **A Glossodynamic View of Language Teaching** 172
7.3 **A Concluding Pedagogical Summary** 174
7.4 **Suggestions for Further Reading** 176

APPENDICES 177
A: The Major Symbols of the IPA 178
B: Lenneberg's Description of Language Development with Respect to Motor Development 179
C: Summary of the Biological and Maturational Factors in Language Acquisition 182
D: Values of t 184
E: Values of F at the $p < 0.01$ Confidence Level 185
F: Values of χ^2 186
G: Summary of Statistical Techniques 187

GLOSSARY 189

REFERENCES 197

INDEX 215

Preface

The learning of a language is a complex neurological and psychological feat. Even though psychologists and psycholinguists have been investigating and documenting the patterns which characterize verbal learning for some time, their findings and insights have generally gone unnoticed by the average classroom language teacher, probably because most of the information on the psychology of verbal learning is scattered in technical journals and monographs which are both difficult to locate and difficult to read. Of the many excellent introductory manuals on applied linguistics and language-teaching methodology, relatively few focus on the research into the psychology of verbal learning and its relevance to the pedagogical domain.

The purpose of this book is to provide the language teacher with an up-to-date survey of the psychological theories and research on the nature of language learning in the hope that a basic understanding of the psychological mechanisms involved in this process will allow the teacher to make informed choices vis-à-vis teaching strategy. This is not a book about how to teach languages; rather it is about the contribution that a knowledge of psycholinguistic research can make to the teaching of language.

The book is divided into seven chapters. Chapter 1 explains some basic concepts about language design and use and provides a general characterization of scientific linguistics. The second, third, and fourth chapters focus on the parameters which make up the language-learning process; Chapter 5 examines the possible applications of the insights gleaned from psycholinguistic research to language teaching. Chapter 6 describes some rudimentary techniques in statistical measurement, testing, and research that are germane to the possibility of evaluating teaching models and learning behaviors. Chapter 7 proposes a psycholinguistically based model of language learning and teaching which derives from the findings and insights of one of the authors (e.g., Titone 1977a). Each chapter contains a 'Pedagogical Summary' section which aims to delineate briefly the main implications of the theories and research for teaching, a 'Signposts' section which describes concisely new trends and directions in the research area that is discussed in the chapter and their relevance to language pedagogy, and a 'Suggestions for Further Reading' section. A glossary of technical terms is included at the end of the book for easy reference.

Needless to say, it is not possible to cover all the topics and issues involved in as vast a field as the psychology of verbal learning. We have had to make choices about what to treat in detail, what to emphasize, and what to mention only briefly. Nevertheless, it is our sincere hope that this book will give the language teacher a 'taste' of the subject and will prove to be both an accessible introduction to current issues in the field and a convenient reference volume.

RENZO TITONE
MARCEL DANESI

Acknowledgments

We wish to express our sincere appreciation to Dr Albert Valdman of Indiana University and Dr Henry Schogt of the University of Toronto for having read over the manuscript. Their valuable commentary has allowed us to improve this book vastly. We also wish to thank Dr Ron Schoeffel of the University of Toronto Press for his expert editorial guidance which he gave so generously during the writing of this book. Needless to say, we alone are responsible for any infelicity that this book might contain.

APPLIED PSYCHOLINGUISTICS

1
The Scientific Study of Language

A human language is a system of remarkable complexity. To come to know a human language would be an extraordinary intellectual achievement for a creature not specifically designed to accomplish this task.
(Chomsky 1975:4)

1.0 Introduction

The logical point of departure in any investigation of how language is learned is the scientific study of language itself. Since the goal of *linguistics* is to describe accurately natural language in all its dimensions, a familiarization with some of its general principles is of obvious importance to the language teacher. As Corder (1975:5) emphasizes: 'In the case of language teaching it is true to say that we cannot teach systematically what we cannot describe.'

In this chapter we will discuss some general concepts of language structure from the standpoint of two main schools of linguistics: *structuralism* and *transformationalism*. A brief description of *speech acts* is also included. In general the term 'speech acts' is used in a technical sense, as will be discussed later. Finally, we will define the relationship between *scientific linguistics* and *applied linguistics* on one side, and between 'general' *psycholinguistics* and *applied psycholinguistics* on the other.

1.1 Language

It has often been said that language is what makes us unique as a species. Language allows us to express *stimulus-free* meanings. This property is not possessed by animal communication systems which are *stimulus-bound*, or fixed to a given situation, even though the well-known work with chimpanzees (see, for example, Gardner and Gardner 1969 and 1975) has demonstrated that some primates have the ability to learn complex systems. But language in all its multidimensionality still seems to be unique to the human species.

What is language? There are many definitions of language; no one all-embracing definition can describe it adequately. However, some of its more salient characteristics are easily identifiable (see, for example, Brown 1980:5). Above all else, language is a communication system that allows humans to express thoughts. This implies that language is not made up of a random assortment of speech symbols, but rather that the symbols of language form an interlocking set of relations and patterns. Language consists of a set of conventionalized and arbitrary symbols (vocal and visual). This means that there is no direct link between speech symbols and the world of objects and ideas which they represent. Language operates in a speech community and is culturally transmitted; i.e., people acquire language through their culture.

It is also important to note that language and language learning both have *universal* characteristics. The research on the universal properties of human language has shown, in fact, that there are some features which all languages apparently share (see, for example, Greenberg 1966 and Willis 1972:7). For example, it has been found that all languages have nominal and verbal phrases. Moreover, all languages have modifiers which correspond to adjectives and adverbs. All languages have structures equivalent to transitive and intransitive statements. All languages have ways of turning verbal phrases into nominal ones and of forming adjective phrases from other structures. And all languages possess ways of turning simple declarative sentences into interrogative, negative, and imperative ones. Many more cases of language universals have been examined and documented. The point is that human languages exhibit remarkable similarities.

1.1.1 LANGUAGE AS PATTERN

Although the complex code of language is mastered by age two without instruction or conscious effort, it is normal to find that people are generally unaware of its structure or organization. Yet, without structure or pattern verbal communication would be impossible – a fact that is recognized at least intuitively by all speakers of a language. Consider, for example, the following anomalous or 'irregular' English sentences (an anomalous form, such as a word or sentence, is indicated by an asterisk):

1) *Put that ztick away!
2) *John go tomorrow.
3) *Eats the boy the cake.
4) *Tom drank the meat.

Native speakers of English will immediately recognize these sentences as being deviant at different levels. If asked, they will be able to identify the anomalies without difficulty and might also be able to explain them, perhaps simplistically, as structural or semantic irregularities. In (1), native speakers will recognize instantaneously that the word *ztick* is wrong; moreover, they know that no English word would ever begin with *zt*. This structural peculiarity is what linguists call a *phonological constraint*. The appropriate rule may be stated as follows: *z* cannot occur as the first consonant in word-initial consonant clusters in English. In (2), native speakers will recognize a *morphological*, or *morphosyntactic*, anomaly: the future tense in English requires the modal auxiliary *will*. In (3), native speakers will detect a *syntactic* aberration: in English the main verb occurs between the subject and object of a simple declarative sentence. And in (4), a *semantic* irregularity will be easily detected: the object noun phrase which follows the verb *drank* must contain a noun referring to a liquid substance.

Language is, clearly, patterned or rule-governed behavior – a fact that is easily recognized as soon as linguistic rules are violated. To know a language implies that one has internalized the set of rules which specify word and sentence formation, phonetic combinations, etc. The knowledge of linguistic structure is commonly referred to as *competence*, whereas the utilization of this knowledge in speech acts is called *performance*. A similar terminological distinction used in linguistic analysis is between *langue* and *parole*, where *langue* is the knowledge of the rules of a language and *parole* is the realization of those rules in actual speech events.

1.1.2 LANGUAGE AS AN OPEN-ENDED SYSTEM

One of the unique properties of language which deserves a special mention is its *open-endedness* or *creativity*. As used by linguists, 'creativity' designates the ability to produce and understand an infinite variety of stimulus-free utterances. For example, it is highly unlikely that the readers of this book would have previously heard or read the following sentence: *My kangaroo swallowed the pencil that you left on the TV set last night.* Nevertheless, all readers will understand the meaning of this sentence without any difficulty. Clearly, this would be impossible if linguistic knowledge were acquired solely by memorizing all the utterances produced by one's sociocultural environment – a task which would require an infinite storage capacity. Linguistic creativity implies the ability to relate sounds or alphabet characters to meanings by means of formal linguistic mechanisms and operations.

Another important aspect of linguistic open-endedness is the ability of a speech community to formulate new words to designate new concepts. Often this is done by joining words or parts of words that had previously existed, as in the use of classical affixes in scientific terminology (e.g., *television, telephone,* etc.); sometimes this is done by borrowing words from other languages (e.g., *naive, gusto*); and sometimes this is done by inventing totally new vocabulary in accordance with the phonological and morphological constraints present in the language. This property of language allows it to serve any degree of complexity a culture may reach.

1.1.3 LANGUAGE DESIGN AND SCIENTIFIC LINGUISTICS

Although it is beyond the scope of this book to deal with theories and models of linguistic structure in detail, it is obviously essential to provide at least a cursory outline of some of the more significant concepts about language design developed by scientific linguistics. Thus, we will discuss some general features of language structure from the standpoint of two main theoretical schools of linguistics: *structuralism* and *transformationalism*. Preference will not be given to either of these schools in this book, particularly since the psycholinguistic literature on language learning contains findings that relate to both.

Despite the many epistemological and technological differences among the various schools of linguistics, there is one feature that they share in common: they work on the assumption that the central task of linguistics is the development of an analytical apparatus or framework for the description of language design or architecture. The study of how language is used or how it influences behavior is generally considered to be in the domain of interdisciplinary fields such as *sociolinguistics* and *psycholinguistics*. In other words, linguistic theories tend to be models of competence, whereas sociolinguistic and psycholinguistic theories are considered to be models of performance. A terminological distinction that is often used in this regard is that between *microlinguistics* and *macrolinguistics*. The former refers to the scientific analysis of linguistic data proper (sounds, words, etc.); the latter refers to the description of language as it manifests itself in sociological and psychological contexts.

Scientific linguistics is divided into two main branches: *synchronic* (or *descriptive*) and *diachronic* (or *historical*). Synchronic linguistics is concerned with the microlinguistic description of a language at a particular time, usually the present. Diachronic linguistics aims to describe the ways in which a language changes over time. To illustrate the diachronic method, we will look briefly at one classic example of sound change. The Romance languages French, Spanish, and Italian (and others) are related phylogenetically because they derive directly from spoken Latin. Languages related in this way are sometimes called *sister* languages, and the language they derive from is called their *proto-language*. A list of cognate words in French, Spanish, and Italian and their etymological Latin source is found in the accompanying chart.

LATIN	FRENCH	SPANISH	ITALIAN
la*ct*em 'milk'	la*it*	le*ch*e	la*tt*e
o*ct*o 'eight'	hu*it*	o*ch*o	o*tt*o
no*ct*em 'night'	nu*it*	no*ch*e	no*tt*e
fa*ct*um 'done'	fa*it*	he*ch*o	fa*tt*o
te*ct*um 'roof'	to*it*	te*ch*o	te*tt*o
etc.	etc.	etc.	etc.

As can be clearly seen from this chart, a definite correspondence pattern can be established between the Romance words and their Latin source with regard to the consonant cluster *ct*: (1) in French *it* corresponds to *ct*; (2) in Spanish *ch* corresponds to *ct*; and (3) in Italian *tt* corresponds to *ct*. Once historical linguists have identified correspondences such as these, they are able to formulate rules of linguistic change. From the examples above, the rules can be schematized as follows:

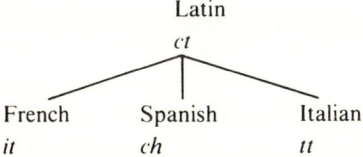

In their search for general patterns of change, historical linguists also assign labels to such changes in terms of the physiological or phonetic phenomena they exemplify. Thus, in the case of French it can be seen that the first member of the cluster *ct* has become a vowel *(it)*, even though in modern French the letters *it* do not represent separate speech sounds. This process is called, therefore, *vocalization*. In Spanish the entire cluster has changed in articulation to a single palatal sound represented orthographically by *ch*, and this process is designated *palatalization*. And in Italian the first consonant has become identical to the second one *(tt)*; hence, the process is referred to as *assimilation*.

The primary goal of diachronic linguistics, then, is the investigation and documentation of language change together with the formulation of general theories to account for change. The aim of synchronic linguistics, on the other hand, is the description of the structure of language at a specific point in time, usually the present. Although a knowledge of diachronic linguistics is of some use to language teachers, it generally does not play an important role in the teaching

8 Applied Psycholinguistics

process itself. A familiarization with diachronic linguistics will, nevertheless, provide teachers with a more global understanding of the object of their teaching, language itself.

1.2 Linguistic Structuralism

Linguistic structuralism dominated synchronic theory until the advent of transformationalism in the 1950s. Of the classical works which describe structural theory and analysis, one can mention, among others, those by De Saussure (1916), Sapir (1921), Bloomfield (1933), Harris (1951), and Hockett (1958).

1.2.1 PARADIGM AND SYNTAGM: TWO BASIC STRUCTURAL CONCEPTS

According to the structuralists, language manifests a hierarchical organization consisting of four main levels: phonological, morphological, syntactic, and semantic. The analysis of each level is carried out in an independent fashion, and if some linguistic phenomenon overlaps two levels then it is referred to with hyphenated terms such as morpho-phonemic or phono-syntactic.

At each level, two formal structural relationships are posited for all units: *paradigmatic* and *syntagmatic*. These two relational dimensions provide a framework for locating and defining a unit or a class at each level. A paradigmatic relationship keeps the members of a class distinct, or in opposition, and also determines class membership. For example, in the sentence frame _____ *boy is eating the cake*, the empty slot can be filled by items which belong to the class known as the *determiner* class:

$$\begin{Bmatrix} \text{The} \\ \text{A} \\ \text{This} \\ \text{That} \\ \text{etc.} \end{Bmatrix} \text{boy is eating the cake.}$$

These items are related to each other paradigmatically, i.e., they are substitutes for each other in a specific structural position and they cannot, as a corollary, occur consecutively.

A syntagmatic relationship specifies the sequential organization, or concatenation, of units and classes at all levels. An example of syntagmatic structure was pointed out in Section 1.1.1; namely that the consonant sequence *zt* is not permitted in word-initial position in English. Another example of syntagmatic relationship is the sequential organization of the determiner (Det), noun (N), and adjective (Adj) in English noun phrases. The order of these morphological classes is given by the formula Det + Adj + N:

Det	Adj	N	
$\begin{Bmatrix} \text{The} \\ \text{That} \\ \text{A} \\ \text{etc.} \end{Bmatrix}$	$\begin{Bmatrix} \text{young} \\ \text{intelligent} \\ \text{lazy} \\ \text{etc.} \end{Bmatrix}$	$\begin{Bmatrix} \text{girl} \\ \text{man} \\ \text{woman} \\ \text{etc.} \end{Bmatrix}$	is eating the cake.

Syntagmatic relationships are determined, therefore, by identifying the permissible combinations of forms at the different levels. Paradigmatic relationships are established by means of so-called substitution, or *commutation*, tests, such as the one used above to establish determiner-class membership.

1.2.2 STRUCTURAL PHONOLOGY

At the phonological level, the commutation test allows the analyst to identify the *phonemes* of a language. These are the basic units of sound which enable the native speakers of a given language to recognize differences of meaning between words. For example, in the word frame, _in, the alternative substitution of the consonants represented by the letters *p, b, t, f* yields differences in meaning:

$\begin{Bmatrix} p \\ b \\ t \\ f \\ \text{etc.} \end{Bmatrix}$ in (i.e., *pin, bin, tin, fin,* etc.)

A symbol which represents a phoneme is put between slashes: /p/, /b/, /t/, /f/, etc. A phoneme is a theoretical construct. Phonemes are realized by positional variants in the chain of speech whose phonetic differences are generally not perceptible to native speakers. The positional variants, or realizations, of a phoneme never contrast with each other; i.e., they are never found in paradigmatic opposition. In other words, the actual pronunciation, or phonetic shape, of a phoneme is determined by its position in what is called a *phonetic environment*. The environmentally conditioned variants of a phoneme are called its *allophones*. For example, in English the phoneme /p/ has two allophones (which are put between square brackets): [p^h] = an aspirated voiceless bilabial stop and [p] = a corresponding unaspirated stop. Both sounds are pronounced in the same way except that in the case of [p^h] the articulation is accompanied by a small puff of air.

[pʰ]	[p]
pin	spin
pat	spat
pun	spun
etc.	etc.

The reader can verify the difference in articulation between [pʰ] and [p] by putting his/her hand or a lit match near his/her mouth during the articulation of these two sets of words. In the pronunciation of *pin, pat, pun*, etc., the puff of air will extinguish the match.

The distribution of these two allophones in English is predictable: (1) [pʰ] occurs before a stressed vowel in word- or syllable-initial position; (2) [p] occurs after /s/ in our examples, but upon consideration of further data it can be shown to occur in all other environments (*play, apron,* etc.). These two allophones are said to be in *complementary distribution*; i.e., they occur in mutually exclusive environments. Complementary distribution is a structural relationship that occurs at all levels and is used to determine the environmentally conditioned variants of a form.

The two-part distributional statement given above is an example of what linguists call a *phonological rule*. Notational devices and systems have been developed for the formalization of such rules. Thus, the distribution of /p/ may be formalized as follows:

$$/p/ \rightarrow \begin{cases} [p^h] \ / \ \# \underline{} \acute{V} \\ [p] \text{ elsewhere} \end{cases}$$

In this rule, the arrow (→) stands for 'is realized as'; the braces enclose the allophones; the slash (/) stands for 'in the environment of'; the symbol # indicates word or syllable boundary; and the symbol V́ stands for any stressed vowel. Thus, this rule is read as follows: 'The phoneme /p/ is realized as [pʰ] before a stressed vowel in word- or syllable-initial position and as [p] in all other environments (elsewhere).'

A consideration of allophones indicates very clearly that there are at least two levels, or strata, in phonology: a phonemic stratum and a lower phonetic one. Briefly, it can be said that all levels contain two such strata: a higher *emic* one (phon*emic*, morph*emic*, etc.) and a lower *etic* one (e.g., phon*etic*). In the case of the phonetic stratum, the descriptive task facing the analyst consists in developing a framework for the classification of sounds. *Articulatory phonetics* describes and classifies speech sounds in terms of the physiological mechanisms involved in their production; *acoustic phonetics*, in contrast, describes the physical properties

TABLE 1.1

English consonants classified by place and manner of articulation

	Place of articulation						
Manner of articulation	Bilabial	Labio-dental	Inter-dental	Alveolar	Palatal	Velar	Glottal
Stops							
Vl	[p]			[t]		[k]	
Vd	[b]			[d]		[g]	
Fricatives							
Vl		[f]	[θ]	[s]	[š]		[h]
Vd		[v]	[ð]	[z]	[ž]		
Affricates							
Vl					[č]		
Vd					[ǰ]		
Nasals							
Vd	[m]			[n]		[ŋ]	
Liquids							
Laterals							
Vd				[l]			
Vibrants							
Vd				[r]			

of sound waves as they are recorded on sound spectrographs. The articulatory classification of sounds is the more common practice in linguistics. For the purpose of sound description, a *phonetic alphabet* is used in which each symbol represents one and only one sound. It should be noted, at this point, that a basic principle of linguistic analysis is the primacy of speech over writing. Writing is simply a method of transcribing speech sounds, and it is not always a reliable one as shown by words such as the following English ones: *knife* = [naif]; *enough* = [inəf]; *light* = [lait]; etc. The symbols in square brackets are phonetic symbols, and these always represent sounds on a one-to-one basis.

Table 1.1 is a typical example of phonetic classification. It contains the major English consonants classified according to the *manner* and *place* of articulation. The categories which refer to manner of articulation may be described briefly as follows. A *voiced* (Vd) sound is produced by vibrating the vocal cords; a *voiceless* sound is produced without this vibration. *Stops* are consonants which are pronounced by cutting off completely the flow of air emanating from the lungs.

12 Applied Psycholinguistics

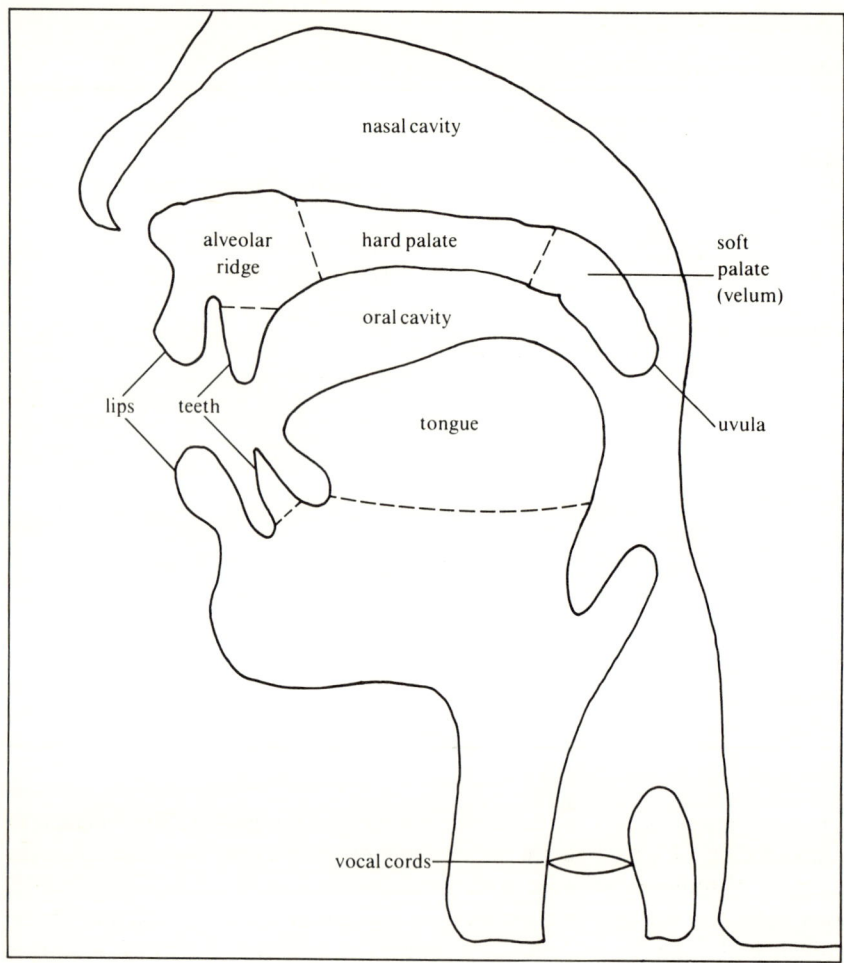

FIGURE 1.1 The organs of speech

Fricatives are produced by allowing the air to escape through a narrow constriction in the oral cavity. *Affricates* are articulated in a combined fashion; they begin as stops and end as fricatives. *Nasals* are pronounced by allowing the air to flow through the nose. The category of *liquids* consists of *laterals* and *vibrants*: laterals are produced by lowering one or both sides of the tongue, and vibrants are articulated by raising the tongue towards the roof of the mouth. The categories which refer to place of articulation (*bilabial*, *labiodental*, etc.) are self-explanatory.

A diagram of the organs involved in the production of speech is given in Figure 1.1. The following examples illustrate the English consonants:

s*p*in	=	[p]	=	voiceless bilabial stop
*b*oy	=	[b]	=	voiced bilabial stop
*t*rain	=	[t]	=	voiceless alveolar stop
*d*rop	=	[d]	=	voiced alveolar stop
*c*at	=	[k]	=	voiceless velar stop
*g*ap	=	[g]	=	voiced velar stop
*f*in	=	[f]	=	voiceless labiodental fricative
*v*ine	=	[v]	=	voiced labiodental fricative
*th*aw	=	[θ]	=	voiceless interdental fricative
*th*e	=	[ð]	=	voiced interdental fricative
*s*ip	=	[s]	=	voiceless alveolar fricative
*z*ip	=	[z]	=	voiced alveolar fricative
*s*ure	=	[š]	=	voiceless palatal fricative
*b*eige	=	[ž]	=	voiced palatal fricative
*h*e	=	[h]	=	voiceless glottal fricative
*ch*in	=	[č]	=	voiceless palatal affricate
*g*in	=	[ǰ]	=	voiced palatal affricate
*m*an	=	[m]	=	voiced bilabial nasal
*n*ame	=	[n]	=	voiced alveolar nasal
si*ng*	=	[ŋ]	=	voiced velar nasal
*l*ad	=	[l]	=	voiced alveolar lateral
*r*ed	=	[r]	=	voiced alveolar vibrant

Most of the phonetic symbols used above are based on the Roman alphabet, and this is the normal practice in phonetic transcription. The phonetic-transcription system that has received the widest acceptance is known as the *International Phonetic Alphabet* (IPA), for which, see Appendix A. Needless to say, a basic understanding of sound classification is of obvious importance to language teaching.

1.2.3 STRUCTURAL MORPHOLOGY

As previously mentioned, in structural linguistics paradigmatic and syntagmatic relationships characterize all the levels of language. At the morphological level, a paradigmatic analysis establishes the *morphemes* of a language, which are its minimal meaningful forms. A consideration of the distributional characteristics of morphemes allows the analyst to identify the *allomorphs*, or *etic* variants, of morphemes. For example, in English both the indefinite and the definite articles have two allomorphic variants, distributed as follows:

1) *a* and *the* = [ðə] occur before a form beginning with any consonant:

$$\left\{\begin{array}{l}a\\the = [ðə]\end{array}\right\} \left\{\begin{array}{l}girl\\boy\\book\\etc.\end{array}\right\}$$

2) *an* and *the* = [ði] occur before a form beginning with any vowel:

$$\left\{\begin{array}{l}an\\the = [ði]\end{array}\right\} \left\{\begin{array}{l}apple\\egg\\orange\\etc.\end{array}\right\}$$

There are several types of morphemes. A word such as *teachers*, for example, consists of three separate morphemes: *teach-*, *-er-*, and *-s*. The first one has lexical or 'dictionary' meaning and is sometimes called a *lexeme*. The *-er-* and *-s* are *affixes*, i.e., they are morphemes which are adjoined to other morphemes. There are three affix types: *prefixes* which are affixed to the beginning of a form; *infixes* which are affixed internally; and *suffixes* which are affixed at the end. In the word *unhappy*, the *un-* is a prefix. In *teachers*, the *-er-* is an infix and the *-s* is a suffix. The *-er-* is also called a *derivational* morpheme because it allows the formation of new words and usually new parts of speech. The suffix *-s* is called an *inflectional* morpheme because it expresses a grammatical category, namely plurality. Affixes and function words (e.g., *the, to, for, which, if*) are sometimes called *system* morphemes.

Basically, then, morphemes are classified as either *bound* or *free*. All affixes are bound morphemes. Function morphemes and most lexemes are free morphemes. However, some lexemes, such as the English *-vene*, occur only as bound forms: *convene, intervene, contravene*, etc. A *word*, then, is defined as a free form. A complex word is a free form made up of more than one morpheme. The complex word *teachers*, as already indicated, has the following morphological structure (note that *-er-* is an infix in this particular case, but may also be a suffix).

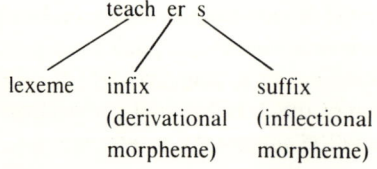

lexeme   infix   suffix
            (derivational   (inflectional
            morpheme)   morpheme)

It is, of course, obvious that an accurate scientific description of morphological structure can be of great pedagogical value. Students will be able to focus on the meaningful 'bits and pieces' of the target language and thus learn to make discriminations more accurately and rapidly.

1.2.4 STRUCTURAL SYNTAX

As may be recalled, in Section 1.2.1 the class of determiners was established by means of the paradigmatic substitution of items in the sentence frame: _____ *boy is eating the cake*. Similarly, the subclass of nouns known as 'animate human' can be determined by the substitution of items in a frame such as *The _____ is reading the book*.

$$\text{The} \begin{Bmatrix} \text{boy} \\ \text{girl} \\ \text{etc.} \end{Bmatrix} \text{is reading the book.}$$

The classes established by this analytical procedure are the basic units, or *syntaxemes*, of structural syntax. Syntagmatic relations at this level are then determined by a consideration of the ways in which syntaxemes are concatenated. For example, in English noun phrases containing a determiner (Det) and a noun (N), it can be shown that the linear order of these syntaxemes is always Det + N.

$$\begin{Bmatrix} Det \\ \text{the} \\ \text{a} \\ \text{this} \\ \text{etc.} \end{Bmatrix} \begin{Bmatrix} N \\ \text{book} \\ \text{table} \\ \text{chair} \\ \text{etc.} \end{Bmatrix}$$

In some versions of structural syntax (particularly in the United States) the process of identifying the basic syntactic units is carried out in a somewhat different fashion than in the procedure outlined above. American structuralism developed a method of syntactic analysis known as *immediate-constituent* (IC) analysis which is also based on a substitution procedure. In order to discuss IC analysis it is necessary to define the terms *construction* and *constituent*. A construction is a group of words or morphemes joined together logically. A constituent is any morpheme, word, phrase, etc., which enters into some larger construction. The ICs of a given construction are the constituents of which it is directly formed. In order to carry out an IC analysis, linguists often use a *tree diagram*. For example, in the sentence, *The boy likes the girl with the green dress*, the ICs can be shown as in the accompanying diagram.

16 Applied Psycholinguistics

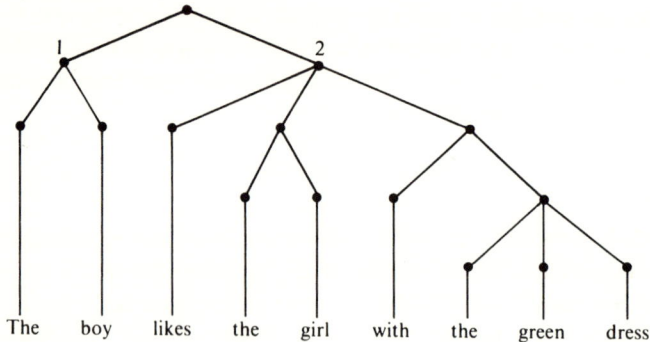

The ICs can be identified in terms of the *nodes* of the tree diagram. Thus, the first ICs are *The boy* and *likes the girl with the green dress*. These ICs are represented by nodes 1 and 2. The determination of these two nodes is, of course, based on the paradigmatic procedure of substitution. *The boy* can be replaced by, say, *Michael (Michael likes the girl with the green dress)*. Similarly, *likes the girl with the green dress* can be replaced by, say, *works (The boy works)*. We have, of course, identified the sentence subject at node 1 and the sentence predicate at node 2. This analytical procedure continues until we cannot segment any further.

With the use of labels for the nodes, this type of syntactic analysis is known as *phrase-structure* analysis (S = sentence, NP = noun phrase, Subj NP = subject noun phrase, Pred VP = predicate verb phrase, Det = determiner, N = noun, V = verb, Prep P = prepositional phrase, Prep = preposition, Adj = adjective).

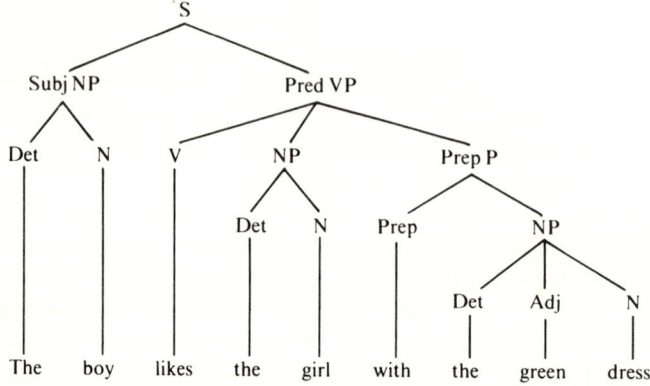

Phrase-structure analysis allows the linguist to determine the basic phrase, clause, and sentence patterns. However, unlike structural phonology and morphology, neither IC nor phrase-structure analysis has received a wide acceptance among linguists. The theoretical problems associated with these two analytical techniques have been discussed frequently in the linguistic literature of the last thirty years. IC analysis in particular has been almost completely abandoned. But, as Palmer (1971:133-4) points out, the phrase-structure method has been extended and developed into more sophisticated versions. The two best known are *tagmemics*, associated with Kenneth Pike (1954), and *stratificational linguistics*, associated with Sydney Lamb (1966). These versions are not, however, simple revisions of phrase-structure analysis. They have, in fact, become separate schools of linguistics with their own technical analytical apparatus and they have had a far-reaching influence on the development of scientific linguistics.

From a pedagogical standpoint, it is almost needless to comment that an understanding of phrase structure will help the student grasp the fundamental principles involved in sentence construction. Even the use of tree diagrams can become a helpful teaching device. As Stockwell, Bowen, and Martin (1965:306) observe, these graphic representations of structure 'utilize the visual capacity for learning which our society in general encourages.'

1.2.5 STRUCTURAL SEMANTICS

The study of meaning has always been a thorny problem for structural linguistics. Some structuralists, in fact, consider semantics to be in the domain of philosophy or psychology, rather than a legitimate area of investigation for linguistics (even though semantic considerations are accepted as part of the process of phoneme identification as discussed in Section 1.2.2). It is not difficult to see why the description of the semantic level poses analytical problems. What are the basic units of meaning and how are they related to other aspects of structure?

The structural method of paradigmatic substitution does allow for the identification of meaning to some extent. For example, in the sentence frame *She lives in a newly built* _____ the items that can fill the empty slot from a strictly semantic (or meaningful) standpoint are lexemes such as *house, home, building*, etc. The basic unit of meaning shared by these lexemes is 'structure for human habitation' (or something similar). This basic unit is known as a *sememe*, in conformity with the terminology used at the other levels for the determination of emic units. A sememe is defined, therefore, as the *denotative* or literal meaning of a morpheme or lexeme. It is important to note, moreover, that when an item is used in different contexts, its semantic range may be extended to cover so-called figurative or *connotative* meanings. Thus, for example, the lexeme *house* can take on the following connotations according to the context: (1) 'dormitory structure': e.g., He sleeps in one of the *houses* at Harvard; (2) 'legislative quorum': e.g., The lower *house* is in session now; (3) 'audience at a place of entertainment': e.g., The *house* roared with laughter.

18 Applied Psycholinguistics

The problems associated with the structural analysis of meaning are obvious. For one thing, it is almost impossible to establish the complete set of sememes. It is, moreover, difficult to relate connotative meanings to sememes. Are they contextualized variants or 'allosemes'? And if so, what kind of distributional process is involved? But perhaps the most obvious problem of all is the actual identification and classification of sememes. Some linguists have attempted to establish a limited number of truly fundamental words (sememes) with which all other words can be defined (e.g., Ogden 1942). Others have tried to define all lexical items in terms of a finite set of abstract markers or *features* such as [animate] or [human]. By marking the presence of a feature with '+' and its absence with '−', it is possible to give a semantic configuration to lexemes. For example, the lexemes *man, woman, child, bull, cow, calf, table* can be defined in terms of the semantic features [animate], [human], [male], [adult] as in the accompanying chart. This procedure is known as *componential* analysis and is used commonly in anthropological studies of kinship terminology. The problem associated with this method is how to determine the set of semantic features needed for the description of a particular language. This is, nevertheless, a very promising approach to the study of meaning.

	man	woman	child	bull	cow	calf	table
[animate]	+	+	+	+	+	+	−
[human]	+	+	+	−	−	−	−
[male]	+	−	+ or −	+	−	+ or −	−
[adult]	+	+	−	+	+	−	−

It is difficult, if not impossible, to assess the value of structural theories of meaning for language teaching. However, there are two significant insights of structural semantics of which the teacher should take note. The first is that in teaching vocabulary the context in which a word occurs is important. The second is that it is practically impossible to learn meaning independently of grammatical structure.

1.2.6 THE STRUCTURAL MODEL OF LANGUAGE DESIGN

In essence, it can be said that the *modus operandi* of structural linguistics consists primarily in the identification and classification of the emic units and their etic variants at all the linguistic levels. The main goal of structural linguistics is, therefore, the development of a set of *discovery procedures* that will enable the linguist to identify the phonemes, morphemes, etc., of a language.

The structural model of language design can be described as a hierarchical arrangement of four basic levels (phonological, morphological, syntactic, and semantic). The phonemes of a language are its basic units. These are linked together into syllables. The phonemes and syllables make up, in turn, the morphemes of the language. The combination of morphemes produces words. Morphemes and words are joined together into syntactic structures such as phrases and clauses. The concatenation of the syntactic units of the language produces sentences and utterances which are then assigned a sememic structure. Meaning and speech production are respectively at the top and bottom of the hierarchy (see Figure 1.2).

MEANING (CONTENT)

Semantic level (sememes)

Syntactic level (syntaxemes/sentences/utterances)

Morphological level (morphemes/words)

Phonological level (phonemes/syllables)

SPEECH PRODUCTION (EXPRESSION)

FIGURE 1.2 The structural model of language design (from the point of view of the speaker)

1.3 Linguistic Transformationalism

Ever since the publication of Noam Chomsky's *Syntactic Structures* in 1957, transformationalism, or *transformational-generative* (TG) grammar, has become the most influential school of linguistic analysis. Unlike structural linguistics, TG grammar has as its goal not the discovery of structure through the direct observation of linguistic data, but rather the justification or evaluation of a linguistic theory. In the structural approach, linguistic analysis begins with the observed data and works upwards from the sound system to syntax and meaning. In contrast, the emphasis in TG grammar is on the nature of the linguistic knowledge that a native speaker possesses. Transformationalists define this knowledge in terms of 'generative' and 'transformational' rules which are directions for constructing and interpreting grammatical (well-formed) sentences. As Allen (1975:42) puts it, the 'grammar "decides" that an utterance is grammatical if a precise relation can be established between the utterance in question and some combination of symbols which is generated by the rules of the grammar.' In constructing rules, transformationalists rely heavily on deduction and the *intuitions* of native speakers. Linguistic intuitions are simply the judgments of native speakers with respect to the acceptability or grammaticality of sentences. The task of the analyst according to TG grammar is, then, the formulation of linguistic rules which reflect the intuitions native speakers have about the structure of their language.

1.3.1 DEEP AND SURFACE STRUCTURE: A FUNDAMENTAL DICHOTOMY

The basic assumption of TG grammar is that language consists of two levels of representation: a *deep structure* and a *surface structure*. These are connected by so-called *transformational rules* which convert deep structures into surface ones. The difference between these two levels can be demonstrated as follows. Consider the phrase *old men and women*. This phrase is ambiguous because it can be interpreted in two ways: (1) old men and old women; (2) old men and women (who are not necessarily old). These interpretations belong to the deep structure, whereas the actual phrase *old men and women* is a surface-structure string. The surface structure is, then, the actual spoken or written form of a sentence. The deep structure, on the other hand, is its underlying form and is the level at which it is interpreted. If symbols are used to represent the two deep structures, then it becomes clear that what has occurred is the process of factorization (X = old, Y = men, Z = women).

1) $XY + XZ \longrightarrow X(Y + Z) \longrightarrow XY + Z$
   (old men and old women) $\longrightarrow$ (old men and women)

2) $XY + Z \longrightarrow XY + Z$
   (old men and women) $\longrightarrow$ (old men and women)

The factorization (or deletion) of X exemplifies a transformational rule which operates on the deep structure sequence $XY + XZ$ and converts it to a derived surface-structure string $X(Y + Z) = XY + Z$. This derived string 'collides' with the isomorphic deep-structure sequence of (2) causing the ambiguity.

The basic assumption in transformational analysis is, therefore, that there are two types of strings or sentences: *kernels* and *transforms*. The kernels are unambiguous declarative sentences which are found in the deep structure, and the transforms are all other sentence types which are derived from kernels by means of transformational rules. Thus, for example, sentences such as *The cake is eaten by the boy.*, *Is the boy eating the cake?*, and *The boy does not eat the cake.* are all derived transformationally from the kernel sentence *The boy eats the cake.* The first one is a passive transform; the second is an interrogative transform; and the third is a negative transform.

In its original and simplest form, TG grammar can be described in the following manner. The deep structure contains a *base component* consisting of *phrase structure* and *lexical insertion* (or *subcategorization*) rules. In addition, it contains a *lexicon* and a *semantic component* which assign a meaning to the output of the phrase structure and lexical insertion rules. The surface structure contains a *phonological component* which assigns a pronunciation to a string. These two levels are connected by transformational rules (see Figure 1.3). In our discussion we will describe only the main features of the *standard* version of transformational theory.

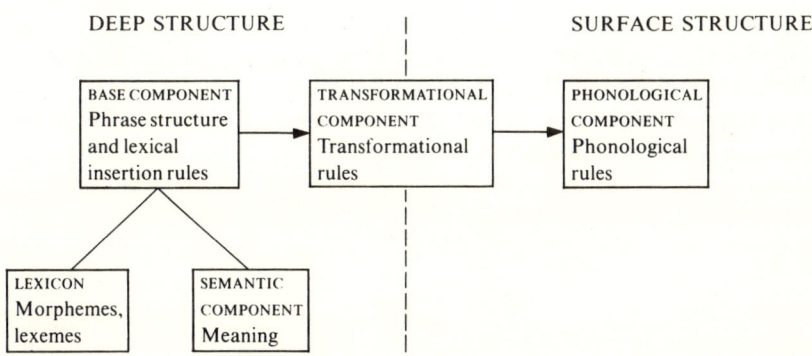

FIGURE 1.3 The transformational model of language design

1.3.2 THE BASE COMPONENT

The rules of the base component generate kernel sentences. There are two types of rules for this purpose: *phrase structure* and *lexical insertion* rules. *Phrase structure* (PS) rules contain the same type of information as IC analysis, i.e., they specify the constituent structure of kernels. To illustrate the form and operation of PS rules, we will analyze the simple kernel sentence *The girl reads the book*. An IC analysis of this sentence reveals the following syntactic information: the sentence consists of a noun phrase *(The girl)* followed by a verb phrase *(reads the book)*; the verb phrase can be broken down further into a verb *(reads)* and a noun phrase *(the book)*; both noun phrases consist of a determiner *(the)*, which is a definite article, and a noun *(girl, book)*. PS rules specify this syntactic information in the form of 'rewrite' rules (or formulas) (S = sentence, NP_1 = first noun phrase, NP_2 = second noun phrase, VP = verb phrase, Det = determiner, Def = definite article, N_1 = first noun, N_2 = second noun, V = verb)

1) S → NP_1 + VP
2) NP_1 → Det + N_1

22 Applied Psycholinguistics

3) Det → Def
4) Def → *the*
5) N$_1$ → *girl*
6) VP → V + NP$_2$
7) V → *reads*
8) NP$_2$ → Det + N$_2$
9) Det → Def
10) Def → *the*
11) N$_2$ → *book*

The arrow in these rules stands for 'rewrite.' Thus, the above PS rules are read as follows: '(1) rewrite S as NP$_1$ followed by VP; (2) rewrite NP$_1$ as Det followed by N$_1$; (3) rewrite Det as Def; etc.' When these rules are applied consecutively, their output is the kernel string *The girl reads the book*, which can be represented with a tree diagram as illustrated.

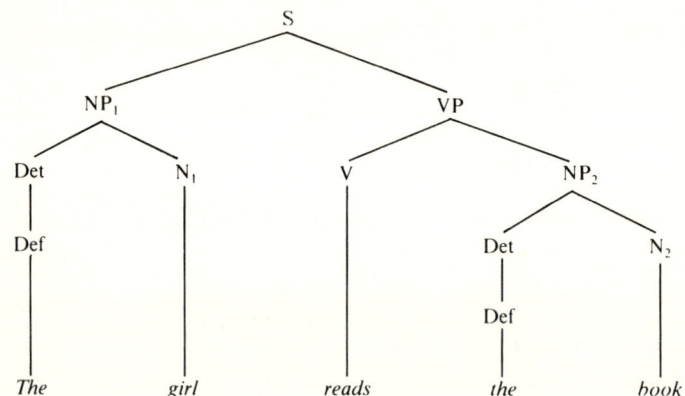

Rules (4), (5), (7), (10), (11) are actually lexical-insertion rules, i.e., they insert an item from the lexicon into the PS rules. Clearly, then, an item listed in the lexicon must have associated with it a specification of the grammatical categories (e.g., N or V) into which it can be inserted. In early versions of TG grammar, these rules operated in an ad hoc fashion: an item was extracted from the lexicon and inserted into its appropriate slot in the PS rules. However, it soon became obvious that, without any selectional constraints operating on lexical insertion, nonsensical strings could be generated by the grammar (e.g., *The table reads the book*; *The silkworm reads the book*). In *Aspects of the Theory of Syntax* (1965), Chomsky added rules to the base component to remedy this situation. He analyzed lexical items in terms of *distinctive-feature matrices*. For example, the nouns *girl* and *book* can be represented with the following features:

girl   *book*

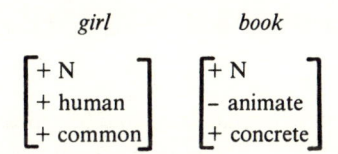

$$\begin{bmatrix} + N \\ + \text{human} \\ + \text{common} \end{bmatrix} \quad \begin{bmatrix} + N \\ - \text{animate} \\ + \text{concrete} \end{bmatrix}$$

Verbs are then specified in terms of co-occurrence restrictions with respect to nouns. Thus, the verb *read* – which must be preceded by a [+ human] noun and followed by a [− animate, + concrete] one – can be represented as follows:

read

$$\begin{bmatrix} + V \\ + [+ \text{human}] \underline{} \\ + \underline{} [- \text{animate}, + \text{concrete}] \end{bmatrix}$$

This matrix specifies the environment in which *read* can occur; i.e., the choice of *read* from the lexicon carries with it certain selectional constraints with respect to N.

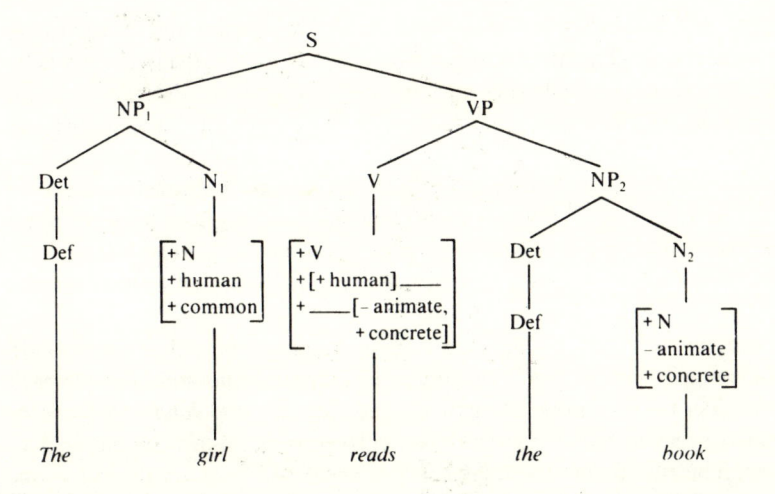

```
                        S
                    /       \
                  NP₁         VP
                 /  \       /    \
               Det   N₁    V      NP₂
                |    |     |     /   \
               Def  [+N]  [+V]  Det   N₂
                    [+human]         [+N]
                    [+common] [+[+human]__]  Def  [−animate]
                              [+__[−animate,         [+concrete]
                                   +concrete]]
                |    |     |      |      |
               The  girl  reads  the   book
```

By specifying the domain of selectional constraints of lexical items, the deep structure also functions as a semantic, or interpretive, component.

1.3.3 THE TRANSFORMATIONAL COMPONENT

Transformational (T) rules operate on the kernel strings generated by the base component. In the standard version of TG grammar these rules are meaning-preserving, i.e., they transform a kernel into a surface-structure form without changing its underlying meaning.

There are three types of transformational processes covered by T rules: addition, deletion, and transposition. To exemplify both addition and transposition we will analyze the process of passivization in English, i.e., the process whereby active sentences are converted to corresponding passive ones. Consider the passive form of the kernel generated by the base component in Section 1.3.2 *(The girl reads the book)*: *The book is read by the girl.* There are four structural differences between the two strings: the order of the two NPs is inverted; the agent word *by* has been added; the verb has been changed to a past participle (PP); and the verb *to be* has been added. A T rule for passivization will give this information:

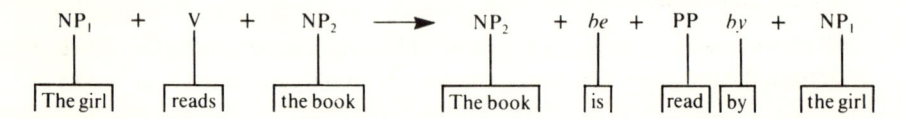

$$NP_1 + V + NP_2 \longrightarrow NP_2 + be + PP + by + NP_1$$

| The girl | reads | the book | The book | is | read | by | the girl |

The left side of this rule is sometimes called the *structural index* and the right side, the *structural change*. The structural index specifies what the order of the syntactic symbols (NP, V, etc.) of a kernel must be in order for it to undergo a certain transformation. The structural change specifies the end result of the application of a T rule.

The difference between T rules and PS rules is obvious. A T rule operates on a completed kernel string. A PS rule expands syntactic symbols in terms of other syntactic symbols, and the expansion process terminates in lexical insertion. In other words, a T rule changes the structural makeup of the kernel string generated by PS rules without a change in meaning.

The vast literature on T rules and general transformational processes indicates that some T rules do not apply independently but rather interact with each other. Consider the sentences *John gave the book to Mary* and *John gave Mary the book*. Native speakers will immediately recognize these two as acceptable equivalent forms. The two forms are related transformationally by two T rules: one changes the order of the two phrases following the verb, and another deletes the preposition *to*. The first rule may be called indirect-object movement and the second *to*-deletion:

1) Indirect-object movement (Prep Phrase = prepositional phrase):
    T rule: NP + V + NP + Prep Phrase → NP + V + Prep Phrase + NP
    Structural index: John (NP) + gave (V) + the book (NP) + to Mary (Prep Phrase)
    Structural change: John (NP) + gave (V) + to Mary (Prep Phrase) + the book (NP)

2) *To*-deletion:
   T rule: X + V + *to* + Y → X + V + ϕ + Y
   Structural index: John (X) + gave (V) + to *(to)* + Mary the book (Y)
   Structural change: John (X) + gave (V) + Mary the book (Y)

The *to*-deletion rule uses general symbols or variables rather than specific syntactic symbols. Thus, the X stands for any syntactic symbol or symbols which precede V, and Y stands for any syntactic symbol or symbols which follow V and *to*. The ϕ symbol shows that one of the symbols in that position has been deleted. The essence of this rule is to show that *to* is deleted when it occurs right after V. Notice that *to*-deletion applies *after* the indirect-object movement rule. This implies that these rules are ordered with respect to each other. The view that posits ordering for all transformations *(cyclical theory)*, while very interesting, is beyond the scope of the present discussion.

The general implications of TG grammar for language teaching are obvious. For one thing, it suggests that *what* is acquired is as important as *how* it is acquired. Language competence is a creative ability and the memorization of sentence patterns is not a means of acquiring it. It also suggests that some types of sentences (transforms) can perhaps be best learned as derivatives of simpler, more basic sentences (kernels).

1.3.4 THE PHONOLOGICAL COMPONENT

The output of the transformational component is assigned a phonetic interpretation by the rules of the phonological component. The system of phonetic classification employed by transformationalists is based on *distinctive articulatory features* (Chomsky and Halle 1968). These define sounds in terms of the presence (+) or absence (−) of certain phonetic categories. For example, the English consonants can be classified in a matrix with fourteen distinctive features (see Figure 1.4): [consonantal] and [vocalic] are self-explanatory (notice that semiconsonants are marked as [− consonantal, − vocalic]); [sonorant] refers to consonants such as nasals and laterals which are produced without an obstruction or constriction to the air flow; [continuant] distinguishes stops and affricates from 'continued' sounds such as fricatives; [lateral] and [nasal] obviously refer to lateral and nasal articulations; [delayed release] distinguishes affricates from stops; [strident] distinguishes those affricates and fricatives which are noisier than others; [voice] indicates whether the sound is produced with or without the vibration of the vocal cords; [anterior] refers to sounds produced in the front of the mouth; [coronal] stipulates whether the tip of the tongue is involved in the articulation; and [high], [low], [back] all refer to tongue position.

	p	t	k	b	d	g	f	θ	s	š	v	ð	z	ž	č	ǰ	m	n	ŋ	w	y	h	r	l
consonantal	+	+	+	+	+	+	+	+	+	+	+	+	+	+	+	+	+	+	+	−	−	−	+	+
vocalic	−	−	−	−	−	−	−	−	−	−	−	−	−	−	−	−	−	−	−	−	−	−	+	+
sonorant	−	−	−	−	−	−	−	−	−	−	−	−	−	−	−	−	+	+	+	+	+	+	+	+
continuant	−	−	−	−	−	−	+	+	+	+	+	+	+	+	−	−	−	−	−	+	+	+	+	+
lateral	−	−	−	−	−	−	−	−	−	−	−	−	−	−	−	−	−	−	−	−	−	−	−	+
nasal	−	−	−	−	−	−	−	−	−	−	−	−	−	−	−	−	+	+	+	−	−	−	−	−
delayed release	−	−	−	−	−	−	−	−	−	−	−	−	−	−	+	+	−	−	−	−	−	−	−	−
strident	−	−	−	−	−	−	+	−	+	+	+	−	+	+	+	+	−	−	−	−	−	−	−	−
voice	−	−	−	+	+	+	−	−	−	−	+	+	+	+	−	+	+	+	+	+	+	−	+	+
anterior	+	+	−	+	+	−	+	+	+	−	+	+	+	−	−	−	+	+	−	−	−	−	−	+
coronal	−	+	−	−	+	−	−	+	+	+	−	+	+	+	+	+	−	+	−	−	−	−	+	+
high	−	−	+	−	−	+	−	−	−	+	−	−	−	+	+	+	−	−	+	+	+	−	−	−
low	−	−	−	−	−	−	−	−	−	−	−	−	−	−	−	−	−	−	−	−	−	+	−	−
back	−	−	+	−	−	+	−	−	−	−	−	−	−	−	−	−	−	−	+	+	−	−	−	−

FIGURE 1.4 Distinctive feature matrix of English consonants

The Scientific Study of Language 27

The rules of the phonological component provide a phonetic representation for both phonetic and morphological structure. To illustrate how these rules work, we will analyze the following case of so-called *sequential redundancy* in English (Whitley 1978:17–18). The members of the class of voiceless fricatives /f, s, š, θ/ generally contrast with each other (e.g., *fin, sin, shin, thin*). But in front of a non-sonorant consonant (e.g., stops and affricates) in word-initial position only /s/ can occur: *spin* but not *fpin, shpin, thpin*. In fact, it can be said that of the entire class of fricatives /f, s, š, θ, v, z, ž, ð/, only /s/ can occur in this environment. This fact can be expressed in terms of distinctive-feature matrices.

$$\begin{bmatrix} + \text{ consonantal} \\ - \text{ sonorant} \\ + \text{ continuant} \end{bmatrix} \rightarrow \begin{bmatrix} + \text{ strident} \\ - \text{ voice} \\ + \text{ anterior} \\ + \text{ coronal} \\ - \text{ high} \end{bmatrix} / \# \underline{\quad} [- \text{ sonorant}]$$

The matrix on the left side of the arrow specifies those features necessary to distinguish the class of fricatives from all other sounds (see Figure 1.4); the matrix on the right side specifies the features required to distinguish /s/ from the other fricatives. Thus, this rule is read as follows: 'The class of fricatives is realized only as /s/ before a non-sonorant consonant in word-initial position.'

The rules of the phonological component also cover morphemic structure (inflection, derivation, etc.). It is not, however, necessary to deal in detail here with the form of morpheme-structure rules. They operate in a similar way to the fricative rule above; however, morphological markers (N, Plural, etc.) are part of the distributional statement. The main point to bear in mind about phonological rules is that they map syntactic and lexical representations of words and sentences into phonetic representations. Thus, the phonological component is connected to the other components in a direct linear manner. As Grinder and Elgin (1973:203) observe, the forms that serve as input to the phonological component 'undergo modification by the phonological rules, and ultimately are spelled out in their final surface forms as the morphemes of the language.'

1.3.5 SOME RECENT DEVELOPMENTS

The standard theory of TG grammar is based on the view that transformations are meaning-preserving. In recent work on this theory (e.g., Jackendoff 1972, Chomsky 1980) some aspects of semantic interpretation are related to the surface structure after transformations have occurred. But the fundamental dichotomy between deep and surface structure is still maintained. This version of TG grammar has come to be known as the *extended-standard theory*. However, some transformationalists (e.g., McCawley 1968) have rejected this dichotomy and have proposed the view that the surface structure is related directly to semantic interpretation by transformations without the intermediate level of deep structure. This alternative model of TG grammar has come to be known as *generative semantics*. It is, however, beyond the scope of this brief discussion to deal with the many interesting aspects of the debate between generative semanticists and proponents of the extended-standard theory. The point is that transformational theory is in a state of flux.

Two other alternatives to the standard version of TG grammar worthy of note are known as *case grammar* and *relational grammar*. Briefly, case grammar posits a small universal set of relations (cases) in the deep structure which hold between a verb and any NP (Fillmore 1968). Relational grammar, which is associated with Perlmutter and Postal (e.g., 1977), claims that sentences can be represented by 'relational networks' or 'graphs' which specify functional relations (subject, object, etc.) at different levels or strata corresponding more or less to the three basic components of standard TG grammar.

Finally, it should be mentioned that TG theories have recently come under criticism from several points of view. Among other things, it is often pointed out that transformational theory is too reductive – reducing everything in language to a series of states and processes as expressed by the TG rules themselves. Moreover, TG theory tends to be restricted to models of competence rather than to encompass both competence and performance.

1.4 Language and Communication

The main concern of scientific linguistics is the development of theories to account for the native speaker's unconscious knowledge of language structure and pattern. Linguistics has, therefore, concentrated traditionally on microlinguistic matters. Neither structural linguistics nor TG grammar has dealt in any significant way with language as a communicative phenomenon. This aspect of language has been investigated from two interdisciplinary points of view known as *sociolinguistics* and *psycholinguistics*. Sociolinguistics aims to describe primarily the functions and patterns of language use in different social settings. One of the original aims of psycholinguistics was the description of the behavioral aspects of verbal communication, although this field has now been expanded to cover such interesting areas as language acquisition and language pathology. As Greenberg (1977:9) observes, developments in such interdisciplinary fields are bringing about the realization that only a multifaceted theory will 'do justice to the existence and interconnection of the many aspects of language – as system, as historical product, and as an adaptation, both to the internal physical and mental endowments of human beings and to their external sociocultural environment.' We will now look very briefly at some of the more common sociolinguistic and psycholinguistic aspects of verbal communication.

1.4.1 THE SOCIOLOGY OF VERBAL COMMUNICATION

Needless to say, one of the main functions – if not the primary function – of language is human interaction. The use of language as a communicative instrument is clearly of central importance for language teaching. There would be no point in learning language structure without knowing how to use it.

In all languages speech acts are subject to social conventions and constraints which are extremely important for successful verbal communication to occur. A starting point for the sociological study of language is to determine and classify speech acts according to well-defined social conventions. Sociolinguists often use the term *register* (or *style*) when referring to the specific form a speech act takes in a specific social context. A classic work on this subject is the one by Martin Joos (1967). According to Joos, there are five registers, or levels of formality, in the use of English: (1) *oratorical* or *frozen*, which is used for public speaking and is characterized by careful planning in advance, exaggerated intonation, and the utilization of many rhetorical devices; (2) *deliberative* or *formal*, which is also used in addressing audiences, but is less formal than the frozen style (e.g., a university classroom lecture); (3) *consultative*, which is a formal dialogue style used in business transactions, board meetings, etc.; (4) *casual*, which is marked by very few stylistic formalities and is the register used in communicating with friends, colleagues, etc.; (5) *intimate*, which is a style exhibiting no sociolinguistic inhibitions or formalities whatsoever and is used among close friends, family members, loved ones, etc. Strevens (1964) has exemplified these five registers in a humorous way: (1) *frozen*: 'Visitors should make their way at once to the upper floor by way of the staircase.' (2) *formal*: 'Visitors should go up the staircase at once.' (3) *consultative*: 'Would you mind going upstairs right away, please?' (4) *casual*: 'Time you all went upstairs now.' (5) *intimate*: 'Up you go, chaps.' It should also be mentioned that formality varies according to medium. It seems to be a universal characteristic that written language is more formal than spoken language.

In addition to registers, speech acts manifest special purposes or functions. Halliday (1973) has identified seven functions which he considers to be typical of most speech acts: (1) *instrumental*, which serves to bring about or influence certain events (e.g., 'Eat the cake!'); (2) *regulatory*, which serves to control or regulate events and social encounters (e.g., speech protocols of approval, disapproval); (3)

representational, which implies the making of statements for the purpose of conveying information; (4) *interactional*, which serves to establish social roles and contact (also known as *phatic communion*); (5) *personal*, which permits the expression of feelings, emotions, etc.; (6) *heuristic*, which involves the use of language to acquire knowledge; (7) *imaginative*, which functions to create imaginary or ideational systems (e.g., poetry). This classification paradigm, as Brown (1980:195) observes, covers most patterns of verbal interaction including: greeting, parting, inviting, flattering, seducing, charming, bragging, interrupting, requesting, evading, lying, shifting blame, changing the subject, criticizing, reprimanding, ridiculing, insulting, threatening, warning, complaining, accusing, denying, agreeing, disagreeing, arguing, persuading, insisting, suggesting, reminding, asserting, advising, reporting, evaluating, commenting, commanding, ordering, demanding, questioning, probing, sympathizing, apologizing, making excuses.

Austin (1962) and Searle (1969) have developed four categories of speech acts which have received wide acceptance. The first category is known as an *utterance act*. This refers simply to the act of uttering sounds, words, sentences, etc. The second category is referred to as an *illocutionary act*. This is an act performed *in* uttering something. Such acts as promising, reporting, stating, asking, telling, threatening, asserting, requesting, suggesting, ordering, and proposing are classified as illocutionary. These acts are crucial to verbal communication. They make up most of our conversations. The third category is called a *perlocutionary act*. This is an act performed *by* uttering something which produces an effect on the hearer. Some typical perlocutionary acts are: inspiring, impressing, embarrassing, intimidating, persuading, deceiving, misleading, irritating. The fourth category is referred to as a *propositional act*. This is an act of referring and predicating.

In addition to the classification of registers and speech acts, another important area of sociolinguistics is the study of language variability. This refers to the study of language in terms of how it changes from individual to individual and from group to group. Basically, there are three concepts that are relevant to this area of investigation: (1) *idiolect*: the unique and peculiar language used by each individual in a speech community; (2) *dialect*: the form of language according to geographical space; (3) *sociolect*: the form of language according to socioeconomic level. Although dialectal and sociolectal manifestations of language overlap considerably, a *dialectal variant* refers traditionally to microlinguistic differences (phonological, morphological, etc.) between the standard language and a dialect, whereas a *sociolectal variant* is the particular form of language used in a certain socioeconomic group (often called *social dialect*).

Although it is not the purpose here to deal in any detail with the sociological study of language, some familiarity with speech acts and language variability is of obvious importance for language teaching. A knowledge of speech-act typologies, for example, will be extremely useful in organizing speech encounters in the classroom. As Corder (1973:49) eloquently puts it, language teaching is concerned with teaching the learner 'not just to produce grammatically acceptable strings of words, but also to use language to some purpose, to communicate and be communicated to, to assume certain roles.'

1.4.2 THE PSYCHOLOGY OF VERBAL COMMUNICATION

It is not widely known that the interest in the psychological aspect of verbal communication can probably be traced back to the writings of Wilhelm von Humboldt (see 1935) who viewed language as *enèrgeia* (i.e., as a manifestation of personality and general behavior) rather than just form, or *ergon*. Nevertheless, the paths of psychology and linguistics remained divergent until the turn of the present century when psychologists began to investigate the interconnection between language and psychological mechanisms such as association (e.g., Wundt 1901, Mead 1904, Ginniken 1909). One of their primary aims was to discover which psychological processes, if any, triggered or influenced language change. The journal *Zeitschrift für Völkerpsychologie und Sprachwissenschaft* (1860-90) was founded by Moritz Lazarus and Heymann Steinthal for such investigations.

With the rise of synchronic linguistics in the early part of this century, models of language design soon came to be investigated from the point of view of psychological theories of behavior. Concepts such as paradigmatic opposition sought corroboration in corresponding psychological theories of opposition. Although European linguistics was influenced to some degree by 'mentalistic' theories of verbal behavior (e.g., Delacroix 1930; Bühler 1934; Kainz 1941, 1946), on this continent it was the *behavioristic* mode of thought which shaped linguistic theory (e.g., Allport 1924, Weiss 1925, Kantor 1936, Skinner 1957). Among the notable exceptions to this trend, one can cite Miller (1951), Carroll (1953, 1958), Roback (1955), and Reiss (1959). Today, it is *cognitive* psychology that is in the forefront vis-à-vis linguistic theory.

To the best of our knowledge, the term *psycholinguistics* was coined by Proncko in 1946. However, it was not until 1951, with Miller's pioneering study on language and communication, that psycholinguistics emerged as a new interdisciplinary mode of thought. With the publication of the proceedings of the Indiana University conference on psycholinguistics in 1953 (Osgood and Sebeok 1954), this fledgling science established itself as an autonomous branch of both linguistics and psychology. In the last two decades, psycholinguistics has been one of the more productive branches of language study; a lot of research has been directed towards the investigation of the psychological reality of linguistic rules. For a detailed historical survey of the relationship between schools of psychology and linguistics, see Titone (1964b:37–62).

As Haden Elgin (1979:134) observes, psycholinguistics can be defined simply as the 'study of the relationship between human language and the brain.' This implies, of course, a very large territory of investigation, containing such areas as language learning, language processing, speech pathology, etc. The principal areas of study were perhaps first outlined in the 1961 anthology of papers edited by Sol Saporta, *Psycholinguistics: A Book of Readings*. Saporta classified the studies under eight categories which indicated specific domains of psycholinguistic research: (1) the nature and function of language; (2) approaches to the study of language; (3) speech perception; (4) the sequential organization of linguistic events; (5) the semantic aspect of linguistic events; (6) language acquisition, bilingualism, and language change; (7) pathologies of linguistic behavior; (8) linguistic relativity and the relation of linguistic processes to perception and cognition. In the last decade or so, several other areas of investigation, such as animal, mass, and non-verbal communication, have been added to the ever-broadening field of psycholinguistics. The focus has been, however, on two areas: (1) the psychological reality of grammatical models of language competence and of theories of performance (see, for example, Jakobovits and Miron 1967, Slobin 1971:21–38, and Cairns and Cairns 1976:95–185); (2) child language (e.g., Smith and Miller 1966, Slobin 1971, Brown 1973).

Before dealing with some specific aspects of psycholinguistic research in subsequent chapters, we will give here a brief characterization of the psycholinguistic study of verbal communication. One of the more important influences on this line of investigation has been information theory (see Shannon and Weaver 1949). There are two postulates that underlie the informational view of verbal communication: (1) language is an instrument for communication; (2) communication is defined as a system for transmitting information. In line with this theory, the model of communication consists of a *source* which transmits a message to a *destination* by means of the manipulation of the alternative signals which can be selected from the connecting *channel*. A *transmitter* emits the signals and a *receiver* receives them. Any interference in the channel is referred to as *noise* (see Figure 1.5). In the case of human communication several psychological components are added to this 'engineering' model. For one thing, both the source and destination are contained in the speaker who is a transmitter and receiver at the same time, capable of controlling and regulating a message. Thus, a human communication system contains a *feedback* mechanism. Moreover, within a stimulus-response (S-R) framework it can be said that speech perception or

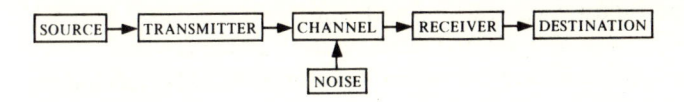

```
SOURCE → TRANSMITTER → CHANNEL → RECEIVER → DESTINATION
                          ↑
                        NOISE
```

FIGURE 1.5 The informational model of communication

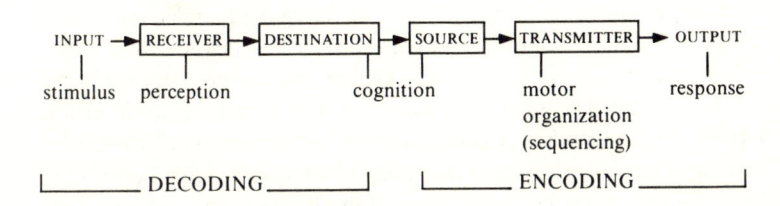

```
INPUT → RECEIVER → DESTINATION → SOURCE → TRANSMITTER → OUTPUT
  |         |            |          |          |            |
stimulus perception  cognition           motor         response
                                      organization
                                      (sequencing)

        |_____ DECODING _____|    |_____ ENCODING _____|
```

FIGURE 1.6 An informational model of verbal communication

comprehension occurs in the receiver and that the motor organization of a speech event occurs in the transmitter, while cognition of speech occurs in both the source and destination (see Figure 1.6).

Osgood and Sebeok (1954:4) define psycholinguistics from the standpoint of this model as follows: 'the scientific study of the processes of encoding and decoding in the act of communication as they relate states of messages to states of communicators.' Thus, psychologically, verbal communication can be characterized as the process by which thoughts are transformed into the signals of a socially established code *(encoding)* and as the process by which these signals are given a meaning or interpretation *(decoding)*. Clearly, a knowledge of how speech is encoded and decoded is fundamental to the language-teaching process.

1.5 Linguistics and Language Teaching

We will discuss learning theory and language teaching in subsequent chapters. It is important to emphasize here, however, that (in our opinion, at least) two general principles underlie these two interacting processes: (1) Language learning is a complex psychological process. It involves such mechanisms as memory, recall, acquisition, reinforcement, perception, cognitive organization, and learning style. (2) Language teaching should be synchronized with the psychological conditions underlying the learning process, i.e., teaching strategies should take into account those psychological mechanisms involved in language learning *(ars docendi imitatur artem discendi)*. As a corollary, it can be said that language teaching should be a feedback or self-regulating process, i.e., language teachers should modify and adjust their teaching techniques in accordance with the reactions of learners, so as to guide and facilitate the learning process.

This point of view is, surprisingly, not shared by all linguists and psychologists. Chomsky (e.g., 1966), for one, has always maintained that linguistic and psychological models of language behavior are not germane to language teaching. However, it is our firm belief – and that of many scholars and educators – that effective language teaching will benefit from an integrated understanding of language design and use, of the psychological aspects of language learning, and of the human relationship that exists between teacher and learner. As one of the writers (Titone 1964a:5) has previously stated, 'the building of a sound and efficient methodology depends not only on the clear perception of the educational goals to be achieved in language teaching nor exclusively on an up-to-date linguistic analysis of the materials to be taught, but also on a comprehensive and thorough-going analysis of the psychological process of second-language learning.'

1.5.1 APPLIED LINGUISTICS AND APPLIED PSYCHOLINGUISTICS

There is little agreement on what the term *applied linguistics* means (see Kaplan 1980). This term is often considered to be synonymous with language teaching. Basically, the difference between theoretical and applied linguistics is – as the terms imply – one of theory and application. A good definition is provided by Allen and Corder (1975:xi): 'Our aim in applied linguistics is to make use of the knowledge and insights gained from scientific investigations into the nature of language, in the hope that we may solve some of the problems which arise in the planning and implementation of language teaching programmes.' Spolsky (1978) has proposed the term *educational linguistics* because it conforms more with isomorphic applied disciplines in psychology (educational psychology) and sociology (educational sociology).

In this book we will use the term *applied psycholinguistics* in an analogous fashion, i.e., as the study of the pedagogical implications arising from the research into the psychology of language learning. Actually, the applications of psycholinguistic research are not restricted to the pedagogical domain. As Koplin (1968) points out, research into speech pathologies can have applications in therapeutic ways. Or, research into child language development can help in cases of language-learning disabilities (see also Titone 1974a). However, in this book the term 'applied psycholinguistics' is used only in the specific way mentioned above, namely as the study of the pedagogical applications of the psycholinguistic research into language learning.

Actually, applied linguists have always shown considerable interest in the psychological aspects of language learning. In 1964, for example, Rivers analyzed the psychological bases of the audiolingual method (see Chap. 5). But, in general, they have concentrated their efforts on examining the relationship between scientific linguistics and language teaching and on identifying the linguistic problems that emerge during the teaching process. Less attention has been devoted to the psychological mechanisms underlying language learning and their implications for language teaching.

1.6 A Pedagogical Summary

What do the linguistic theories and research findings discussed in this chapter imply for language teaching? It is perhaps useful to list in point form some of the possible implications this domain of scientific knowledge has for the average classroom practitioner.
1) Even a rudimentary knowledge of linguistics will inevitably help the teacher understand the ways in which languages work and therefore how to prepare appropriate 'grammatical' explanations, exercise materials, etc.
2) Linguistic theories provide the teacher with systematic ways of classifying and organizing the linguistic facts to be taught. The division, for example, of language into phonological, morphological, syntactic, and semantic levels may be of use in providing a framework for developing, say, drills on pronunciation, word-formation, etc. Transformational theory suggests that some language processes are best handled by rules that relate complex structures to simpler ones: e.g., interrogative, passive, and negative sentences can be derived simply from corresponding kernels.
3) It goes without saying that the more teachers know about language, the better prepared they will be to handle all kinds of classroom situations: e.g., 'grammatical' queries by students or confusions arising from poor textbook explanations.

In essence, then, some knowledge of theoretical linguistics is as important for the language teacher as the knowledge of geometry is for the draftsman or architect. The idea is that practitioners can become truly effective by insuring some familiarity with the theoretical aspects of their trade.

1.7 Signposts

Where is linguistics going? For what concerns us here, it is useful to point out that the main trend in linguistics during the last few decades has been a gradual movement away from the narrow, microlinguistic view of language design to a broader one that incorporates into linguistic methodology the changing shapes of language as it occurs in diverse spatial, social, and psycho-communicative contexts. The concepts 'native-speaker intuition' and 'ideal speaker-hearer' are being largely abandoned in favor of a more empirical, or ecological, linguistics. Through the influential work of methodologists such as Labov (e.g., 1966, 1970, 1975), mainstream linguistics is becoming gradually more macrolinguistic in its focus (see also Danesi 1982). What this probably means for language-teaching methodology is that it too will become increasingly ecological. Classroom practice is already starting to stress communication much more than structure as the primary objective of language learning. As will become clear throughout this book, it is our view that language teaching is heading towards an amalgamation of structural and communicative objectives, i.e., it will probably become more and more eclectic in its attempt to respond adequately to the psychological reality of language learning.

1.8 Suggestions for Further Reading

There are many excellent introductions to the field of linguistics. Still basic is Gleason (1961). Other widely used ones include Lyons (1968), Bolinger (1968), and Wardhaugh (1977). A comparative study of the major schools of linguistic analysis can be found in Davis (1973).

Some very good introductions to applied linguistics and language pedagogy can be found in Brooks (1964), Titone (1966, 1974b), Chastain (1971), Corder (1973), Wardhaugh (1974), Allen and Corder (1975), Brown (1980), and Stern (1983). A detailed bibliography of this field can be found in Mollica, Danesi, and Urbancic (1983).

Works on psycholinguistics which may be of interest to language teachers include: Penfield (1959), Carroll (1964), Lenneberg (1964, 1967), Rosenberg and Koplin (1968), De Vito (1970), Marshall (1977), Titone (1977c), Smith (1979), Fillmore, Kempler, and Wang (1979), and Paivio and Begg (1981).

2
The Language-Learning Process

Language is a highly complicated activity, and it is wholly learned. It involves both neural and muscular tissue, and it has psychological, interpersonal, and cultural aspects that are indispensable to its acquisition and use. (Brooks 1964:48)

2.0 Introduction

In the next three chapters we will be looking at the psychological aspects of language learning. In Chapter 3 we will discuss first-language acquisition, and in Chapter 4 we will examine second-language learning. In this chapter we will look at language learning as a general neurological and psychological phenomenon.

2.1 Verbal Behavior

Before exploring how verbal behavior is learned, we will outline some of the distinguishing features which set it apart from other forms of human behavior.

2.1.1 A REPRESENTATIONAL MODEL OF VERBAL BEHAVIOR

Perhaps the most important characteristic of verbal behavior is that it is *symbolic* in nature. This implies that some form of conscious control is involved on the part of the human organism. Verbal symbols may be oral, written, or gestural. They are abstract representations of objects, concepts, emotional states, etc. Almost fifty years ago, Karl Bühler (1934) proposed a very interesting model of verbal behavior in terms of its primarily representational nature. According to Bühler, all speech acts consist of three concomitant functions: (1) *representation (Darstellung)*, i.e., the referential function of speech (a speech act refers to something); (2) *expression (Ausdruck)*, i.e., the subjective function of speech (reference to the speaker); (3) *address (Appell)*, i.e., the interpersonal function of speech (reference to the hearer).

Bühler eventually replaced these terms with *symbol, symptom,* and *signal,* respectively. Thus, when someone utters 'It is raining,' he/she is verbalizing a meteorological event with oral verbal symbols (symbolic function); in addition, he/she is expressing an emotional state or attitude (symptomatic function) and may evoke some response from a hearer (signalling function). Figure 2.1 is used

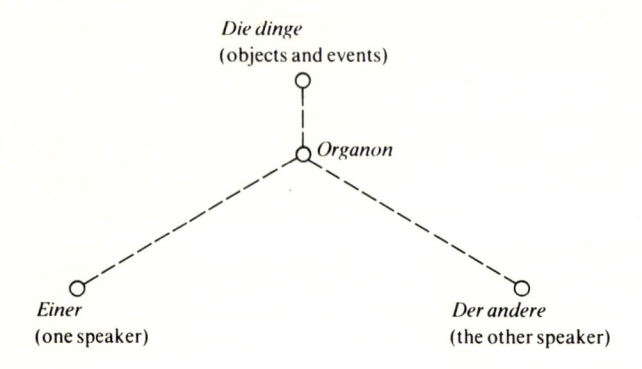

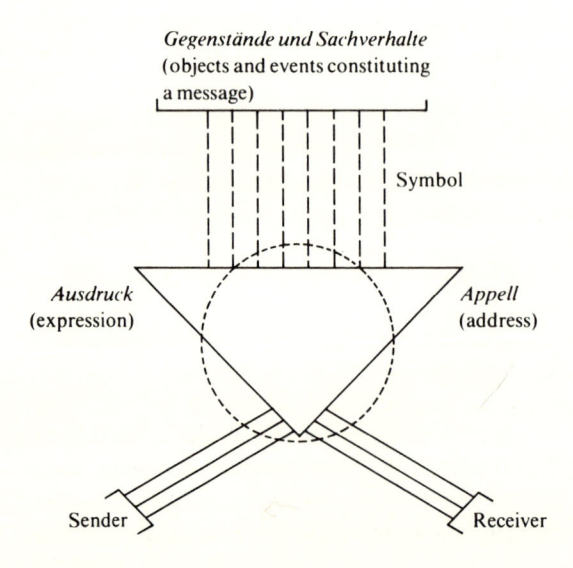

FIGURE 2.1 Bühler's model of verbal behavior

by Bühler to illustrate his model of verbal behavior. The triangle stands for the three functions, and the circle and triangle taken together represent a speech act as it is produced and perceived.

2.1.2 AN INFORMATIONAL MODEL OF VERBAL BEHAVIOR

A second characteristic of verbal behavior is its *communicative* nature. As discussed in the previous chapter (see Section 1.4.2), this feature inspired the first attempts to investigate language from a psycholinguistic perspective. The theoretical framework within which research on this aspect of verbal behavior is conducted is *information theory* (Shannon and Weaver 1949). According to this theory, the information of a message has nothing to do with its content but is defined in terms of its *predictability*. If an outcome is totally predictable, the message carries no information; but, if it is unpredictable, the degree of information it carries is related to the degree of predictability. The measurement of information is in *binits* (or *bits*) and it is based on a binary system of probable choices: a code with two alternative signals, both equally likely, has an information value, or *capacity*, of one binit per use; a code with four alternative signals, all equally likely, has a capacity of two binits per use; a code with eight alternative signals, all equally likely, has a capacity of three binits per use; and so on. In general, the capacity in binits of a code, or the amount of information in a code where each signal has equal probability, is defined as the logarithm to the base 2 of the number of alternative signals:

$I = \log_2 N$ (I = information, N = number of signals)

Such ideal communication situations rarely occur mainly because some signals have a higher probability of occurrence than others. As Gleason (1961:373-90) points out, in a communication system such as an alarm device the probability of occurrence of the signal 'silence' is greater than the 'alarm' signal. But the latter signal obviously carries more information (because it is unpredictable). Mathematically, the amount of information is related inversely to the probability *(p)* of occurrence of a signal; i.e., the amount of information is the logarithm to the base 2 of the reciprocal of *p*:

$I = \log_2 1/p$

This is a very important insight of information theory, and although the mathematical details of the complete theory are of no direct interest here, the concept that information and predictability are inversely related is pivotal. The overall or average information of a code is called *entropy* which is defined by Hockett (1961:49) as the 'actual rate at which a source generates information, on the average.'

Another important finding of information theory is that in order to combat or diminish the effect of interference, or *noise*, in the channel, *redundancy* is either present or introduced into a communication system. Redundancy is, in fact, found at all levels of language (e.g., the predictable occurrences of morphemes in certain syntactic frames or slots, complementary distribution). As Gleason (1961:384) emphasizes, redundancy 'is not an imperfection in language, but an essential feature, without which language would be inoperative.' In 1929 Zipf demonstrated that any element of speech which occurs in language more frequently than some other similar element demands less emphasis or conspicuousness than any other element which occurs less frequently. Information theory has confirmed this fact for the linguist.

As discussed in the previous chapter (see Section 1.4.2), verbal communication can be considered to have the following components: (1) an information *source* consisting of a message which a speaker wishes to convey, and which depends on the neurological apparatus of the human organism as well as on the experience and personality of the speaker; (2) a *code* which is an arbitrary, prearranged set of verbal signals available to the human organism; (3) a *transmitter* capable of encoding the message, i.e., the vocal organs which are controlled by the cortical centers of the brain; (4) a *channel* which transmits the encoded information through time and space; (5) a *receiver* who decodes the message by means of auditory and neurological mechanisms.

The communicative nature of verbal behavior forms the nucleus of another interesting model proposed by Friederich Kainz (1946). According to Kainz, speech acts can be classified as either *dialogues* or *monologues*. In dialogue form, speech has three functions: manifestation, address, and information. The first function is characterized by Kainz as being self-directed, or ego-oriented; the second is described as other-directed because it reflects the tendency to communicate something to someone; and the third is described as pure linguistic expression which may, for example, take on the form of words or physical behavior (gestures, facial expressions, etc.). Kainz also includes what he calls 'interior address' which involves such verbal acts as repeating encouraging words to oneself during the performance of difficult tasks. Thus, verbal communication is a means of supporting or stimulating one's thoughts or reflections. Both the dialogue and monologue aspects of verbal behavior are primary; there also exist secondary aspects which have an ethical or esthetic function, e.g., a tone change from violent to soft, the poetic use of words, and sounds to create harmonic effects.

This model of verbal behavior, therefore, includes three general functions: (1) *communicative* (other-directed or objective), e.g., the transmission of information, ideas, emotions, attitudes, beliefs; (2) *expressive* (self-directed or subjective), e.g., the babbling of children, phatic communion; (3) *reflective*, e.g., repeating concepts just learned to oneself, writing down one's thoughts.

2.1.3 LINGUISTIC RELATIVITY

A third feature which distinguishes verbal behavior is its highly abstract, or *cognitive*, nature. Language is, in fact, at the root of cognitive organization. Words allow children to discriminate among objects and to perceive a shared property of a group of objects. According to the well-known *linguistic-relativity hypothesis*, or *Sapir-Whorf hypothesis* (Whorf 1956), it is claimed that one's perception of the world, or *Weltanschauung*, is influenced totally by the language one speaks. This is, of course, an extreme point of view, since it is probably more accurate to say that only part of one's *Weltanschauung* is determined by language structure. Two favorite examples used by the proponents of linguistic relativity are: (1) Inuit have many different words for different types of snow and consequently *perceive* different realities with regard to snow; (2) all languages show lexical differences in color terminology which affect the perception of 'color.' However, as Greene (1975:70) points out, the question that immediately comes to mind is 'whether it really is a matter of *perceiving* things differently or whether it is just that we talk about them differently.'

From many experimental studies on language and perception, it appears that the discriminations and objects which are important to a certain group of people who speak the same language are simply named and differentiated by that language. As Roger Brown (1958:262-3) observes, languages differ in the categories they name or label and code grammatically *(codifiability)*, in addition to obvious phonological, morphological, and syntactic differences. Children learn these categories through their parents and their environment. However, the codifiability of a language has been shown to be separate from perception and cognition by Piaget (1968) and his followers who have continually shown that it is impossible for a child to understand a verbal expression until the underlying concept or logical operation has been mastered.

In a recent study, Fishman (1980) gives six reasons that weigh against the relativistic hypothesis: (1) *difference*: How can we tell whether language structures are significantly different? It certainly cannot be done, as Whorf maintained, by simple literal translations which show only surface differences in the ability to perceive certain phenomena; (2) *language-in-society*: Whorf based his theory on the view that speech communities are naturally monolingual. But even in monolingual societies, there are many structural varieties within the one language; (3) *alterability*: Language is not fixed, as Whorf assumed. If a language structure impedes what speakers want or need to say, it *can* and sometimes is changed in order to make that possible; (4) *directionality*: While language does reinforce a certain prior reality, it is insufficient to bring about that reality by itself. Morpholexemic changes, such as from *chairman* to *chairperson*, for example, have not in themselves brought about social change; (5) *human communication*: The human species is more versatile in coping with the limits of communication systems than Whorf admitted. We use all kinds of non-verbal cues and symbologies (e.g., gestures, looks, etc.) in order to communicate; (6) *cognition*: There is a vast experimental literature that supports the separation of language and cognition. From studies on brain-damaged people, for example, Gazzaniga (1973:600) observed that there are data which 'suggest that there exists in the brain a conceptual system that is separate from the natural language system.'

However, as Fishman also points out, there have been some beneficial by-products resulting from the debate connected with the relativistic hypothesis. For one thing, the ethnosciences have become more sensitive to the intricate relationship between language and culture. Moreover, Whorf's emphasis on language differences has engendered a plethora of research in the opposite direction, namely on language universals. Finally, the relativistic view of language and society has stimulated sociolinguistic research on the relationship between language structure and sociological variables.

From a pedagogical standpoint, Carroll (1973:144) observes that linguistic relativity has at least one clear implication: the systematic differences between the representational system of the source and target languages do not add up to differences in mental outlook. 'This is not to say that the speakers of a language may not have a particular world view, but if they do have one, it is more likely to have arisen from social and historical factors which have nothing to do with language.'

2.2 Neurological and Psychological Components of Language Learning

Human learning is characterized, in general, by such features as perception of pattern, cognitive organization, practice, personality, motivation, storage and memory, and neuropsychological mechanisms. Psychological research into learning aims to answer such general questions as: How do humans learn? Are there any universal patterns inherent in human learning? It also aims to answer some specific questions: What effect does the *entry behavior* (what the organism already knows) have on the learning process? What are the goals of a specific learning event? What training methods are best suited for a specific learning task?

What is learning? Mednick et al. (1973:16–17) point out that learning has at least four defining characteristics: (1) it generally causes a change in behavior; (2) it comes about as a result of practice or experience; (3) it is a relatively permanent change; (4) it is not *directly* observable, although the only way to ascertain if learning has occurred is through the observation of behavior.

In the case of language, it is convenient to make a terminological distinction between learning and acquisition. Krashen (e.g., 1976, 1977) defines language *acquisition* as the *subconscious* creative construction process used by children in acquiring first and second languages, as well as by adults. Language *learning*, on the other hand, is the *conscious* process by which explicit rules are assimilated and monitored. Adult learners are more likely to 'learn' the second language during the initial stages by consciously monitoring their speech through the knowledge of rules. Only later does acquisition take place. A difference between the two can be illustrated by comparing the speech of second-language learners in 'structured' and 'free' learning situations. In such structured learning situations as drills and exercises, learners are capable of using with a high degree of accuracy what they have 'learned.' But in free learning situations (e.g., spontaneous oral conversation), language learners will produce only what they have 'acquired' to any degree of accuracy. In other words, language acquisition is 'automatic' while language learning is 'controlled' (see also Carroll 1981).

In this section, we will examine the neurological and psychological mechanisms which underlie both language acquisition and language learning. In Chapter 3 we will focus on language acquisition and in Chapter 4, on language learning.

2.2.1 LANGUAGE AND THE BRAIN

Many fascinating neurological questions arise from the study of language acquisition and language learning: Where is language localized in the brain? How is language encoded and decoded? That branch of linguistics which deals with such questions is known as *neurolinguistics*.

Neurologists have discovered that the brain can be divided, or 'mapped,' into areas with specialized functions, such as motor activities (movements) and sensory perceptions (see Figure 2.2). The brain consists of approximately ten billion nerve cells, known as *neurons*, which are connected by fibers. The intricate network of neurons is called the *gray matter* which forms the surface, or *cortex*, of the brain. The connecting fibers are found under the cortex in the so-called *white area*. The cerebral cortex is the decision-making organ of the body, receiving sensorial messages and initiating all voluntary actions. It is, moreover, the storehouse of memory. The brain is divided into two parts, or *cerebral hemispheres*, one on the right and one on the left. These are connected by the *corpus callosum* which permits the two hemispheres to be in communication with each other. The left hemisphere controls movements on the right side of the body, and the right hemisphere controls movements on the left side.

44 Applied Psycholinguistics

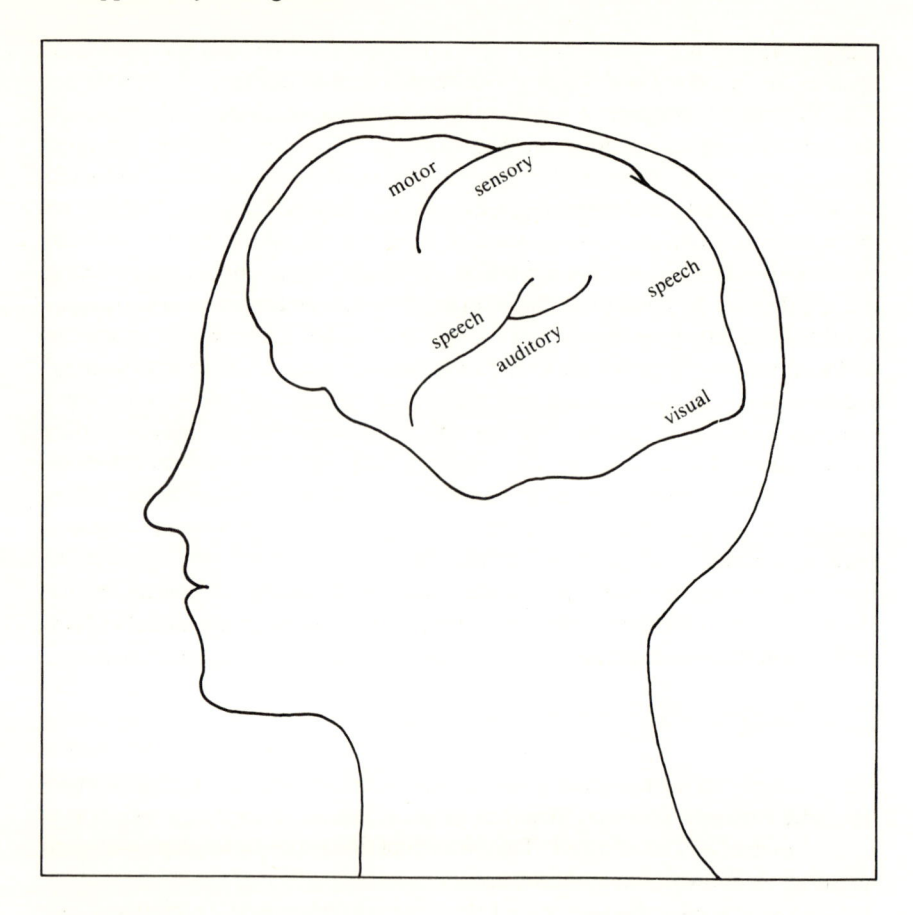

FIGURE 2.2 Specialized areas of the brain

It is now an established neurological fact that in most people the left hemisphere is responsible for speech. More specifically, language is located in two areas of the left hemisphere known as *Broca's area* and *Wernicke's area* (see Figure 2.3). However, the localization of language is related to an individual's handedness: right-handed people have speech controlled by the left hemisphere; 60 percent of left-handed people also have the language function in the left hemisphere (Gazzaniga 1973:135). Research on brain-damaged people (Gazzaniga 1970, 1973:600–4) suggests that the right hemisphere is able to take over the left-hemisphere functions to some degree.

The Language-Learning Process 45

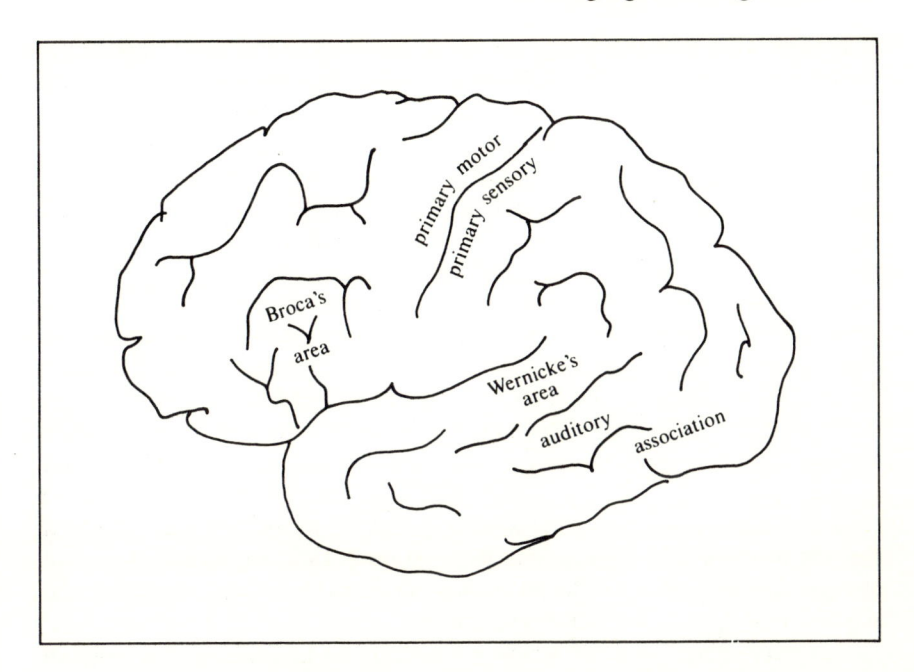

FIGURE 2.3 Speech areas in the left hemisphere (adapted from Whitaker 1971:181)

The study of pathological speech has provided most of the information vis-à-vis the localization of language. Lesions in Broca's area or near Wernicke's area in the left hemisphere produce defects in the utilization and understanding of language. Such impairments are known as *aphasias*. Damage to corresponding sites in the right hemisphere do not usually produce aphasic symptoms. As Akmajian, Demers, and Harnish (1979:308) point out: 'Approximately 70 percent of all individuals with damage to the left hemisphere will experience some type of aphasia, as compared with only 1 percent of those with right hemisphere lesions.'

The major aphasias include: (1) *auditory*, or *Wernicke's aphasia*, i.e., difficulty in comprehending spoken or written language; (2) *dysgraphia*, i.e., a disturbance of the ability to express thoughts in writing; (3) *dyslexia*, i.e., an impairment of the ability to read; (4) *dysphasia*, i.e., a partial loss of the ability to use language (a synonym for general aphasia); (5) *motor*, or *Broca's*, *aphasia* or *apraxia*, i.e., an impairment in the execution of the physiological movements necessary for speech production; (6) *anomia*, i.e., a difficulty in finding or recalling words.

Experimental evidence for the localization, or *lateralization*, of language is provided by a research technique known as *dichotic listening* which uses auditory signals to explore how stimuli are processed by the individual hemispheres. Subjects are given two different auditory signals simultaneously through earphones. For example, the right ear (left hemisphere) may be given the word 'cat' and the left ear (right hemisphere) the word 'dog.' Or, the subjects may hear a bell in one ear and a horn in the other. The subjects are then asked to identify what they hear. Responses to right-ear (left-hemisphere) stimuli are generally more correct if the stimuli are linguistic in nature. On the other hand, responses to left-ear (right-hemisphere) stimuli tend to be more correct if the signals are non-linguistic. These experiments show that the left hemisphere is not superior for processing *all* sounds, but only those which are verbal.

Of special significance to the language function is the *left thalamus* which receives nerve-fiber projections from the cortex and the lower nervous system and radiates fibers to the entire cortical region. It is believed that the thalamus is responsible for the interaction between language and memory. It is also believed that the processes of encoding and decoding result from an integrated cortical and subcortical system; i.e., language depends on the interconnection of neural sensory, motor, and associative mechanisms.

The neurological findings which are relevant to language acquisition and learning may be summarized as follows (see Krashen 1975, Schnitzer 1978, Taylor 1978). Although there is some disagreement as to the exact age when lateralization occurs, there is no doubt that it occurs sometime during childhood, probably by age six. From birth to age six the brain is undergoing rapid maturation and it is very *plastic*; it can, therefore, reorganize its functions in the event of damage. After puberty the brain has reached its full weight and has all but lost its neural plasticity. After puberty aphasias tend to be permanent.

Languages seem to be acquired most efficiently while the brain is plastic, i.e., during childhood. This period is referred to as the *critical period*, during which language is acquired effortlessly and relatively permanently. Lenneberg (1967) has shown that, from 21 to 36 months, language acquisition and hand preference occur and that cerebral dominance is established by age five. From ages eleven to fourteen foreign accents emerge and from then on the acquisition of languages becomes more difficult. After puberty approximately 97 percent of the population has language lateralized to the left hemisphere.

2.2.2 LANGUAGE AND PERCEPTION

In general, psychologists define *perception* as the experience of the objects and events in the environment upon stimulation of the sense organs. In the case of verbal stimuli, *auditory speech perception* (hearing) or *visual speech perception* (reading or sign language) are involved. Cairns and Cairns (1976:120-1) define auditory speech perception as 'the process that takes the sensation produced by the sound wave in the auditory system and produces a perceptual representation of the linguistic characteristics of utterances.'

The ability to perceive speech signals correctly is a fundamental step in learning a language. When we listen to a language that we do not know, all we hear is a linear string of sounds and tonal changes which seem to have no meaning. But when we listen to our own language being spoken, we hear a series of structured, meaningful, and frequently predictable verbal stimuli. In fact, we are able to *reconstruct* grammatically or phonologically defective messages instantaneously. Even interrupted sentences such as 'The gir_ was rid_ her b_ke' can be reconstructed easily ('The girl was riding her bike'). In other words, we do not process speech signals as separate discrete sounds but as emic categories; i.e., we discriminate among the meaningful or constant (emic) cues in the flow of speech and concomitantly group sounds into meaningful structures.

In any model of speech perception (e.g., Ervin, Walker, and Osgood 1965), there are at least three components which interact simultaneously during the decoding process. First of all, the perception of speech involves the psychophysical ability to *discriminate* speech sounds from other stimuli in the environment. Speech discrimination is part of the *projective* component. This component also allows us to *recognize* the constant or emic cues of the speech stimulus *(perceptual constancy)*. This implies the presence of perceptual *schemata* or 'mapping' mechanisms which relate the incoming speech sounds to our knowledge of linguistic structure and pattern. The second component is the *integrative* one. This component allows us to group speech sounds into units (phonemes, phrases, sentences, etc.). Perceptual integration, or *analysis by synthesis* (e.g., Halle and Stevens 1964), allows us to reconstruct broken messages and to correct automatically in our minds the pronunciation errors that a foreign speaker makes. We adjust such aberrations to fit our perceptual schemata. And finally, in the *representational* component the speech signal is assigned a semantic configuration or reading *(interpretation)*, and this is stored *(storage)* in the form of images or concepts for early retrieval (see Figure 2.4).

Some interesting experiments suggest that the basic perceptual unit is the phrase. For example, Fodor and Bever (1965) devised an ingenious experiment to show the presence of phrase boundaries in speech perception. Immediately after the subjects listened to a sentence during which a click occurred, they were asked to write down the sentence and to indicate where the click occurred. Fodor and Bever found that subjects were more inclined to be accurate in locating the locus of the click if it occurred between phrases (i.e., at a phrase boundary). They

48 Applied Psycholinguistics

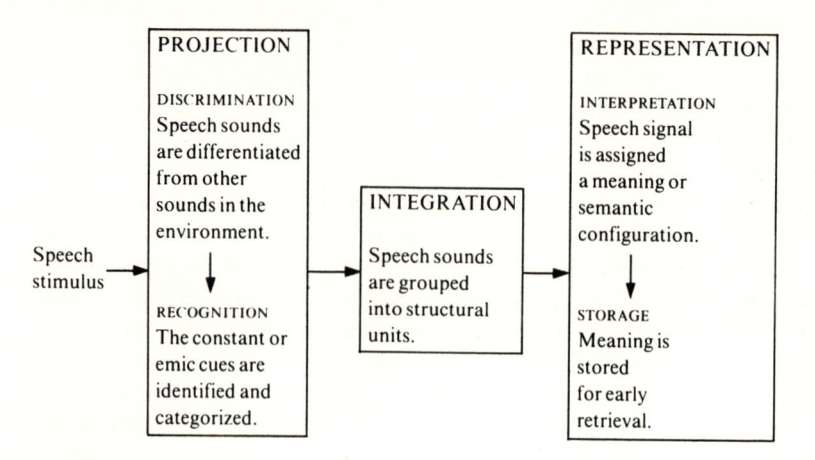

```
                    ┌─────────────────┐                        ┌─────────────────┐
                    │  PROJECTION     │                        │ REPRESENTATION  │
                    │                 │                        │                 │
                    │ DISCRIMINATION  │                        │ INTERPRETATION  │
                    │ Speech sounds   │                        │ Speech signal   │
                    │ are differen-   │                        │ is assigned     │
                    │ tiated from     │     ┌─────────────┐    │ a meaning or    │
                    │ other sounds    │     │ INTEGRATION │    │ semantic        │
                    │ in the envi-    │     │             │    │ configuration.  │
    Speech          │ ronment.        │     │Speech sounds│    │                 │
   stimulus  ─────▶ │      ↓          │ ──▶ │ are grouped │──▶ │      ↓          │
                    │ RECOGNITION     │     │into struct- │    │ STORAGE         │
                    │ The constant or │     │ural units.  │    │ Meaning is      │
                    │ emic cues are   │     └─────────────┘    │ stored          │
                    │ identified and  │                        │ for early       │
                    │ categorized.    │                        │ retrieval.      │
                    └─────────────────┘                        └─────────────────┘
```

FIGURE 2.4 An elementary model of speech perception

concluded that the smallest unit of speech perception is the phrase. Garrett, Bever, and Fodor (1966) subsequently showed that the major syntactic break could not have been signalled by an acoustic cue. Experiments such as these suggest that we perceive speech in terms of our structural and lexical knowledge. As Slobin (1971:26) remarks: 'the hearer assigns a perceptual structure to speech sounds on the basis of his knowledge of the rules of language.'

Speech perception (or decoding) is intrinsically connected to speech production (or encoding). One assumes the other. Speech production involves the same ability to integrate sounds into structural 'packages.' In addition, it involves verbal motor skills (articulation). One theory of speech perception – the 'motor theory' – goes so far as to claim that for the perception of speech the hearer actually reproduces 'silently' the speech signal by making active use of the internal knowledge of the speech-production apparatus. However, there is no direct experimental evidence that this is so (see Lieberman [1972:21–31] for an assessment of the motor theory).

There are several salient implications for language teaching that can be derived from a consideration of language and perception. For one thing, if speech is in fact perceived in terms of perceptual schemata which correspond to higher-level structures, then too much use of such devices as nonsense syllables or mimetically oriented drills will probably be a waste of time. Learners must have some control over structure and some lexical data stored away before they can perceive or understand the verbal stimuli to which they are being exposed. Moreover, since integration is an essential component of perception, the teaching process should be based on larger units rather than on isolated sounds.

2.2.3 LANGUAGE, MEMORY, AND COGNITION

After speech signals have been processed by perceptual mechanisms, they are somehow stored for possible retrieval. Thus, another crucial component of verbal processing and learning is *memory*. The memory system consists of three main stages. There is, first of all, a *sensory storage* stage which involves little more than direct perception. The verbal information in this stage is generally lost within seconds unless the information content captures one's attention, in which case the information is transformed into a more stable form and passed on to a second stage, *short-term memory*. Much less information is processed at this stage, but it has a longer life (around seventeen seconds). It is at this stage, as Miller (1956) found out experimentally, that information is preserved in familiar *chunks*: letters are easier to remember than nonsense forms, words easier than anagrams, etc. Chunk formation implies that previous learning, or cognitive structure, is involved. According to Miller, the maximum number of chunks that can be stored in our short-term memory is seven, plus or minus two. Thus, for example, it is easier to remember seven letters as seven chunks of information, say as seven words (*p – party*, *c – cat*, etc.), than it is to remember, say, ten random letters. If the verbal information in short-term memory is then coded or organized, it is then transferred to the third state of the memory system, *long-term memory*. Once here, it remains indefinitely, although it is not always easily retrievable (see Figure 2.5).

SPEECH STIMULUS → Sensory storage → attention → Short-term memory → cognitive organization → Long-term memory

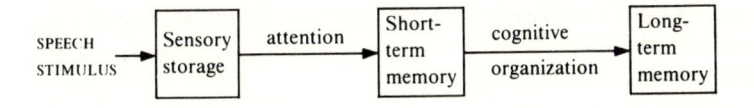

FIGURE 2.5 A basic memory system (adapted from Zimmerman and Whitehurst 1979:6)

The storage of any kind of information in long-term memory is enhanced by verbal labeling or naming. It is believed, in fact, that early-childhood memories are harder to recall, not because they are easily forgotten, but because they were not always stored by means of the sophisticated verbal labeling techniques available to older children and adults.

The coding or organizing of verbal information into a permanent form in long-term memory clearly involves *cognition*. This is simply the ability to form thoughts and ideas. Cognition implies four basic mechanisms: *grouping, differentiation, concept formation*, and *association*. Grouping is the ability to recognize pattern, i.e., to see a property shared by a group of objects. Differentiation, or discrimination, is the ability to distinguish differences between stimuli or objects. Concept formation is the process of learning concepts; it involves the ability to abstract a property of objects or events and then generalize that property to the appropriate class of objects or events. Association is the ability to form a connection between stimuli or objects. These interacting cognitive functions are involved in the coding of verbal information into long-term memory. More will be said about language and cognition in Section 2.3.2 and in subsequent chapters.

The pedagogical implications of the foregoing discussion are obvious. Mnemonic tasks (e.g., the learning of new vocabulary items or of new structural information) should be performed in meaningful chunks (not to exceed seven, plus or minus two). Rote-memorization procedures may be useful for short-term retrieval, but for long-term learning a permanent change in cognitive structure is involved. This may require some rule learning so that this type of information can be sorted indefinitely for future retrieval.

The discussion of perception, memory, and cognition can now be summarized as follows: All three psychological mechanisms interact in language decoding and encoding. During perception, sounds are grouped into meaningful phrases and stored in short-term memory. Some speech stimuli are coded and stored in long-term memory. In both instances a knowledge of linguistic structure is involved. In the case of speech production, a control of the verbal motor skills is also involved. Therefore, language learning is governed by perceptual schemata in both comprehension and production, as well as by cognitive ones. Comprehension can, of course, be both aural and visual (e.g., writing), and production can be both oral and visual (e.g., writing or sign language). The ability to store verbal information on a long-term basis implies that language learning involves some form of cognition. The ability to extrapolate concepts, code them, and store them is at the core of the language-learning process.

2.2.4 LANGUAGE AND PERSONALITY

The *personality* of the learner is an extremely important component of the language-learning process. In fact, the view that personality contributes significantly to the success or failure of second-language learning is gaining wide support in language-teaching circles.

Early theories of personality were often crude attempts to categorize individuals into types *(type theories)*. W.H. Sheldon (1940, 1954), for example, proposed a typology based on physical constitution and temperament. The three main physical types were: endomorphic (heavy), mesomorphic (muscular), and ectomorphic (thin). The three main temperament types were: viscerotonic (easy going), somatotonic (aggressive), and cerebrotonic (intellectual, artistic). Clearly, theories based on discrete categories such as these are subject to many criticisms. How does one decide, for example, which type is appropriate for a specific individual? From a pedagogical standpoint, type theories have little or no value.

Of more interest are theories which attempt to identify personality characteristics by means of measurement. These theories are known as *trait theories*, and they are based on the measurement of individual differences. They rely, therefore, on statistical techniques, like *correlation* and *factor analysis*, for the identification of traits. It is claimed that the same underlying factor controls characteristics that are interconnected *(correlation clusters)*. For example, an individual's performance on a series of verbal tests will tend to be consistent; and the factor responsible for this consistency is designated 'verbal ability.' Once these factors, or *source traits*, have been isolated and measured, an individual's personality is assessed in accordance with them. A language teacher might wish to know what a learner's measured verbal ability is in order to formulate a specific teaching strategy. However, one should always be wary of 'measured' characteristics, for they are always subject to error and misinterpretation. Moreover, one's abilities can always be improved.

Personality theories that derive from clinical psychology are known as *psychodynamic theories*. The most influential of all these theories was, of course, the one developed by Sigmund Freud. According to Freudian theory, there are three basic psychological structures which control the various personality functions: (1) The *id* is viewed as the core of personality. It constitutes the instinctive, primitive, and animal basis of human beings. The id seeks pleasure by means of the immediate gratification of the instinctive impulses. (2) The *ego* restrains the id and aligns human instinctive behavior with socially acceptable behavior. It is a pivotal structure in human personality. (3) The *superego* is the conscience of human beings. Freud maintained that these structures are normally in conflict and that, therefore, an individual's personality is governed by the dynamic interaction of the *id*, *ego*, and *superego*. The basic patterns of personality dynamics are, moreover, established during childhood. Psychodynamic theories of personality are of obvious interest to language teachers. Language learning is dominated by a person's ego which brings together perceptual and cognitive structures. It is responsible for synthesizing them during the learning process. To learn a second language involves the restructuring of one's personality in line with the new patterns of verbal behavior.

The systematic study of the learner's personality and social background leads to a better understanding of the psychological learning apparatus brought to a learning situation. Among the many personal and social factors that a teacher may wish to consider are *egocentric*, *motivational*, and *cognitive* factors.

Experiments on the relationship between self-esteem and language learning have tended to show that they correlate positively (e.g., Gardner and Lambert 1972, Brodkey and Shore 1976). The pedagogical implication is that a teacher should instill confidence in every learner. Egocentricity is a central component of learning. In addition, the learner who is motivated to perform some learning task will probably achieve a higher success rate than one who is not. More will be said about motivation in language learning in Chapter 4. Learning, or *cognitive*, style is particularly relevant for language teaching. For example, it has been found that individuals tend to develop either a *field-independent* style or a *field-dependent* one: the former refers to the ability to perceive a particular item in a field of distracting items; the latter refers to the converse tendency to depend on the total field so that parts within it are not easily perceived. The interesting point is that classroom learning environments seem to require a field-independent style (see Naiman, Fröhlich, and Stern 1975). This implies that in classroom situations one should focus on the relevant variables in a field of distracting stimuli. Thus, it is pedagogically important to identify precisely the phonological, grammatical, and semantic patterns of the language and to practice them by the use of exercises and drills. Many other variations in learning style play a part in language learning (reflectivity vs. impulsivity, tolerance vs. intolerance, etc.). While it is not known exactly how they affect the language-learning process, they certainly cannot be ignored.

2.3 Theories of Language Learning

Language teachers have much to gain from a knowledge of the psychological theories of language learning. Some aspects of language learning may require a behavioristic approach, others, a cognitive one. In fact, there is no exact theoretical formula for language teaching. As Robert Gagné (1965) has convincingly argued, human learning varies according to the context and subject matter being learned.

In this section, we will look at three main theories of language learning: *behavioristic*, *cognitive*, and *humanistic*.

2.3.1 BEHAVIORISTIC THEORIES

At the turn of this century, the famous psychologist and physiologist Ivan Pavlov conducted a series of experiments which appeared to show that some human learning results from the process of *conditioning*. In order to discuss the theory of *Pavlovian*, or *classical*, *conditioning*, an understanding of the following terms is essential: (1) *stimulus* (S): 'a physical aspect of the environment that is capable of exciting an organism's sense organs' (Gazzaniga 1973:380); (2) *unconditioned stimulus* (US): a stimulus which consistently elicits a response; (3) *conditioned stimulus* (CS): the stimulus which, when paired with an unconditioned stimulus, elicits the conditioned response; (4) *response* (R): the behavior elicited by a stimulus or set of stimuli; (5) *unconditioned response* (UR): the response elicited by the unconditioned stimulus; (6) *conditioned response* (CR): the response produced by a conditioned stimulus used in conjunction with an unconditioned stimulus.

In his experiments, Pavlov (1902) exposed a hungry dog to meat powder (the unconditioned stimulus) while simultaneously ringing a bell (the conditioned stimulus) in order to elicit salivation (the unconditioned response). After repeated pairings of the meat powder with the sound of the bell, he then removed the meat powder and found that the sound of the bell alone elicited salivation (the conditioned response). These experiments showed that a conditioned response is learned by *associating* the conditioned stimulus with the unconditioned one; i.e., a previously neutral stimulus (the sound of a bell) acquires the power to elicit a response (salivation) that is normally associated with an unconditioned stimulus (the sight or smell of meat powder). Figure 2.6 illustrates the conditioning process.

DURING CONDITIONING | AFTER CONDITIONING

US (meat powder) ⟶ UR (salivation) | CS (bell) ⟶ CR (salivation)

↑↓

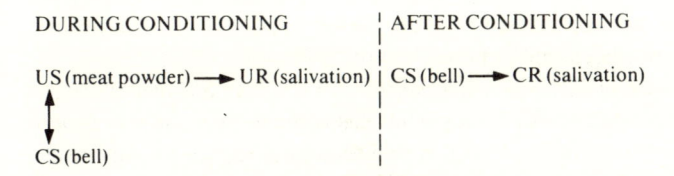

CS (bell)

FIGURE 2.6 Schematization of Pavlovian conditioning

Pavlov maintained that the learning process consisted in the formation of *associations* of this type. In a later stage of conditioning, the initial conditioned stimulus, CS_1, is associated with a second neutral stimulus, CS_2, which, after repeated pairings in close temporal contiguity, will evoke the CR when presented alone. This is known as *higher-order conditioning*, and the overall theory of learning is known as *contiguity theory*. According to this theory, the CR is elicited by the nth CS by the contiguous pairing of consecutive conditioned responses, $CS_1, CS_2, CS_3, \ldots, CS_n$. In other words, according to this theory learning results from a *chain* of stimulus-response (S-R) associations or connections (see Figure 2.7).

It was John B. Watson (1913) who probably first coined the term *behaviorism*. Watson claimed that Pavlovian conditioning explained all human learning. He believed that by the process of conditioning we build up an array of S-R connections and that complex behaviors are learned by higher-order conditioning. Along with other behaviorists, he maintained that *frequency* of conditioning affects the learning process, and that a CR may become weakened or extinguished if, over a protracted period of time, it is not reinforced by association. It is claimed, however, that extinction is prevented if *stimulus generalization* has

PAIRING OF CS$_1$ AND CS$_2$	PAIRING OF CS$_2$ AND CS$_3$	CONTIGUOUS PAIRINGS CONTINUED	PAIRING OF CS$_{n-1}$ (PENULTIMATE CS) AND C$_n$
CS$_1$ → CR ↓ CS$_2$	CS$_2$ → CR ↓ CS$_3$	...	CS$_{n-1}$ → CR ↓ CS$_n$
RESULT AFTER CONDITIONING	RESULT AFTER CONDITIONING		FINAL RESULT AFTER n PAIRINGS
CS$_2$ → CR	CS$_3$ → CR	...	CS$_n$ → CR

FIGURE 2.7 Schematization of higher-order conditioning

occurred, i.e., if the learned behavior is generalized to similar, or isomorphic, stimuli which have not been encountered before.

With the publication of *Behavior of Organisms* in 1938, B.F. Skinner charted a new course for behaviorism, establishing what has come to be known as *neobehaviorism*. According to Skinner, Pavlovian conditioning explained only a specific type of learning which was more indicative of animal learning, but which played only a small part in human conditioning. He proposed instead the theory of *operant conditioning* (also known as *instrumental learning*). According to this theory, which is based on Thorndike's *Law of Effect*, it is claimed that an organism maintains only a response that has been confirmed, or reinforced, by a reward.

Skinner distinguished between two types of responses; *respondents*, which are sets of responses elicited by recognizable stimuli (e.g., physical reflex actions), and *operants*, which are classes of responses elicited and governed by *consequences*. The former type is produced by classical conditioning, whereas the latter is produced by consequences or rewards. For example, if a dog is rewarded consistently with a piece of meat when it sits up *(positive consequence)*, it will probably exhibit that behavior again. However, if the dog receives an electric shock for its efforts *(negative consequence)*, it will eventually cease to sit up. Thus, in operant conditioning, a behavior is elicited and maintained by its consequences, whether positive or negative.

Neobehaviorists claim that learning occurs as a result of three main procedures. (1) *Simple reinforcement*: This is a consequence that increases the probability of the response being learned. If one wants a dog to continue to sit up, then a reward of meat should always accompany its action. If one wishes to extinguish this behavior, then repeated applications of electric shocks should be given.

(2) *Shaping*: This is a technique for reinforcing approximations to a final learning goal. For example, if one wishes to teach a child the word 'mama,' then a response such as 'ma' is *shaped* by reinforcing closer and closer approximations to the final response, 'mama.' (3) *Chaining*: This technique is similar to shaping in that it involves reinforcing the stages which will eventually lead to a final response. However, in this case each stage is a complete behavior in itself, and the final behavior involves *chaining* all the separate behaviors together. For example, in learning how to play the piano, one must learn to read notes, to use the correct fingering, etc. By reinforcing these separate behaviors at each appropriate learning stage, the end result will probably be the ability to play the piano.

Such theories of learning are, obviously, hard pressed to explain 'mental' phenomena such as concept formation, deductive reasoning, and problem solving. For this reason, behavioristic psychology has developed so-called *mediation theory* to account for processes of abstraction. In brief, this theory maintains that there exist implicit associative responses that mediate between an overt stimulus and an overt response. For example, when given the letters l, r, i, g to unscramble and to form a word (an anagram stimulus), one first pauses before uttering 'girl' (response). Mediation refers to what occurs during the pause between the stimulus and the overt response (e.g., Mowrer 1954).

In the case of verbal meaning, the mediation process can be illustrated as follows. (1) The referent of a word (what it refers to) elicits a response, R_t. (2) Some portion of R_t becomes 'detached' and can be labeled as r_t. (3) The referent and word are associated together by repeated pairings. (4) The word finally acquires a meaning when it evokes r_t, the detachable portion of R_t. In other words, the meaning of the word *cat* is understood when it elicits a portion of the total behavior elicited usually by a cat (the animal) (see Figure 2.8). Mowrer's

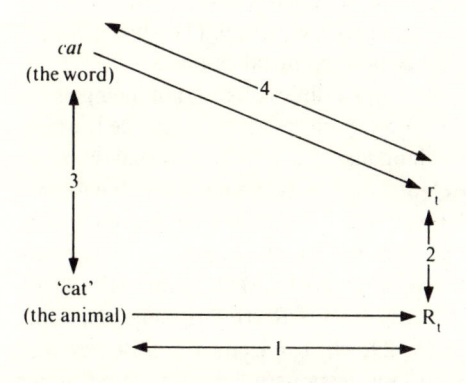

FIGURE 2.8 A schematization of Mowrer's mediation theory

56 Applied Psycholinguistics

theory was refined further by Osgood (e.g., 1953, 1957). According to Osgood a stimulus Ṡ (e.g., a cat, the animal) elicits a total behavior R_t. The word *cat*, which is originally a neutral stimulus [S], is paired with Ṡ; i.e., the word and the animal are associated together. Part of the R_t is detached and is symbolized as r_m, which is the *representational mediation response*: representational because it 'represents' the behavior produced by Ṡ and mediational because it 'mediates' between [S] and the responses it evokes, symbolized as R_x. The r_m then elicits s_m, which is a type of 'self-stimulation' or conscious awareness of meaning; it is an 'internal' stimulus which leads to R_x. Finally, R_x is one's observable behavior to [S] (see Figure 2.9). In 1963, Osgood elaborated the theory further into a *three-stage*

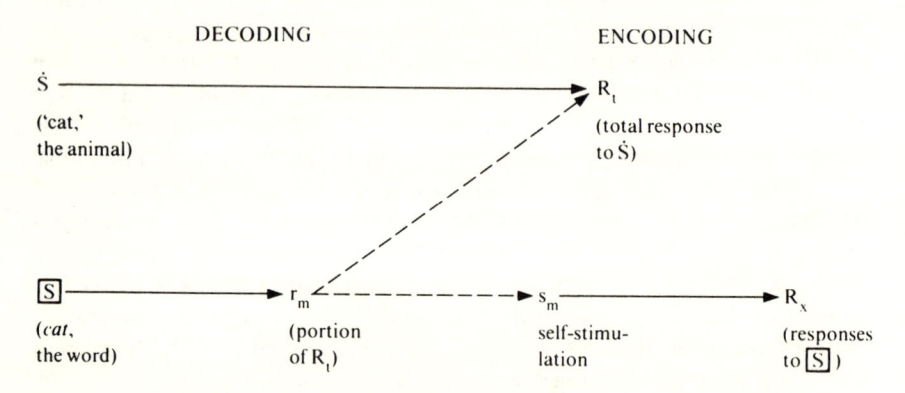

```
              DECODING                              ENCODING

Ṡ ─────────────────────────────────────────► R_t
('cat,'                                        (total response
the animal)                                    to Ṡ)



[S] ──────────────► r_m ◄─ ─ ─ ─ ─ ─ ─ ► s_m ──────────────► R_x
(cat,              (portion              self-stimu-         (responses
the word)          of R_t)                lation             to [S])
```

FIGURE 2.9 A schematization of Osgood's mediation theory

mediational model. In this model, there are three levels: (1) *projection*, where the neural relay system is involved in eliciting an automatic response to a stimulus; (2) *integration*, where S-R events are paired together frequently; (3) *representation*, where the connection between a word and its referent takes place.

The behaviorists' view of language learning is a direct offshoot of their general learning theories. In *Verbal Behavior* (1957), Skinner described language learning as operant conditioning. He argued that language is a system of verbal operants that become habitualized by means of associative chaining. In behavioristic theory, a verbal *habit* is considered to be an instrumentally and/or osmotically learned response that occurs regularly. This model of language was severely criticized by Chomsky (1959) but defended staunchly by MacCorquodale (1970).

The view that language learning is a result of S-R conditioning has come frequently under attack. R. Clark (1975: 293–9), for example, observes that behavioristic theories are concerned with how responses are formulated rather than with how they come to be produced in the first place. In an influential article,

Miller (1965) points out that behaviorism cannot explain the following features of language: (1) some physical features of speech are not significant for communication, and not all significant features have a physical representation. This implies that language is not completely observable; (2) the meaning of an utterance is not equivalent to its reference; (3) the meaning of an utterance is not the sum of the meanings of the words which comprise it; (4) the syntactic organization of sentences governs their meaning; it is abstract and not directly observable; (5) there is no limit to the number of sentences and meanings that can be expressed; (6) the description of language and the description of a language user are different; (7) there is a large biological component to the human capacity for speech. This implies that language learning is not totally acquired from environmental stimuli.

Although strictly behavioristic approaches to language teaching are being abandoned in large scale, it is our opinion that some aspects of behavioristic learning theory should be retained if they are shown suitable to some specific learning task. For example, the acquisition of motor verbal skills is naturally instrumental. The teacher should select a teaching strategy on the basis of a particular learning situation.

2.3.2 COGNITIVE THEORIES

The experimental literature on behavioristic learning theory shows quite clearly that some aspects of behavior can be observed, controlled, and studied directly. On the other hand, there is a side to human behavior that is not directly observable: thinking, the organization of knowledge, etc. The theory that seeks to explain such behavior is known as *cognitive theory*. Like the Gestalt psychologists (e.g., Koffka 1935, Köhler 1947), cognitive theorists focus on thoughts, ideas, and images as the basic units of learning. *Cognition* is a general term that designates the various modes of knowing: reasoning, remembering, forgetting, recognizing, perceiving, conceptualizing, imagining, etc. The study of cognition involves, therefore, such areas as information processing, perception, storage and retrieval.

One of the basic views held by cognitive psychologists is that what an organism knows about its environment has been transformed not only by the sense organs but also by complex structures or systems that process, interpret, and reinterpret the sensory input. The organism is thus considered an active participant that selects only the meaningful stimuli from its environment.

Two of the most influential cognitive theories of learning have been proposed by Piaget (e.g., 1962, 1968) and Bruner (e.g., 1956, 1960, 1964, 1966). According to Piaget, there are four basic features underlying cognition. (1) *Assimilation*: This refers to the ways in which information is acquired by the brain. Thinking is a function not only of input stimuli, but also of what is already present in the brain. (2) *Accommodation*: This refers to the ways in which the brain accommodates, or accumulates, incoming environmental stimuli. (3) *Schema*: This refers to a structural unit of cognitive capacity in an existing framework onto which sensory data are inserted. (4) *Equilibration*: This is the process by which schemata, or cognitive structures, change from one state to another.

In contrast to Piaget, Bruner stresses environmental and experiential factors in learning. He distinguishes among three modes of representing, or symbolizing, in human thought: (1) *enactive*: this refers to amplifiers of human motor capacities (e.g., tool using); (2) *iconic*: this refers to amplifiers of sensory capacities (e.g., radar); (3) *symbolic*: this refers to amplifiers of reasoning capacities (e.g., language).

It is perhaps in the area of *concept learning* that cognitive psychology has made its most significant contribution. Concept learning is the acquisition of the capacity to discriminate and generalize the properties that objects or events have in common. The ability to distinguish between relevant and irrelevant properties is known as *discrimination*. For example, the concept 'triangle' is learned when the property 'three sides of any length meeting at three vertices of any angular degree' is discriminated.

Bruner et al. (1956) observed that people use different learning strategies in concept formation. In one experiment, it was noticed that some subjects developed logical strategies that depended mainly on memory. To reduce this dependence, some of the subjects concentrated on a single property at a time. For example, if the stimuli varied in shape, size, and color, the subjects would focus on only one of these until they decided whether it was useful to the discovery of the concept that was being sought. In contrast, other subjects focused on two properties at a time, thus increasing their risk: if the choice was incorrect, they gained almost nothing from the trial. This strategy was more common in subjects who were forced to work under time pressure. Bruner and his colleagues suggested that both thinking and planning play a part in concept learning. In other words, concept learning is not a passive activity, but rather a deliberate and conscious one.

In the area of language learning, cognitive psychology has received most of its theoretical thrust from transformational linguistics. Cognitive psycholinguists maintain that language learning cannot be explained solely as the acquisition of a set of habits by the process of conditioning, as the behaviorists would have it. As Ausubel (1968:108) points out, the type of rote learning stressed by behaviorists is valid only for short-term memory, whereas for long-term memory *meaningful* learning is almost always involved. Meaningful learning is the process of relating new material to the relevant schemata or areas of cognitive structure. As new material enters the cognitive field, it interacts with the existing schemata. Rote learning, on the other hand, involves the mental storage of items without connecting them to existing cognitive structure.

Two classic experiments on meaningful language learning were conducted over thirty years ago by Noble (1952a, 1952b). He constructed a long list of two-syllable words which contained ordinary English words and nonsense words (or paralogs). He obtained an index of meaning for each word by counting the average number of associations given by the subjects to each word in a sixty-second time interval. The indices ranged from a low of 0.99 associations for the paralog *gojey* to 9.61 associations for the word *kitchen*. The subjects were then compared on their rate of learning the words by the method of *serial anticipation*. This is a learning method in which items are arranged in a series and the subjects must anticipate the next item in the series; i.e., the subjects must respond with one word when presented with another word. Noble found that the authentic English words were easier to learn than the paralogs, thus showing that it is easier to retain meaningful material.

The relevance of cognitive theory to language learning is obvious. As Brown (1980:74) puts it: 'Too much rote activity, at the expense of meaningful communication in language classes, could stifle the learning process.' According to cognitive learning theory, rote-learning procedures such as repetition and imitation have only a small role to play in language learning and teaching. Too much use of grammatical explanation, moreover, can be counterproductive, unless it is made meaningful. As Chastain (1971:92) observes: 'The role of the teacher is to recognize the importance of mental activity in learning and to organize the information presented in such a way that the new material is easily assimilated into the learner's existing field of knowledge.'

2.3.3 HUMANISTIC THEORIES

The term 'humanistic' has two meanings as employed in the field of language teaching. It refers, first of all, to the interpersonal and student-centered approaches which sprung up in the late 1970s. Second, it refers to the integrated, or 'eclectic,' methodologies which have also sprung up in the past decade.

The interpersonal approach has probably been influenced, to some extent, by the client-centered psychology of Carl Rogers (e.g., 1951, 1961). In such an approach the personality of the learner plays a more important part in the language-teaching process. The focus is on affective, rather than on instrumental or cognitive, variables in language learning. According to Rogers, all human motives derive from the drive towards self-actualization, not from the instincts. He maintains that all persons have a natural urge to realize their potential and to function autonomously. This tendency will flourish under conditions of warmth and acceptance by others and by oneself. But when these conditions are lacking, people tend to distort their experiences in order to avoid the discomfort they may cause. In Rogers' client-centered approach, people are helped to remove whatever obstacles lie in the way to self-actualization. His psychoanalytic therapy focuses on the client's present feelings, emotions, and attitudes.

Rogers' psychoanalytic theory has one important implication for language education: it shifts the focus away from teaching towards learning. One of the best ways to facilitate the learning process, according to Rogers, is to establish an interpersonal relationship with the learner. The teacher should always respect and appreciate the individual learner as a human being. The development of an open attitude is therefore essential. The teacher should also try to 'humanize' the learning atmosphere. The teacher should be perceived as a 'facilitator' in the learning process. Some educators involved in this field suggest that teachers place themselves among the learners in a classroom situation rather than at the head of the class. This creates a less formal learning context.

Clearly, the creation of a personal and congenial learning environment is a desirable thing. But the lack of explicit, or formal, learning-teaching procedures could lead to a lack of direction and eventually to frustration. Some educators have therefore suggested that interpersonal techniques be integrated with cognitive ones, especially at the beginning of the learning process. Moreover, if the teacher finds the interpersonal approach uncomfortable, this could lead to serious pedagogical problems. But despite such misgivings, the interpersonal approach in language teaching, when put into a broader perspective, can be conducive to successful language learning. Affective variables play an extremely important role in language learning. The role of motivation, for example, should not be underestimated. More will be said about affective variables in Chapter 4.

The recent trend towards 'eclectic' methodologies – the other meaning of 'humanism' in language teaching – has had at least one beneficial effect: it has instilled more flexibility in language-teaching methodology. Some language-learning tasks may require a behavioristic approach (e.g., articulation); others, a more cognitive one (e.g., word order); still others may require an interpersonal approach (e.g., free speech exercises).

One of the first attempts to integrate behavioristic and cognitive viewpoints can be found in Levelt (e.g., 1974). Levelt distinguishes three factors in language acquisition: (1) *process factors*, the general possibilities and limitations of information processes (perception, storage, etc.); (2) *semantic factors*, the intention of a sentence; (3) *conceptual factors*, the system of concepts present in the human organism. According to Levelt, elements of both behaviorism and cognitive psychology should be integrated into a truly explanatory model of language acquisition. The activation of process, semantic, and conceptual factors in language acquisition depends both on environmental stimulation and on conceptual or semantic processing. The human organism disposes of little or no foreknowledge of the grammar it is acquiring, but it can deduce it by means of strong heuristic principles. As Levelt puts it (1974:161), grammars 'are learnable by means of a certain S-R mechanism in which correct responses are confirmed and incorrect responses are not confirmed.' However, he cautions that such an explanation 'does not increase our insight into what actually happens during learning' (1974:161). He suggests that a good model would also contain a description of the cognitive-inference mechanism. In essence, Levelt attempts to show that both the behavioristic and cognitive viewpoints are only partially explanatory. A more comprehensive model would be one in which elements of both have been integrated.

An attempt to integrate behavioristic, cognitive, and humanistic (affective) theories can, in fact, be found in the work of Titone (e.g., 1977a). His so-called 'glossodynamic' model will be examined in Chapter 7.

2.4 A Pedagogical Summary

We can now summarize some of the obvious pedagogical implications that can be derived from a consideration of the psychology of verbal learning. (1) There is a difference between language acquisition and language learning. The former is automatic; the latter is controlled. The language teacher can intervene primarily to facilitate learning. However, the goal should always be acquisition. A study of the acquisition patterns of children learning their first language will obviously provide some useful pedagogical insights. Language acquisition will be discussed in Chapter 3. (2) The teacher should always keep in mind that there is a neurological limitation to the learning of language after the age of puberty. Since by this time the language function has been lateralized and the brain has all but lost its plasticity, the teacher should expect, and consequently tolerate, many errors. More will be said about this in Chapter 4. (3) Since language learning involves, a priori, the ability to perceive the meaningful emic cues in the flow of speech, the teacher should concentrate during the initial learning stages on exposing the learner to many examples of the language. However, since perception involves control over structure and lexical data, the teacher should make sure that structural and lexical features are explicitly presented from the very beginning. (4) For short-term recall, mimetic and repetition exercises can be used profitably. But for long-term storage and retrieval, the psychological literature shows clearly that 'meaningful' learning tasks should be involved. More will be said about this in Chapter 5. (5) The teacher should expect comprehension to precede production. This is probably due to the psychological fact that the ability to perceive emic cues develops prior to their effective use in production. (6) The personality and cognitive style of the learner play a crucial role in the learning process. Teachers should synchronize their teaching strategies with the personality of their learners, otherwise they will probably find that their efforts will turn out to be fruitless. The educational background, motivations, attitudes, etc., of the learners should be assessed and taken into account in the development of a pedagogical program. More will be said about this in Chapter 4. (7) The behaviorist, cognitive, and humanist viewpoints of learning can all contribute in helping the teacher select an appropriate teaching strategy for a specific learning task. Those tasks requiring motor development may benefit from behavioristic rote-learning procedures. In contrast, those tasks which involve cognition might benefit from problem-solving techniques.

In essence, therefore, the literature on the psychology of language learning provides the teacher with several general pedagogical insights. These may relate to the teacher's expectations and attitudes vis-à-vis the possibilities and limitations of the learning task; or they may help the teacher formulate both a general and a specific teaching strategy.

2.5 Signposts

Perhaps the line of investigation that is receiving the greatest amount of attention at present in the area of the psychology of language learning is the theory of the critical period and lateralization in general. Some researchers are beginning to cast some doubt on the role of the critical period in determining successful language learning. For one thing, it is becoming clearer that the right hemisphere of the brain has considerable 'competence' with respect to the comprehension of language. Indeed, several studies in Scarcella and Krashen (1980) suggest that the right hemisphere might be involved directly during the initial learning stages, whereas conscious monitoring of the input – a left-hemisphere function – occurs later on. If this is the case, then the pedagogical implications are obvious: teaching methods should vary according to the stage of learning with more 'oral' and 'creative' tasks preceding those that are more formally oriented. But much more research in this area is needed.

Recently, Krashen (1982:9) has suggested that the ability to communicate in the new language develops in accordance with what language material the learner needs and is ready to acquire. As Krahnke and Christison (1983:627) put it: 'it is hypothesized that learners can acquire language when they have to use it to communicate their wants and needs, when the focus is on *what* they need to say rather than on *how* they should say it.'

2.6 Suggestions for Further Reading

A good general introduction to the psychology of learning is found in Marx (1964). More detailed treatments of language learning can be found in Chastain (1971), Oldfield and Marshall (1968), Allen and Corder (1975), Miller and Johnson-Laird (1976), Mowrer (1980), and Studdert-Kennedy (1983). A good collection of studies on cognition and language learning is Piattelli-Palmarini (1980).

3
First-Language Acquisition

> *By investigating how children acquire their native language, the linguist, as well as the psychologist, expects to find evidence about the nature and properties of the human mind.*
> (Falk 1978:317)

3.0 Introduction

By the end of their first year, children are already attempting to imitate speech sounds and words. At eighteen months, their words having multiplied considerably, they start trying to communicate one-, two-, and three-word sentences. By age three, they have an incredible control over the perception and production of speech. The child discovers very soon that the ability to speak plays a central role in life at home. Perhaps the most intriguing question asked by psycholinguists is: How is language acquired? Until recently, the research on first-language acquisition was practically limited to diary-like recordings of observed speech. But in the last couple of decades giant strides have been taken towards understanding the psychological mechanisms that underlie this unique phenomenon.

Our purpose in this chapter is to describe some of the theories and research on first-language acquisition. An understanding of how children learn to speak may offer some valuable insights into how language is learned in general, a subject that has obvious pedagogical implications.

3.1 Patterns of First-Language Acquisition

The first noises an infant makes are *cooing* sounds. These have been examined on *sound spectrographs*, which produce visual representations *(spectrograms)* of the acoustic properties of sounds. These spectrograms show quite clearly that infant cooing sounds are acoustically quite different from the sounds of ordinary language, that is, vowels and consonants (see Liebert, Poulos, and Strauss [1974:290–6] for a detailed description of the cooing stage). However, during the *babbling* stage (from around six to twelve months), attempts to imitate adult speech patterns, especially intonational ones, emerge (e.g., Weir 1962, Miller and Ervin 1964). Soon after the first year, children start to utter one-word sentences, or *holophrases*; i.e., they use one word to express the meaning of an entire phrase, sentence, or utterance. Two-word sentences start to appear near the second birthday, and these are soon followed by three-word utterances. From then on, the control of language increases dramatically until, by the age of six, children have acquired their native language (see Appendix B for a time chart comparing motor and verbal development as described by Lenneberg [1967]).

In this section, we will examine some of the patterns that characterize phonological, grammatical, and semantic development as they have been reported in the vast literature on this subject.

3.1.1 PHONOLOGICAL DEVELOPMENT

W.R. Miller (1963:863) provides us with the following typical humorous observation: 'Recently a three year old child told me her name was Litha. I answered "Li*th*a?" "No, Litha." "Oh, Lisa?" "Yes, Litha."' The child in this anecdotal account is obviously able to perceive the phonemic difference between /s/ and /θ/ but is not able to produce it phonetically. This shows quite clearly that the ability to perceive or comprehend speech precedes production or motor development. Perhaps the most dramatic example of perceptual priority has been provided by Lenneberg's (1962) case study of an anarthric (speechless) child. This child was able to understand stories perfectly and to answer questions about the stories by pointing to pictures or by nodding his head. However, he could not produce normal articulated speech.

The literature on articulatory development is large, and it would be out of place to describe it in detail here. We will limit our discussion, therefore, to a general overview.

Kaplan and Kaplan (1970) point out that five main stages have been documented with regard to the perception and processing of speech sounds during the first six months of life: (1) during the first few weeks, the infant is able to localize sounds and perceive differences of frequency, temporal patterning, and duration; (2) the infant can discriminate speech stimuli from others in the environment from about two weeks on; (3) from about two months on, the infant starts to respond to affective voice patterns and to distinguish familiar from unfamiliar voices; (4) at about five or six months the infant starts to recognize suprasegmental features: (5) from six months on, the infant starts to perceive segmental contrasts.

Some recent studies on infant perception have shown, however, that segmental discrimination may occur at a much earlier stage. Using a heart-rate measure, Moffitt (1971) showed that five-month-old infants could discriminate the difference between /b/ and /g/ in monosyllabic forms; Morse (1972) found the same in seven-week-old children; and Mehler and Bertoncini (1979) have discovered, amazingly, that infants only a few days old already have the ability to process speech in a different manner from the way in which they process other acoustic stimuli. It seems that perceptual speech schemata emerge very early indeed in infancy.

One of the early interesting descriptions of phonological development was undertaken by Jakobson (1941) who studied the chronological development of discrete phonemes vs. phonological categories. According to Jakobson, phonological development follows a universal pattern: children distinguish among phonological categories first and then proceed to make finer discriminations among single segments within each category. He called this phenomenon *progressive differentiation*. Thus, for example, a child acquiring English will learn to discriminate between stop and fricative sound classes before learning to distinguish between any two stops or any two fricatives. This was corroborated by Leopold (1953–4) who observed that children learn to distinguish low vowels from high vowels first, then mid vowels, and eventually more refined subcategories (front *vs.* back, etc.). Jakobson postulated, in effect, a universal hierarchy among distinctive features so that the distinction between high and low in a vowel system is higher ranked than in mid range – a point borne out in part by studies of language families and types.

However, as Velten (1943) has shown, there are some doubts about the 'universality' of Jakobson's theory. Velten noted that the monosyllabic forms [ba], [da], and [za] produced by his daughter stood for different concepts: [ba] = 'bottle'; [da] = 'down'; [za] = 'that.' These forms were, in effect, minimal pairs showing a contrast among [b], [d], and [z]. Moreover, he found minimal pairs in which corresponding voiceless consonants, [p], [t], [s], also contrasted phonemically among themselves. However, he could not determine if contrasts existed between corresponding voiced ([b], [d], [z]) and voiceless ([p], [t], [s]) consonants. But he did find that the voiced consonants always occurred in initial position (e.g., [ba], [da], [za]) and the voiceless ones in final position (e.g., [ap], [at], [as]). These consonants obviously were in complementary distribution and the pairs [b, p], [d, t], [z, s] could probably be ascribed to single phonemes each. What Velten found, in other words, was that his daughter had learned to discriminate between single phonemic segments first before having learned to perceive the difference between the phonological categories marked *voiced* and *voiceless*.

However, it must be kept in mind that observational studies of this sort are always subject to various interpretations. A summary of experimental control procedures is given in Chapter 6. It is, in fact, quite difficult to sort out what the child actually perceives. As E.V. Clark (1977:45) remarks: 'Even if the infant does discriminate differences between one sound and another, one does not know which parameter and which combination of parameters are necessary for the child to do this. Nor does the fact of discrimination alone tell us how the child goes from discrimination among speech sounds to recognition of their meaningfulness in speech.'

Despite such reservations, several patterns of phonological development have been identified in psycholinguistic research. (1) In order to discriminate phonemic differences, the child must obviously learn to discriminate differences in meaning as signaled by different words; i.e., phonology does not develop independently of other parts of language. (2) Despite Velten's findings, it seems to be true that in general children learn sounds by first distinguishing maximal differences (e.g., vowels vs. consonants) and then proceed to differentiating smaller ones (e.g., front vs. back). (3) Children perceive many more phonological contrasts than they are at first able to produce.

The development of phonology in children has at least one salient implication for second-language teaching. As language teachers continually discover, beginning learners seem to have little or no difficulty comprehending elementary speech patterns in the target language. But their efforts to articulate words always seem to be arduous. In second-language learning, as in first-language acquisition, there seems to be little doubt that comprehension precedes production. The teacher should accept this fact as a basic heuristic principle. Second-language learners will be able to perceive the phonemic cues of the target language much more easily than they will be able to produce those contrasts which are not operational in their own native language.

3.1.2 GRAMMATICAL DEVELOPMENT

Shortly after the babbling stage, children start to produce *holophrastic* (one-word) utterances. These are their first acts of communication implying that a huge amount of conceptual learning has occurred. It is at this point in their verbal development that they somehow start to perceive the phonemic cues in the flow of speech and start to relate, in an overt manner, sounds to meanings. Thus, for example, an utterance such as 'Up!' could stand for 'Get me up!' or, 'Do!' could stand for 'I will do it!' These holophrases serve three basic communicational functions: (1) naming an object or event; (2) expressing an action or a desire for some action; (3) conveying emotional states. Holophrases are typically monosyllabic reductions of adult words, e.g., *da* for *dog* or *ca* for *cat*. The holophrastic stage normally appears around the first birthday and lasts between three and nine months. Psychologically, this stage suggests that the child's conceptual ability is not yet manifested in speech. The child can obviously think about ideas and concepts, as the holophrases attest, yet lacks the ability to verbalize about them in a full way.

It is around the age of eighteen months that one begins to notice the emergence of two-word utterances. This period of development is often referred to as the *telegraphic stage*. The important feature about telegraphic utterances is that their constituent words are not put together in a haphazard fashion. They exemplify word order and structural function. For example, in utterances such as 'More milk' or 'Hat off' there is no pause between the words, showing both a breath group and phrase structure; and, more importantly, the constituent words belong to different paradigmatic classes. Some psycholinguists refer to the grammatical structure of these utterances as *pivot grammar*. Words such as 'more' and 'off' are called *pivots* (Braine 1963) because they belong to a small fixed class of grammatically functional or operational words. The other words are known as *open* words because they belong to a larger class of words which were previously holophrases. One can make an analogy to adult grammar by comparing pivots to grammatical morphemes and open words to lexemes. Thus, 'more' is a pivot in '*More* milk' or '*More* hot' and 'off' is a pivot in 'Hat *off*' or 'Tape *off*.' A pivot grammar, therefore, can take one of three forms (S = sentence): (1) S → Pivot + Open (e.g., 'More milk'); (2) S → Open + Pivot (e.g., 'Hat off'); (3) S → Open + Open (e.g., 'Milk hot') (see Figure 3.1).

```
        S                      S                       S
       / \                    / \                     / \
    Pivot Open             Open Pivot              Open Open
      |    |                 |    |                  |    |
    More  milk              Hat  off               Milk  hot
      |    |                 |    |                  |    |
    More  hot              Tape  off                Hat  big
     etc.  etc.             etc. etc.              etc.  etc.
```

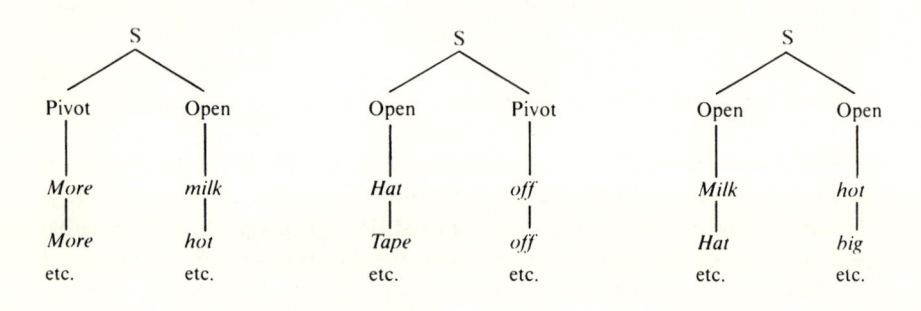

FIGURE 3.1 A typical pivot grammar

Roger Brown (1970) found in his research that the forms of a pivot grammar have various types of structural meaning. In general, the words of a pivot grammar are typically referential or relational. Referential operations include naming an object or event (nomination), indicating the presence (notice) or absence (nonexistence) of certain objects or events, and requesting that an action be repeated (recurrence). Relational operations include attribution, possession, location, agent-action, and action-object. Referential utterances consist of a pivot word followed by an open word; relational utterances consist instead of two open words (see Figure 3.2).

I. OPERATIONS OF REFERENCE
Nominations: *That* (or *It* or *There*) + *book, cat, clown, hot, big*, etc.
Notice: *Hi* + *Mommy, cat, belt*, etc.
Recurrence: *More* (or *'Nother*) + *milk, cereal, nut, read, swing, green*, etc.
Nonexistence: *Allgone* (or *No-more*) + *rattle, juice, dog, green*, etc.

Form of the grammar: S → Pivot + Open

II. RELATIONS
Attributive: *Big train, Red book*, etc.
Possessive: *Adam checker, Mommy lunch*, etc.
Locative: *Sweater chair, Book table, Walk street*, etc.
Agent-Action: *Adam put, Eve read*, etc.
Agent-Object: *Mommy sock, Mommy lunch*, etc.

Form of the grammar: S → Open + Open

FIGURE 3.2 The first sentences in child speech (adapted from Brown 1970:220)

When children start to use utterances of more than two words, they are beginning to approximate the constituent structure of adult grammar. Braine (1963) has shown that the number of two-word utterances increases rapidly between the ages of 18 months and 24 months (see Figure 3.3). Shortly thereafter, three-word sentences (e.g., 'Johnny eat that') characterize a child's speech; and by the age of four years the child has a grammar very similar to that of an adult.

During the holophrastic and telegraphic stages, the child's utterances lack morphological markers; i.e., they have no affixes or morphemes designating number, person, tense, etc. But shortly thereafter children start to acquire the inflectional and derivational morphemes of their language. By the age of four, most children exhibit a firm control over morphological structure. In a classic experiment, Jean Berko (1958) showed that preschool children have not merely

70 Applied Psycholinguistics

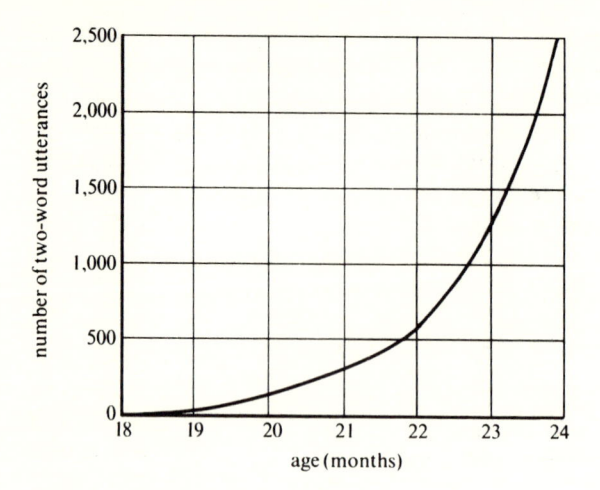

FIGURE 3.3 Number of two-word utterances as the child approaches two years of age (after Braine 1963)

FIGURE 3.4 Example of Berko's (1958) technique

memorized morphologically different forms but have instead internalized the rules of morphological construction. To show this, she presented a series of pictures of nonsense objects. She subsequently gave these objects nonsense names which the children could not have possibly heard before. Thus, for example, she would say 'This is a *wug*.' Then she would show two such objects and say 'These are two _____' (Figure 3.4). She found that her subjects did remarkably well in giving the correct response *(wugs)*. Correct responses were frequent for other morphological categories (past tense, present progressive, etc.). Clearly, these children had internalized the rules of morphological construction in English and were able to apply them to novel linguistic situations. In one longitudinal study of three children, Roger Brown (1973) found, moreover, that there is a chronological pattern to the acquisition of English morphemes. He discovered that the suffix morpheme *-ing*, designating the present-progressive form of verbs, is the earliest one to be acquired. The acquisition of the prepositions *in* and *on* follows next, and then (in order) the plural, possessive, uncontractible copula, article, third person, and uncontractible auxiliary morphemes.

In learning morphological structure, the child shows the ability to induce specific units of constant grammatical value by analogic reasoning. Braine (1963) calls this psychological phenomenon *contextual generalization*. When children hear a new sentence or form, they learn that it occurs in certain positions. They then generalize the observed distributional structure to novel utterances. This tendency often manifests itself in 'erroneous' forms such as *goed* for *went* in which the child has extended by analogic reasoning the past-tense morpheme *-ed* to an irregular verb.

As children become older, their utterances start to expand and they acquire the ability to form questions, to make negative statements, to embed clauses, etc. by the age of five, children have acquired most of the morphological and syntactic patterns of their language.

The main pedagogical implication that can be derived from the investigation of grammatical development is that human beings have in-built mechanisms that are 'programmed' to search out syntactic and morphological patterns. Teachers often encounter errors similar to the child's *goed* in their classrooms. The teacher should consequently expect and tolerate many errors of this type. More will be said about this in Chapter 4. Another pedagogical inference is related once again to the superiority of comprehension over production. Like children acquiring their native language, second-language learners are capable of understanding more complex sentences than they are able to produce. They often 'simplify' their utterances in ways similar to telegraphic speech. It appears to be a natural process in grammatical development to go from the simple to the more complex and refined.

3.1.3 LEXICAL AND SEMANTIC DEVELOPMENT

The first words that children produce are conspicuous signs that they are beginning to acquire meaning. By the age of 24 months, children have a vocabulary that numbers in the hundreds of words. Thereafter, their vocabulary expands at a very rapid rate. By the third year, they possess a one-thousand-word vocabulary (see Figure 3.5). The central question that arises in the study of semantic development is whether the learning of word meaning is connected to concept formation. At first it seems that children use words in response to immediate needs and interests. But in a very short time they somehow start to abstract the concepts represented by their words.

According to Bowerman (1977:253), the study of semantic development revolves around three key issues: (1) the kinds of cues children use as a basis for

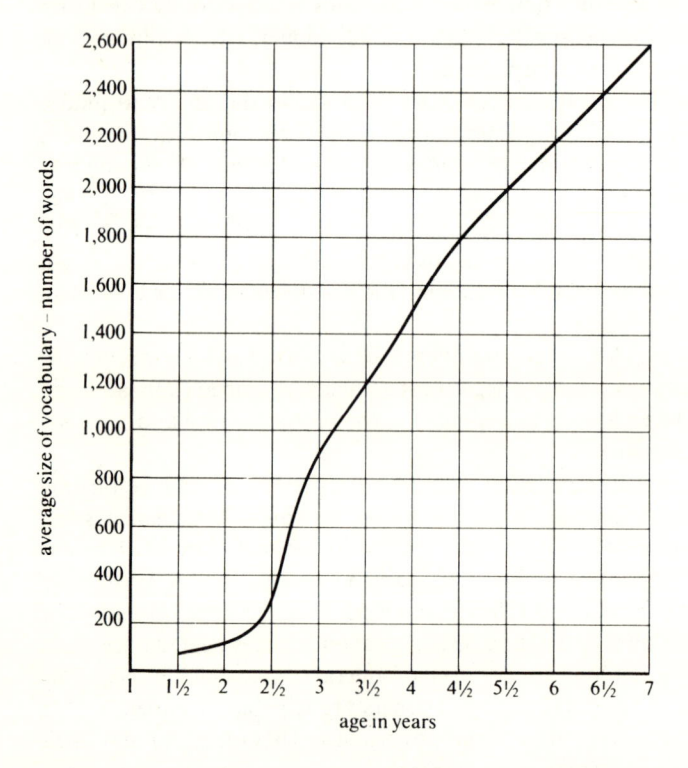

FIGURE 3.5 Size of average vocabulary of children (adapted from Liebert, Poulos, and Strauss 1974:299; based on data from Smith 1926)

extending words to novel referents early in development; (2) the semantic features that children ascribe to words; (3) the ways in which children organize and store word meanings. The research on these, and related areas, of semantic development is often ambiguous and contradictory. It is clear that no one theoretical approach can properly investigate all facets of the acquisition of meaning.

The research does, however, suggest that the acquisition of meaning is a gradual cumulative process; i.e., the relevant semantic components of a word are attached to it through experience (Clark 1973, 1975). This becomes obvious when children *over-extend* the use of a word because they may not have as yet delimited its semantic space. Thus, for example, if they learn at first that round tasty objects are called *apples*, they may use this lexical label to describe an orange or a pear. Eventually, they refine their semantic hypothesis, through experience, and are able to distinguish different genera of round tasty objects. Psychologically, two mechanisms are conspicuously at work here: *generalization* and *differentiation*. The interaction of these two mechanisms leads eventually to the appropriate delimitation of the semantic spaces covered by individual words. DeVito (1970:135) illustrates the hypothetical development of the word *daddy* in terms of four gradual stages which show the interaction of generalization and differentiation mechanisms (Figure 3.6). Semantic development thus implies that the human

STAGE 1	STAGE 2	STAGE 3	STAGE 4
(large)	(large)	(large)	(large)
	(animate)	(animate)	(animate)
		(human)	(human)
			(male)

FIGURE 3.6 Hypothetical development of a dictionary entry for the word 'daddy' (from De Vito 1970:135)

organism is somehow programmed to process and organize the incoming environmental information and then to store it in the form of permanent lexical entries. Clark (1977:22–3) observes that there are six main perceptual categories that influence semantic development, as witnessed in over-extensions: shape, size, movement, sound, texture, and taste (see Table 3.1). Thus, according to some researchers, it appears that semantic development depends on a trial-and-error process during which the child is continually adjusting hypotheses about the semantic organization of experience. This view has, however, been challenged by other researchers (e.g., Nelson 1974) who maintain that children do not analyze experience in terms of perceptual categories, but rather in terms of wholes, which

74 Applied Psycholinguistics

TABLE 3.1

Some examples of over-extensions (adapted from Clark 1977:23)

Category	Lexical item	First referent	Extensions and over-extensions
SHAPE	mooi	moon	cakes, round marks on windows, writing on window and in books, tooling on leather book covers, round shapes in books, round postmarks, the letter 'o'
SIZE	fly	fly	specks of dirt, dust, all small insects, his own toes, crumbs of bread, a toad
MOVEMENT	sch	sound of train	sound of all moving machines
SOUND	fafer	sound of trains	steaming coffee pot, anything that makes a hissing sound or any noise
TEXTURE	bow-wow	dog	toy dog, fur piece with animal head, other fur pieces without heads
TASTE	candy	candy	cherries, anything sweet

are then classified in terms of the actions and relationships associated with them, i.e., in terms of their functional similarity.

With respect to phonological and grammatical development, one thing is clear about the acquisition of meaning: it occurs much later. In fact, a refined and sophisticated semantic system does not emerge until the child is eight or nine years old. Semantic development continues through the school years and even later. This is probably due to the fact that the semantic organization of experience is a very complex phenomenon.

What insights can the language teacher glean from the research on semantic development? Although the research in this area is often obscure, there emerges at least one general pattern that is normal to the learning of words and their meanings, namely that the process of delimiting the appropriate semantic space occupied by a lexical item is a gradual one involving generalization and differentiation mechanisms. What this means for language teaching is clear: the learner will need to be exposed to the vocabulary of the target language in its proper context so that its semantic space can be arrived at by approximations. Isolated vocabulary lists will probably prove to be worthless in the teaching of words. The teacher will find, moreover, that learners tend to superimpose the semantic space occupied by their native-language words onto the semantic space occupied by corresponding target-language words. When these two do not coincide, typical errors in usage (e.g., over-extensions, under-extensions, etc.) will characterize the speech patterns of the learner.

3.2 Factors Influencing Language Development

We will now look briefly at the types of factors which shape and influence first-language acquisition. These factors fall into three broad categories: neurological, psychological, and environmental.

As in all developmental processes, neurological and physiological factors play a determining role in the development of language. The human organism is designed and programmed biologically to learn language. At birth, infants cannot make certain kinds of speech sounds because their neurological and anatomical apparatus is not yet ready for speech production. A certain amount of physical maturation must occur before language can be produced. As pointed out in the previous Section 2.2.1, most of the language function is lateralized early in life, certainly by puberty. During childhood the plasticity of the brain is at a maximum, and this may explain why children can learn to speak several languages without any trace of an accent. After puberty, languages are almost invariably spoken with an accent derived from the native language.

Using data on brain-damaged children, Lenneberg (1967) concludes that lateralization is completed around puberty. This conclusion is prompted by three kinds of evidence: (1) damage to the right hemisphere is connected to language disorders more often in children than in adults, indicating a greater right-hemisphere contribution to language in children; (2) unilateral hemispherectomies (removal of a hemisphere) performed during childhood do not appear to result in aphasia, regardless of which hemisphere is removed; (3) the chance of recovery from acquired aphasia resulting from unilateral lesions is much better in children. Lenneberg gives a time chart relating the data on hemisphere lesions to the neurological and maturational factors involved in language acquisition (see Appendix C). Krashen (1973, 1975), however, interprets the same data considered by Lenneberg differently and suggests that lateralization occurs as early as five years of age. Krashen also cites evidence from dichotic-listening experiments which shows that lateralization occurs much earlier than at puberty. If Krashen is correct, then investigators will have to look for explanations other than neurological ones to account for differences in child and adult language-learning patterns. Krashen's age-five hypothesis is certainly consistent with the fact that children have acquired most of their language by the age of five. The point of such neurological investigations into language acquisition is that lateralization is a process that occurs during childhood, even though there may be some disagreement as to when it is completed. The role of neurology in second-language learning will be discussed in Chapter 4.

As pointed out for the development of morphology and meaning, there are two basic psychological mechanisms at work in language acquisition: generalization and differentiation. These mechanisms interact with perceptual ones in both the processing and eventual production of speech. Another mechanism of early language development is integration (Brown and Bellugi 1964). This refers to the development of phrase structure in children who are apparently able to develop hypotheses about grammatical rules and then construct their own grammar in successive stages which approximate adult grammar. As Griffin (1968:51) puts it: 'in the production of syntactic structures children's development toward adult norms is not a smooth progression but resembles a "damped oscillatory function".' Another psychological mechanism worth mentioning here, and which has not received much attention, is the *metalinguistic awareness* of children, i.e., what they know about language as a system. In a recent study, Gleitman, Gleitman, and Shipley (1972), observing that children often ask questions about language, conducted an experiment in which five- and eight-year-old children were given deviant sentences and then asked to make judgments about them. They found, to no one's surprise, that most of the subjects were able to supply correct forms. But what was more interesting was the finding that most of the subjects provided rather sophisticated explanations about the deviant structures. In Section 3.3 we will look at psychological explanations of first-language acquisition more closely.

In connection with the environmental input in first-language acquisition, the main question that comes to mind is: What is the nature and effect of the linguistic input to children? At first, children seem to be merely imitating what they hear until they start producing telegraphic speech. But imitative behavior alone, although useful for language learning, is not necessary. Some children never seem to imitate at all, yet develop language normally anyway. The spontaneous imitation of what they hear in their environment is only one of several strategies employed by children in acquiring their language. Perhaps the most significant environmental factor influencing language development is the language used by adults when speaking to children. Adults typically use three types of communicative strategies: *expansion*, *modeling*, and *reduction*. If a child says 'Johnny eat,' then the mother might answer him by saying 'Does Johnny want to eat?' Such expansions are clearly intended to provide the child with an exemplary version of adult grammar. For this reason, research (e.g., Waterson 1971, Halliday 1975) has shown that the speech used by adults to children, although very simple, is perfectly grammatical. A modeling strategy is employed when adults speak normally when responding to child speech. For example, in response to 'Johnny eat' the mother might answer: 'Ok, we will have lunch together.' A reduction strategy is a simplification of the language used in line with the stage of development of the child. This may consist in the use of simple sentences resembling telegraphic speech, a slower rate of speech, a limited vocabulary, exaggerated stress and intonation patterns, etc. (Farwell 1973). The question that comes to mind is whether adults actually reduce and simplify fully formed sentences, or whether they reduce the scope of speech acts. Parents soon learn that complex sentences produce no response from their children if they are beyond the possibilities of their stage of development. Thus, reduction strategies may be ways of making sure that children will understand the message, as well as the form, that is being communicated to them. Thus, it is not unusual to find that adults adjust their speech patterns to the stage of language development manifested by their children. Children at the pivot and telegraphic stages respond best to telegraphic speech. As children respond to adult speech with increasing complexity, adults also seem to increase gradually the complexity of their own speech. In this way, adults are continually estimating the level of comprehension of their children and making the necessary adjustments. It seems more likely that reduction is an adaptive strategy; i.e., adults adapt their speech to fit the child's linguistic, cognitive, and experiential makeup.

3.3 Theories of First-Language Acquisition

There are two main theoretical positions that have been put forward to account for first-language acquisition. The behaviorists claim that the child starts tabula rasa and that the acquisitional process depends entirely on environmental conditioning. This is known as the *empircist* hypothesis. Cognitive psychologists, in contrast, maintain that the child has an innate predisposition towards the acquisition of language. This is known as the *nativist* hypothesis.

Actually, the development of language is a combination of both genetic and environmental factors. The mechanisms of speech perception and production are probably biologically determined. But the child would not be able to construct the intricate symbolic system of language without a linguistic environment. This environment is crucial to the shaping, or 'fine tuning,' of such psychogenetic mechanisms (see Figure 3.7).

In this section we will outline the views of both theoretical positions and then we will return briefly to this topic in Chapter 7 where we will offer our own glossodynamic interpretation.

3.3.1 BEHAVIORISTIC THEORIES

According to most behaviorists, linguistic competence results from integrating the linguistic events that have been observed in one's environment. As Cairns and Cairns (1976:191) note, extreme behaviorists go so far as to claim that 'at birth the infant's mind is a blank slate to be written on by experience.'

78 Applied Psycholinguistics

BIOLOGICAL FACTORS	ENVIRONMENTAL FACTORS	
Neurological and physiological apparatus involved in language	Samples of the language	
	Input strategies used by adults	
Psychological mechanisms involved in the perception and processing of language data	The conditioning process involved in making associations between verbal responses and environmental stimuli	PRODUCTION
Psychological mechanisms involved in the cognitive organization of language data and in the building of comprehension	Other influencing factors present in the environment	

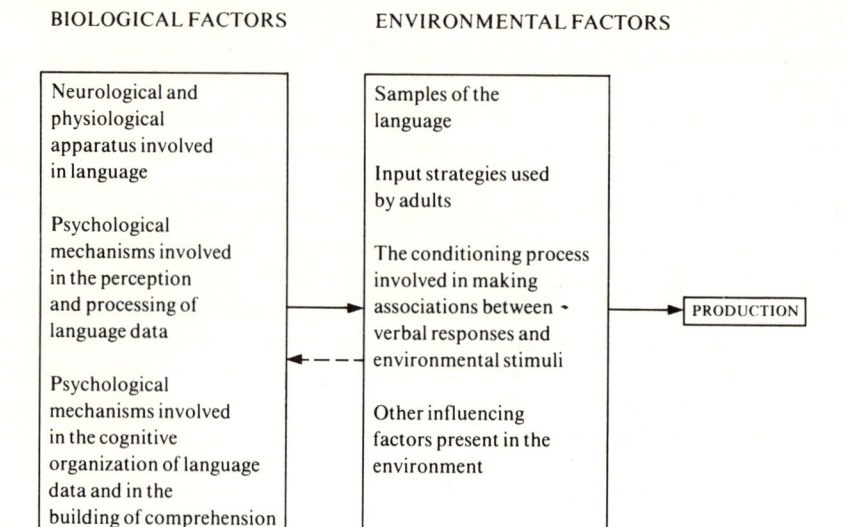

FIGURE 3.7 The conditions necessary for language acquisition

In most versions of behavioristic theory, the development of one's native language results directly from the conditioning process coupled with positive reinforcement; i.e., the child learns to make only those verbal responses which will be rewarded. According to Skinner (1957) – the chief spokesman for the empiricist viewpoint – there are three verbal operants that are significant for language development: (1) *Tacts*. These are responses to particular environmental stimuli. Children naming the objects of their environment ('Kitty', 'Doggy', etc.) are employing tact responses. (2) *Mands*. These are responses produced by the child to verbalize a need ('Milk', 'Cookie', etc.). (3) *Echoics*. These are responses that manifest themselves as repetitions or imitations of the sounds heard in one's environment. Eventually, each verbal operant that the child produces serves as a stimulus for the next verbal response so that sentence structure, for example, is learned by means of chains of associations of this type. In other words, according to behaviorists, the acquisition of language is an environmentally conditioned associational process. Stimuli and responses are linked together in a learning chain, and these S-R associations are reinforced by the linguistic community of the child.

A mediation account of language acquisition has also been proposed. As discussed in Section 2.3.1, the main idea in mediation theory is that what becomes conditioned is a fractional, or detachable, part of the response (r_m), rather than whole overt responses. This little r_m then elicits an internal stimulus, s_m, which in turn mediates a new overt response to a word (see Figure 2.9). For example, when we hear the word *food* just before being served actual food, we respond to it with a mediating response, r_m. This is not the whole response but a detachable portion of it. This means that all sorts of associations among objects are established through the mediation of words. Mediation theorists claim that children build up a chain of r_ms and s_ms to verbal stimuli which will be capable of being enacted independently of these verbal stimuli.

Perhaps the most controversial aspect of mediation theory is that it attempts to account for abstraction by a notion – the mediating response – that cannot be put under the empirical psychologist's microscope. And this, as H. Douglas Brown (1980:20) points out, is 'a cardinal sin for dyed-in-the-wool behaviorists!'

3.3.2 COGNITIVE THEORIES

The behavioristic model of language acquisition has been severely criticized by many psycholinguists and developmental psychologists. Some of the weaknesses of this model can be summarized as follows. (1) Very little verbal behavior actually takes place in the form of tacts and mands. (2) Mediation accounts are limited to simple declarative sentences. Other behavioristic accounts cannot explain the acquisition of word meaning at all. (3) Children learn language in universal stages. If behavioristic theories were totally true, then one would expect to find large variations in the learning rate, which, of course, is not the case. (4) Children learn much more about language than what they are exposed to in their environment. (5) Children are able to construct novel utterances. This cannot be explained by means of imitation or S-R models. (6) Language is not an observable phenomenon; it is a mentalistic one. Therefore, language acquisition is beyond the theoretical perimeter of behaviorism. (7) Language is acquired in a very short period of time. This could not happen if conditioning alone were involved because it would be too time-consuming. (8) Children who are unable to speak for neurological or physiological reasons are still able to understand the language spoken to them. This certainly cannot be explained by any S-R model of language acquisition.

The main alternative to the behavioristic model of language acquisition that has been proposed is the nativist hypothesis. This holds that the human organism is already filled at birth with theories and hypotheses which allow it to impose a structure upon the environment. In other words, children possess a species-specific strategy that allows them to construct a theory of their language solely by being exposed to it. The difference in the two viewpoints is illustrated in Figure 3.8.

80 Applied Psycholinguistics

EMPIRICIST MODEL

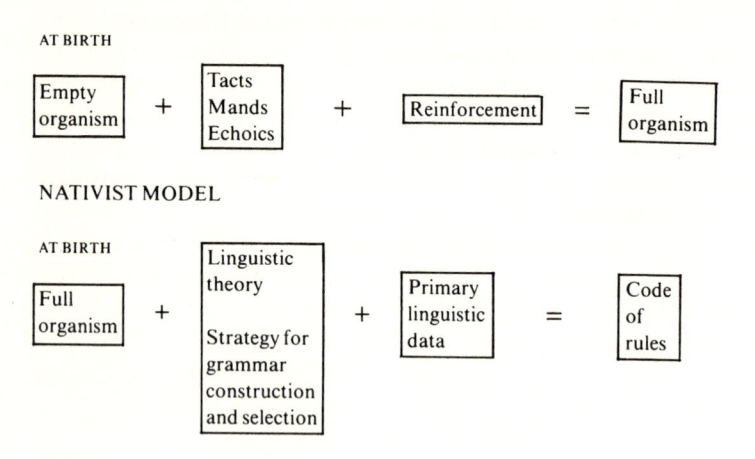

AT BIRTH

| Empty organism | + | Tacts Mands Echoics | + | Reinforcement | = | Full organism |

NATIVIST MODEL

AT BIRTH

| Full organism | + | Linguistic theory / Strategy for grammar construction and selection | + | Primary linguistic data | = | Code of rules |

FIGURE 3.8 Competing models of first-language acquisition (adapted from Gazzaniga 1973:114–15)

What are some of the aspects of language acquisition that seem to favor a nativist viewpoint? As already mentioned, Lenneberg (1967) points out, for example, that certain language milestones are reached in a fixed sequence and that these milestones are synchronized closely with motor development and with those that are known to be biologically determined (see Appendix B and Appendix C). McNeill (1966) outlines, moreover, four unique features which make language acquisition a species-specific phenomenon: (1) the ability to discriminate speech stimuli from other sounds in the environment; (2) the ability to organize linguistic events into categories and hierarchies which can be refined later; (3) the knowledge that only a certain type of linguistic system is possible and that other types are not; (4) the ability to construct the linguistic system out of the data that are encountered.

The cognitive view of language development maintains, in essence, that we are all born with a *language acquisition device* (LAD) that has the four properties mentioned by McNeill. The acquisitional process is considered, therefore, to be a special case of data-processing. In fact, McNeill uses a 'flow' diagram to represent this process (Figure 3.9).

Corpus of speech → LAD → Grammatical system

FIGURE 3.9 The language-acquisition device (from McNeil 1966:35)

First-Language Acquisition 81

But such cognitive theories are not without their weaknesses. For one thing, once we have accounted for the ability to develop language with a LAD, we are left with the problem of accounting for the nature of this LAD and how it is transmitted genetically. Moreover, since cognitive-based research on language development has focused on performance, cognitive psycholinguists are faced with the dilemma of explaining the presence of hesitations, pauses, backtracking, and the like, which characterize child speech because these have relevance to the acquisitional process. In addition, during the earliest stages of language development, there seems to be no more doubt that one of the most frequently used learning strategies is imitation – a strategy which still has no *locus* in cognitive models of language development.

An integrated or eclectic view of first-language acquisition will be proposed in Chapter 7.

3.4 A Pedagogical Summary

What general pedagogical inferences can language teachers draw from a study of first-language acquisition? Are there any parallels between first- and second-language acquisition? As Chastain (1971:115) warns, it must always be kept in mind that 'the two processes are greatly different.' For one thing, the learner is not a developing infant. The environmental conditions are also different. Nevertheless, the systematic study of first-language acquisition reveals, in our mind, some general acquisitional patterns which merit the attention of all language teachers. (1) Since comprehension is superior to production at all stages of development, we should expect this to be true of students learning a second language. (2) Although imitation is involved to some degree in language development, it is always linked to some meaningful experience. Thus, language teachers should always stress meaningful imitation practice, not simple mimetic drilling. (3) Children are being continually exposed to complex utterances which they themselves cannot produce. Similarly, language learners can profit from exposure to language data beyond their productive capacity. (4) Errors are an integral part of first-language acquisition. They reflect the child's approximations to adult grammar. Errors are also typical of second-language learning and should therefore be expected and tolerated. (5) And, since second-language learners already know a first language, second-language teachers should exploit this knowledge.

3.5 Signposts

Research continues to be actively conducted into all aspects of language development. If there is one emerging trend in the literature it is that the theoretical positions of an increasing number of researchers are becoming more eclectic. As Paivio and Begg (1981:252) remark, researchers are beginning to 'converge on language behavior as a specific skill founded on more general cognitive abilities, which in turn come from the infant's exposure to a world of concrete objects and events.' A highly interesting and promising line of investigation is being pursued in the area of computer programming, specifically in the design of computer programs to construct grammars which, in turn, can be used to simulate how grammatical classes might be acquired. But research in this domain is only in its fledgling stages, and no pedagogical implications can be drawn at this point.

3.6 Suggestions for Further Reading

For detailed accounts of first-language acquisition – in addition to the works referred to in this chapter – see Menyuk (1971), Clark and Clark (1977), Bloom (1978), and Tavakolian (1981). Good discussions of language development in older children can be found in Chomsky (1969) and Peterson and McCabe (1983).

4
Second-Language Learning

As interest in second language acquisition grows and more research results appear, it is becoming obvious that in order to make more accurate statements about how a second language is learned, a good deal more must be known about the second language learner.
(Schumann 1976a: 15)

4.0 Introduction

It has often been claimed that second-language (L_2) learning is similar to first-language (L_1) acquisition. This claim is based on the existence of three learning parallels: (1) imitation, repetition, and practice are involved to some degree in both L_1 and L_2 learning; (2) comprehension precedes production in both; (3) listening and speaking skills precede reading and writing ones in both. The view that L_2 learning is similar to L_1 acquisition has been influenced mainly by behavioristic models of language acquisition. These models stress the importance of the environment, rote practice, habit formation, reinforcement, conditioning, and association in L_2 learning and teaching. On the other side of the theoretical arena, cognitive theorists argue that there are many incongruities between L_1 development and L_2 learning. Again, we believe that the 'truth' lies somewhere between these two views. L_2 learning is a complex process which involves the environmental input of the classroom (or context of learning), some imitation and rote memorization, as well as cognitive learning strategies. Schumann (1976a), for one, proposes an integrated model of L_2 learning in terms of three parameters: (1) *initiating parameters*, affective variables which initiate and regulate the learning process; (2) *cognitive parameters*, cognitive operations that a learner performs on the target language input data; and (3) *linguistic product* which results from the operation of the first two (see Figure 4.1).

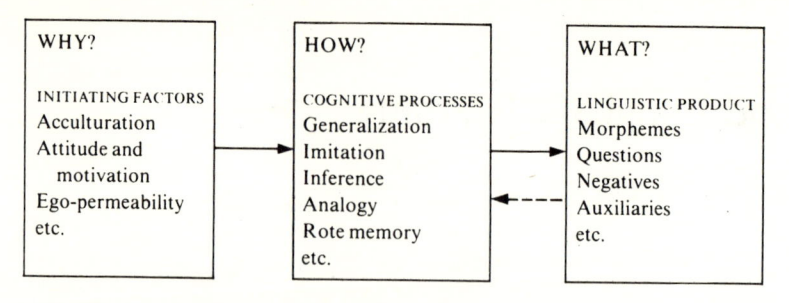

WHY?	HOW?	WHAT?
INITIATING FACTORS Acculturation Attitude and motivation Ego-permeability etc.	COGNITIVE PROCESSES Generalization Imitation Inference Analogy Rote memory etc.	LINGUISTIC PRODUCT Morphemes Questions Negatives Auxiliaries etc.

FIGURE 4.1 L_2 learning (from Schumann 1976a:15)

In this chapter we will discuss some of the differences and similarities that exist between L_1 and L_2 learning. We will also examine some of the variables and constants that characterize L_2 learning. Finally, we will look at bilingualism and multilingualism from both psychological and educational points of view. As in many other treatments of language learning, we will not make any terminological distinction between *second-* and *foreign-*language learning. However, it should be noted that in some contexts – e.g., the Canadian one – where there exists more than one official language, this distinction is, of course, an important one.

4.1 Neurological and Psychological Aspects of Second-Language Learning

In this section we will look briefly at the neurological and psychological components which make up the second-language learning process; i.e., we will discuss some of the research into the neurology and psychology of second-language learning in order to derive some general pedagogical implications from it.

4.1.1 NEUROLOGICAL ASPECTS

The question that has often been asked is whether there is a *critical period* for learning languages. This question can be stated more precisely in neurological terms: What relevance to language learning do cerebral lateralization and brain plasticity have? As Schnitzer (1978:114) states: 'One of the principal sources of interest in the question of cerebral lateralization for language is the fact that children acquire second languages to a degree indistinguishable from native competence, whereas adults do not.'

As pointed out in previous chapters, Lenneberg (1967) has suggested that the lateralization process starts around the age of two and ends around the age of puberty. Krashen (1973, 1975) claims, on the other hand, that it could occur as early as five years of age. In most human beings, the language function is lateralized to the left hemisphere, although in children the right hemisphere will take over the language function if the left one is damaged in any way. This means that the brain is plastic during childhood so that lateralization can be transferred to the right hemisphere in the event of some neuropathological occurrence. Scovel (1969) has suggested that it is this plasticity that allows a child to acquire a second language without difficulty. However, a recent study by Dennis and Whitaker (1976) has cast some doubt on the plasticity theory. They performed detailed verbal tests on nine- to ten-year-olds who had undergone hemispherectomies between the ages of 28 days and 4½ months. They found that in these individuals the right hemisphere (which had presumably taken over some language functions) was deficient at the following skills: (1) comprehending auditory language, especially when it is grammatically complex; (2) identifying and correcting surface structure errors; (3) repeating stylistic variations; (4) forming questions; (5) determining sentence implications; (6) combining syntactic and semantic information for the substitution of missing pronouns; (7) judging word relationships in sentences. In general, Levy (1979) has found that while the right hemisphere can discriminate spoken words and associate those words with meaning, it shows three basic deficiencies: (1) a cognitive deficit and orientation that limit the level of abstraction of concepts that can be acquired; (2) a syntactic deficit that limits the complexity of grammatical structures which can be decoded and encoded, particularly when the words have no persistent spatial referents; (3) an almost total incapacity for phonetic analysis.

As Schnitzer (1978:118) points out, on the basis of findings such as these, 'one must conclude that the left hemisphere is endowed from birth with a greater facility for learning certain crucial aspects of language than is the right hemisphere.' It appears to be the case that although language can be learned by the right hemisphere if necessary, it is not learned as well as it is by the left one. Clearly, the relevance of plasticity and lateralization to the learning of second languages in particular has not as yet been determined.

A related neurological question vis-à-vis L_2 learning concerns the role of the speech muscles. Once again, it seems that skills requiring muscular dexterity, such as playing a musical instrument or controlling the complex phonological system of a language, are dependent upon that mysterious plasticity of the brain. Persons beyond the age of puberty generally find it difficult, if not impossible, to retrain their speech muscles and master the phonological system of another language. Lambert (1956) has, in fact, shown that while second-language learners will improve in most areas of competence in the target language, they will always lag behind in pronunciation.

What implications can second-language teachers derive from a consideration of the neurology of language? There is no doubt that the neurological evidence points to childhood as the optimal period for learning a second language. In adult learners, skills requiring a retraining of muscle coordination, such as pronunciation, may be beyond the reach of most learners. Therefore, it might be a waste of effort to insist on a native-like pronunciation. The emphasis in second-language pedagogy should probably be on communicative and cognitive dimensions. This does not mean necessarily that an adult learner will never learn to pronounce a second language correctly but simply that pronunciation will probably require a lot more time and effort than to master other aspects of the second language.

4.1.2 PSYCHOLOGICAL ASPECTS

Adult second-language learners have already developed one language. This can be both an aid and an obstacle. It can be an aid because second-language learners have already developed some form of metalinguistic awareness which will allow them to construct a theory of the second language in terms of the first without going through the stages of first-language acquisition. It can be an obstacle in those areas where the two languages contrast and where the first language can become a potential source of interference. More will be said about this in Section 4.2.

Perhaps the greatest difference between first-language acquisition and second-language learning is in the *context* of learning. Whereas first-language acquisition occurs normally in a home environment without any pedagogical intervention, second-language learning occurs generally in a classroom environment and is under the control of a teacher. Some knowledge about the perceptual, cognitive, and affective apparatus that a second-language learner brings to the classroom will obviously help the teacher to formulate teaching strategies. The perceptual and cognitive mechanisms will help the teacher understand the 'how' of second-language learning, and the affective variables will help the teacher understand the 'why' of second-language learning.

The perceptual strategies which characterize second-language learning are identical to the ones involved in first-language acquisition. In fact, the first stage or phase in second-language learning is almost invariably marked by the learner's efforts to decipher messages; however, in this case the deciphering process takes place in terms of the first language. As discussed in Section 2.2.2, learning how to perceive speech correctly implies discrimination, recognition, integration, and storage. In the case of second-language learning, the ability to differentiate speech sounds from other sounds in the environment (discrimination) is, needless to say, a firmly established perceptual strategy. Recognition, on the other hand, or the ability to recognize emic cues in the flow of speech, is central to the learning task at hand. The ability to recognize the emic cues of the target language is one of the first clear signs that the learning process has begun. Recognition involves the grouping of sounds into structural units (integration) which are then interpreted semantically and stored for either early or long-term retrieval. Thus, the starting point of the second-language-learning process is the activation of perceptual mechanisms required to decipher the target language. Since the L_2 learner has already established the appropriate schemata to do this, the role of the teacher consists in facilitating the proper perception of the target language. This may require that learners do very little speaking at first and a lot of listening. Since perception invariably involves interpretation, the teacher should always be careful to make the samples of language used as meaningful as possible, relating them perhaps to the experience and intentions of the learners. But in addition to exposing beginners to meaningful chunks of the target language, the teacher could ask them to produce simple one- or two-word responses to verbal stimuli. This will allow learners to monitor their own perceptual learning in terms of their productions, which serve as auditory feedback. Since adults are able to concentrate more than children, they also have a greater capacity for rote learning which can be effective especially for short-term storage. Thus, imitation, repetition, and reinforcement techniques have a role to play during the crucial initial stages of L_2 learning. Teachers will find invariably that a perceptual stage will precede spontaneous production. As Davies (1980) has shown, by emphasizing receptive skills first, a sound basis for production at a later stage will be established.

In regard to the cognitive component of L_2 learning, it is clear that adult L_2 learners are more capable than children of abstracting and understanding abstract grammatical principles and models. By the age of puberty formal thinking transcends concrete experience as a learning strategy. L_2 learners will probably profit somewhat by well-designed grammatical explanations and deductive pedagogical approaches (Ausubel 1964). Such explanations should however take into account the psychological fact that the L_2 learner is making comparisons to L_1. The teacher should realize that comparisons with the native language are unavoidable, particularly in those areas where the target language and native language do not coincide.

As previously mentioned, whereas the perceptual and cognitive mechanisms involved in the learning process help to explain the 'how' of L_2 learning, affective variables constitute the 'why.' Variables such as attitude and motivation, cognitive learning style, and aptitude are crucial to successful language learning.

One of the most important factors in determining successful L_2 learning is *motivation*. Psychologists are not quite sure how to define motivation in this context, but all agree that it is essential to the learning process. Gardner and Lambert (1972) proposed a two-part typology of motivation with respect to L_2 learning: (1) *integrative*, i.e., the motivation to become familiar with, or even a

88 Applied Psycholinguistics

part of, the target culture; (2) *instrumental*, i.e., the motivation to learn a language for utilitarian purposes (e.g., meeting a graduation requirement, fulfilling an occupational need). Of these two, it is believed that integrative motivation is particularly crucial in promoting learning. Pritchard (1952), for example, showed that there is a high positive correlation between the learner's attitude towards the target culture and success at learning the target language. What are some of the components of integrative motivation? According to Gardner and Smythe (1975), there are at least four properties associated with integrative motivation (see Figure 4.2). (1) *Group-specific attitudes*: the attitudes which learners have towards the group that speaks the target language. (2) *Course-related characteristics*: motivational variables which relate directly to the student's response to the classroom situation (e.g., attitudes towards the course, teacher). (3) *Motivational indices*: the amount of effort expended in learning the target language and the desire to learn the target language. (4) *Generalized attitudes*: general attitudes towards foreign languages and cultures. The teacher can clearly intervene to enhance group-specific attitudes and in creating a congenial classroom atmosphere. In fact, since the classroom environment can generate inhibitions, fears,

MOTIVATIONAL CHARACTERISTICS

GROUP-SPECIFIC ATTITUDES
Attitudes towards the group that speaks the target language

COURSE-RELATED CHARACTERISTICS
Attitudes towards learning the target language
Attitudes towards the course
Attitudes towards the teacher
Parental encouragement

MOTIVATIONAL INDICES
Integrative orientation
Motivational intensity
Desire to learn the target language

GENERALIZED ATTITUDES
General attitudes towards the learning of foreign languages

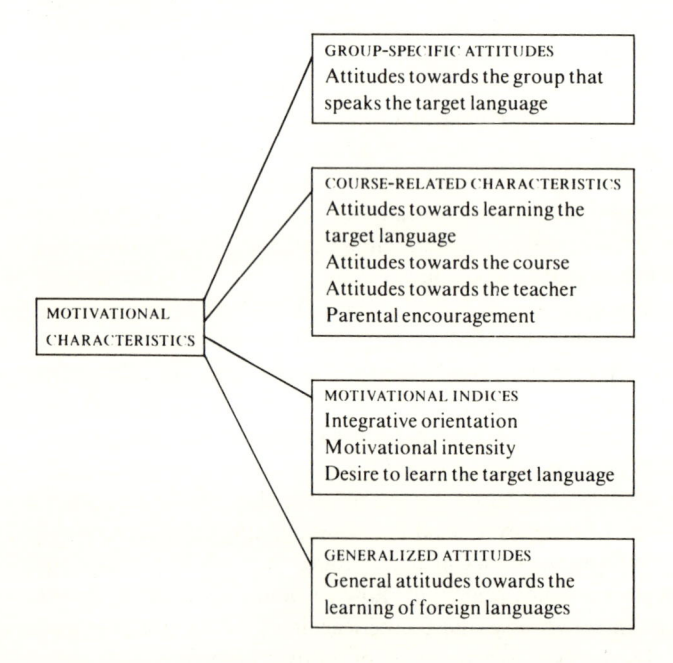

FIGURE 4.2 Aspects of integrative motivation (adapted from Gardner and Smythe (1975:222)

and anxieties which are all detrimental to learning, teachers can contribute significantly to successful language learning by creating as warm and personal a learning environment as possible (Curran 1961, Guiora et al. 1972).

Another important personality variable involved in L_2 learning is *cognitive learning style*. This depends largely on background and motivation. However, when these two variables are kept constant, learning style may become a determining factor by itself. Some researchers (e.g., Carroll 1959, 1961; Titone 1961; Stern 1975) have attempted to describe those traits which characterize a good learning style. There is agreement on four general traits: (1) *Perceptual-motor ability*, the ability to perceive and produce sounds with a high degree of accuracy; (2) *grammatical-cognitive ability*, the ability to recognize the grammatical function and form of linguistic items; (3) *mnemonic-cognitive ability*, the ability to memorize a great number of associations in a relatively short period of time; (4) *generalization ability*, the ability to extrapolate structural patterns from language data. These traits lead to an *aptitude* for language learning which manifests itself in the classroom in such easily recognizable ways as: the ability to imitate sounds and produce phonemic differences; the ability to learn target-language texts easily; a positive approach to a learning task; a tolerant and outgoing approach to the target language and culture; willingness to practice; etc.

From the foregoing discussion we can now summarize the most salient differences between first-language acquisition and second-language learning in terms of four categories: chronological, cognitive, contextual, and motivational. (1) *Chronological differences*: The native language is acquired effortlessly for neurological reasons. After puberty the learning task becomes increasingly harder. (2) *Cognitive differences*: The native language is acquired in an unconscious and automatic fashion. Children are exposed to language data on an unorganized basis and they develop language *in tandem* with cognitive and maturational development. Second-language learning is, in contrast, a conscious and controlled process which occurs on an organized basis. In addition, second-language learners, being older, are more capable of formal grammatical reasoning. (3) *Contextual differences*: The native language is acquired in a 'natural' environment, whereas the second one is generally learned in the 'artificial' environment of the classroom. The acquisition of one's native language occurs without any organized pedagogical intervention, except for the occasionally controlled language input of adults (see Section 3.2). Second-language learning requires direct pedagogical intervention and is characterized by formal learning procedures. (4) *Motivational differences*: In acquiring one's native language, one is striving to cope with the environment. First-language acquisition, therefore, comes naturally and not, as Corder (1973:110) points out, 'as a result of the discovery of its practical utility.' Second-language learners, however, must be motivated to learn the new language.

There are, nevertheless, some striking psychological similarities between first-language acquisition and second-language learning. (1) In both cases, comprehension precedes production. (2) Both processes are marked by typical errors which reveal underlying cognitive processes such as generalization. (3) In both cases, instrumental and meaningful learning strategies are involved concomitantly. More will be said about the interaction of perceptual, cognitive, and affective variables in language learning in Chapter 7.

4.2 Psychopedagogical Aspects of Second-Language Learning

Unlike first-language acquisition, the second-language-learning process takes place in a classroom environment. This raises certain specific questions of a psychopedagogical nature: How are language structures and functions learned and what heuristic role can grammars play in the learning of structures and functions? What kinds of errors typify second-language learning? What is the *locus* and role of translation in second-language learning? In this section we will discuss these questions briefly.

4.2.1 THE LEARNING OF STRUCTURE AND FUNCTION

What does it mean to 'know' the structure of a language? As discussed in Chapter 1, linguists refer to the knowledge of how language is structured and how it is able to convey meanings through its structural framework as linguistic competence. Belyayev (1963) refers to competence as a *Sprachgefühl*, i.e., an unconscious 'feeling' for the general structural properties of language.

Competence may be divided into two categories: conscious *(noetic)* and unconscious *(practical)*. The ability of children to use their native language without any direct awareness of the structural patterns involved is an example of practical linguistic competence. On the other hand, the explanations used by teachers to facilitate the learning of a language exemplify noetic linguistic competence.

How is the linguistic competence of a second language learned? Actually, a more accurate term than *learned* would be *assimilated* since the learning process in this case consists in assimilating the target-language structures into pre-existing native-language ones. In other words, the learning of L_2 (if it occurs separately from L_1) is shaped by the structural framework of L_1; i.e., the assimilation of L_2 structure is influenced by what the learner already knows (practically or noetically) about L_1 structure. This knowledge can obviously be of immense help in learning isomorphic structures *(positive transfer)*; but it can be a source of interference as well in those structural areas where the two languages contrast *(negative transfer)*. It follows, therefore, that the more structurally related L_1 and L_2 are, the easier it is to assimilate the structure of L_2.

Perhaps the main psychopedagogical issue connected to structural assimilation is to decide which teaching strategy is more appropriate: an *inductive* one or a *deductive* one? Historically, the inductive learning of structure has been associated with behavioristic theories of learning, and deductive learning with cognitive and traditional ones. According to many behaviorists, the 'natural' way to learn the structure of the target language is without the benefit of explicit rules; i.e., structure can be learned through induction, the same way that children acquire their native language. On the other hand, cognitivist educators claim that older learners will learn structure more efficiently if rules are used as heuristic devices to help them organize and control structural patterns at a conscious cognitive level (e.g., Chastain 1969, Seliger 1975). Others (e.g., Fischer 1979, Bialystock 1979) suggest that both strategies are involved. Learners will inevitably induce those patterns which are similar to L_1 but will construct hypotheses about the ones which are either different from or non-existent in their native language. It is just these hypotheses which become a potential source of error. The ability to construct hypotheses of this type depends on what Bialystock calls 'explicit' and 'implicit' linguistic knowledge. Learners invariably exploit both kinds of knowledge, in addition to other kinds of available information, in order to infer previously unknown structure and in order to monitor their verbal productions.

From a psychopedagogical standpoint there is one main implication that can be derived from the foregoing discussion; namely, that the older learner's competence in L_1 can be exploited by the use of inductive teaching methods for those areas where L_1 and L_2 are structurally similar. However, deductive approaches might have to be used in areas where the two languages differ or in cases where there are no corresponding L_1 structures. If the learners are very young, then deductive techniques should be avoided because noetic competence has not as yet been developed in the learners, and therefore such techniques will probably not be understood and might even have a negative effect (Wittwer 1959).

Teachers will find that the building-up of competence in L_2 is related chronologically to certain performance variables. This interrelationship can be viewed in terms of four discrete learning stages. The actual amount of time required for each stage obviously depends on the individual learner. (1) There is an initial period during which perception is involved to a greater degree than any other mechanism. During this stage, conditioning techniques (e.g., imitation) can be very useful since the learner is gradually becoming accustomed to the new emic cues. The performance strategies of learners during this stage are typical simple utterances which are produced with much difficulty. These productions are completely conscious and monitored. (2) This stage is followed by one in which productions become more spontaneous and easier to produce. They are still almost completely monitored. During this stage, learners will gain from practice and repetition (reinforcement). (3) The third stage is marked by an increased productive ability which is still being monitored, although to a lesser extent. This is a period during which the learned behavior is being organized cognitively and stored for long-term retrieval. Cognitive techniques, such as the teaching of rules, can be of great benefit during this stage. (4) The final stage is characterized by an automatic unconscious control of the target language. Speech acts are now effortless and totally spontaneous. Competence and performance are now synchronized. This is the period during which learning becomes acquisition. This is a difficult stage to reach for the neurological reasons discussed previously (Section 4.1.1). Nevertheless, this stage is the ultimate goal of all second-language learning.

Needless to say, the learning and teaching of structure should not occur in isolation. Language learning is not a special case of data processing. The goal of second-language learning is the ability to communicate in the target language. This implies a familiarity with its communicative functions. As discussed in sections 1.4.1 and 1.4.2, the ability to use language in different social settings and to express different psychological states is commonly called *communicative competence*. Very little is known about how communicative competence is learned, and it is very difficult to teach speech functions in a formal classroom setting. Some of the ways in which the teaching of communicative competence has been approached can be summarized as follows. (1) Learners can be involved directly in conversational activities. (2) Audio-oral and audio-visual materials (e.g., films, tapes, records) can be used in which native speakers of the target language are involved in some form of discourse (e.g., Wright 1976; Mollica 1978, 1979a, 1979b). (3) Learners can also be presented with humorous events (jokes, cartoons, etc.) or games and problem-solving activities (e.g., Mollica 1976, 1979c, 1981; Danesi 1979, 1980a). (4) Learners can also be encouraged to engage in conversations with the speakers of the target language. More will be said about the teaching of speech functions in Chapter 5.

The foregoing discussion on the assimilation of structure and speech functions leads to the question of the role of *grammars* in second-language learning. As previously mentioned, children have a practical knowledge of their native language. Johnson (1967) refers to this type of grammatical knowledge as *intuitive*. He calls the noetic, or conscious, realization that language is a system of structures *analytical* grammar. Analytical grammars are, therefore, attempts to describe linguistic competence formally. These can be divided into three subtypes (Titone 1969:37). (1) *Traditional*: based on the categories of classical logic and the so-called 'parts of speech.' While they may not always provide accurate descriptions of linguistic competence, traditional analytic grammars are nevertheless 'scientific' attempts to describe language. (2) *Scientific*: as discussed in Chapter 1, these analytic grammars are the formal linguistic characterizations of linguists. (3) *Psychological*: the systematic descriptions of psycholinguists as they aim to relate scientific grammars to psycholinguistic processes. Another major type of grammar is commonly called *pedagogical*. This type lies midway between intuitive and analytical grammars. It is frequently found in the form of foreign-language manuals which attempt to make the target language comprehensible to a specific group of learners. Pedagogical grammars are usually classified as *elementary*, *intermediate*, and *advanced*. These reflect, to some degree, the psycholinguistic learning stages mentioned above. Elementary pedagogical grammars emphasize basic structural patterns and speech functions; intermediate pedagogical grammars review and reinforce the basic material; advanced pedagogical grammars focus on the use of the target language in various settings and media (oral and written). Because pedagogical grammars generally reflect the chronology of second-language learning, they can be very useful, if not indispensable, heuristic aids. They constitute a convenient frame of reference for both teachers and learners.

4.2.2 ERRORS IN SECOND-LANGUAGE LEARNING

The second-language-learning process is frequently characterized by 'systematic' errors, i.e., aberrations or deviations which can be described either in terms of native-language interference or in terms of specific psychological learning strategies. The former are known as *interlinguistic* errors and the latter as *intralinguistic*. Before discussing typical error-producing mechanisms, it is first necessary to make a terminological distinction between mistakes and errors. Mistakes are random performance slips or lapses. They do not result from a defective or approximate knowledge of the target-language structure or vocabulary. Mistakes are recognized immediately by learners who are able to correct them by themselves. Errors are unconscious aberrations in structure or vocabulary that are generated by certain psychological mechanisms within the learner. They are errors in competence.

The language that a learner develops in the course of learning L_2 approximates the target language in successive stages. This language is often referred to as *interlanguage* (after Selinker 1972). It is characterized by many idiosyncratic interlinguistic and intralinguistic errors (see Figure 4.3). Other names that have been used to designate the code which results from the learner's attempts to learn the target language are: *idiosyncratic dialect*, *approximative system*, *transitional competence*, *l'état de dialecte* (Richards and Sampson 1974:5). The applied linguistic technique which aims to describe and classify interlinguistic errors is known as

94 Applied Psycholinguistics

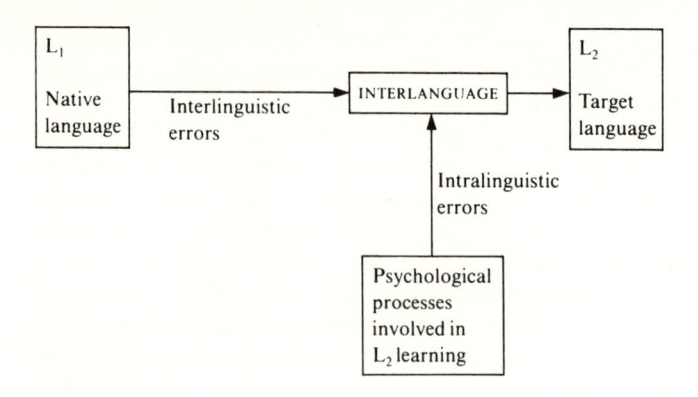

FIGURE 4.3 Interlinguistic and intralinguistic errors

contrastive analysis (CA); the description and classification of intralinguistic errors is commonly called *error analysis* (EA). Both techniques can be designated 'etiological' (Danesi 1980b) because they aim to diagnose those errors that characterize the learner's interlanguage and consequently the second-language-learning process.

We will first look at interlinguistic errors and CA. The automatic and unconscious transfer of the verbal habits of L_1 to L_2 produces many typical interference patterns. According to the strong contrastive hypothesis, it is claimed that a scientific comparison of the two languages in question will pinpoint areas of difficulty where they contrast. In fact, this comparison will yield a hierarchy of difficulties which will allow the teacher to predict, explain, and eventually eliminate interlinguistic errors (Lado 1957). For example, when speakers of English are learning Italian, chances are that they will have difficulty in pronouncing syllable-final /l/ correctly. In English /l/ is velarized to [ɫ] (velar *l*) in syllable-final position (i.e., it is articulated with the back of the tongue arched towards the velum: e.g., *bill* = [bɪɫ], *also* = [ɔɫ - sow]). This is not the case in Italian: *bello* = [bel-lo] 'beautiful,' *alzo* = [al - tso], 'I raise.' In pronouncing the words *bello* and *alzo*, the English-speaking learner will probably use a velar [ɫ] ([beɫ - o], [aɫ - tso]) because of the distributional characteristics of /l/ in English. Unless they are particularly perceptive or are told otherwise, English-speaking learners of Italian will assume that Italian /l/ is like English /l/.

According to CA, such contrasts will prove invariably to be sources of difficulty. These difficulties can be organized into a hierarchy such as the following one (see Brown 1980:152-4). (1) *Level 0 (simple transfer)*: at this level, there is no difference or contrast between the two languages. The learner simply transfers the L_1 item to the target language. For example, the consonant /m/ has the same articulatory and distributional features in both English and Spanish, and therefore the English-speaking student of Spanish will have no difficulty in pronouncing Spanish /m/. (2) *Level 1 (coalescence)*: at this level, two items in L_1 are coalesced into one item in L_2. Students must therefore learn to overlook a distinction they have grown used to. For example, the English-speaking student must learn to ignore gender distinction in third-person possessives *(his/her)* when learning French *(son livre* = 'his/her book'). (3) *Level 2 (underdifferentiation)*: at this level, an item in L_1 is absent in the target language. For example, the English-speaking student of Italian must forget consonants such as /θ/ and /ð/ because they do not exist in Italian. (4) *Level 3 (reinterpretation)*: at this level, an item in L_1 is given a new shape or distribution in the target language. For example, the English-speaking student must learn a new distribution for /d/ when learning Spanish because in Spanish /d/ has both a stop allophone [d] and a fricative one [ð]. The stop allophone is used in initial position, and the fricative one is used in all other phonetic environments. (5) *Level 4 (overdifferentiation)*: At this level, the student must learn an entirely new item. For example, the English-speaking student must learn to include determiners in front of nominals in initial position when learning Spanish *(El hombre es mortal* = 'Man is mortal'). (6) *Level 5 (split)*: at this level, an item in L_1 is split into two or more in the target language. For example, the English-speaking student must learn to distinguish between polite/informal pronouns of address when learning French *(tu/vous* = 'you').

Historically, CA has its roots in behavioristic psychology and is based on two psycholinguistic assumptions: (1) Language learning is habit formation. (2) Old habits in L_1 are transferred automatically to L_2. In addition to the usual arguments that can be voiced against a strictly behavioristic explanation of language learning, there are some psychopedagogical aspects of the strong contrastive hypothesis that can also be criticized (see, for example, Wardhaugh 1970, Whitman and Jackson 1972). For one thing, teachers have been glad to discover that all the learning difficulties predicted by a CA do not always emerge in the learner's interlanguage. In other words, learning difficulties do not necessarily follow from differences between L_1 and L_2. It also does not follow that those difficulties that do emerge in specific instances will form a hierarchy; i.e., there is no evidence to suggest that the difficulties due to, say, overdifferentiation (Level 4) are more troublesome than those at a lower level. Finally, not all the errors that occur in the learner's interlanguage are due to native-language interference. A pedagogically more acceptable version of CA is the weak contrastive hypothesis. This hypothesis claims that CA can be useful in detecting and explaining interlinguistic errors a posteriori; i.e., CA can be used primarily as a diagnostic, rather than predictive, pedagogical tool.

As already mentioned, the second type of error that manifests itself in the learner's interlanguage is the one that results from the learner's attempts to construct a system for understanding and producing utterances in the target language. This type is known as intralinguistic error. A parallel can be drawn between the psycholinguistic mechanisms that produce intralinguistic errors in second-language learning and the mechanisms that produce developmental errors in first-language acquisition. In both cases, there are two main sources of error (see, for example, Richards 1971, Valdman 1975, Schumann 1976b). (1) *Overgeneralization* (or *analogy*): the tendency to apply a certain rule analogically in those areas where it does not apply. For example, learners of English as a second language will typically produce utterances such as *He goed* for *He went*, and *He cans sings* for *He can sing*. In the former example, the learner has overgeneralized the use of the past-tense morpheme *-ed*, and in the latter example the learner has overgeneralized the use of the third-person singular present-tense morpheme *-s* to modal verbs. In other words, the learner has overgeneralized certain rules of English morpho-syntax. Overgeneralization can also result from the failure to observe the constraints on the applications of target-language rules or from the incomplete application of target-language rules. (2) *Simplification* (or *pidginization*): the tendency to reduce complex forms of the target language to simple linguistic models; e.g., *He no home* for *He's not home*. Magnan (1979) identifies six characteristics of pidginized target languages: lexical reduction and the use of paraphrases and circumlocutions; a heavy reliance on extralinguistic features; replacement of inflectional suffixes by free forms; invariant representation of formatives (lexemes); elimination of redundant features such as morphological gender and number agreement; reduction of syntactic structures generally to simple declarative sentences.

Another parallel can be drawn between the second-language learner's interlanguage and the language of children developing their native tongue. In both cases, intralinguistic errors can be generated by the language input. In first-language acquisition (see Section 3.2), the linguistic input is modified and adapted to the child's stage of verbal development. In a similar manner, teachers and foreign-language manuals adapt the language they use to the chronological stage at which second-language learners find themselves. This is, of course, an adaptive strategy which will facilitate and shape the course of the learning process. But it can also lead to pidginization. Moreover, at times the teacher or foreign-language manual may not cover all applications of a certain rule, and this may lead the learner to make a faulty hypothesis about some aspect of the target language (e.g., Stenson

1974). In other words, sometimes intralinguistic errors can be traced to an 'instructional' source.

Overgeneralization and simplification reveal what Dulay and Burt (e.g., 1976) call *creative construction*, a process which characterizes both first- and second-language learning. This process produces errors of addition, omission, substitution, and reordering. It should be pointed out that transfer and interference produce similar types of error. In fact, it can be argued that overgeneralization and simplification are the underlying mechanisms responsible for both interlinguistic and intralinguistic errors. In the former case, the source is the native language; in the latter the source is, in all probability, the cumulative chronological nature of the second-language-learning process which leads learners to construct hypotheses on the basis of incomplete language data and knowledge.

What psychopedagogical implications can be derived from a study of learner errors? Clearly, it would be counterproductive to ignore totally systematic errors because they may become *fossilized*, i.e., permanent. The study of interlanguage also reveals that errors are 'a fact of life' in language learning, and therefore the teacher sould expect and consequently tolerate many errors. The goal in second-language learning should be, as Hendrickson (1978:390) states, 'to communicate *successfully* in a foreign language rather than try to communicate *perfectly* in it.' George (1972:29) even suggests that the tolerance of errors is in itself a factor in their prevention. As Corder (1974:131) points out, errors tend to 'run a course' in second-language learning, and this is generally in line with the chronology of this process. During the *presystematic* stage, learners are unaware of certain rules in the target language and therefore make many random errors. During the *systematic* stage, their errors are regular. During the *postsystematic* stage, they still produce errors, but only inconsistently, and when asked to correct their errors, they can do so and also give an account of the appropriate rule. During these stages it is clearly important never to destroy the learner's self-confidence, otherwise the learner may develop certain 'protective' strategies such as the avoidance of certain structures or lexical items (Schachter 1974), or the use of prefabricated speech patterns that have been memorized (Hakuta 1974). Error-correction strategies should focus on what Hendrickson (1979) calls *global*, rather than *local*, errors. Global errors are those errors which cause a native speaker of the target language either to misinterpret a spoken or written message or else to consider the message incomprehensible; local errors are those which make an utterance appear awkward but which cause little or no difficulty in understanding the intended message.

Another pedagogical implication that can be derived from the study of learner errors is that they can become a valuable source of feedback; i.e., they can help the teacher identify areas which need more elaboration or practice and subsequently to prepare appropriate instructional materials. In fact, this feedback can provide a basis on which to elaborate a 'psychological' pedagogical grammar. Such a grammar would focus on error-producing mechanisms such as interference, overgeneralization, and simplification and develop appropriate explanations and exercises. The elaboration of a grammar of this type would depend clearly on the recognition and description of errors which characterize the learner's interlanguage. One of the most useful 'algorithms' that can be used for this task is reproduced in Figure 4.4.

4.2.3 TRANSLATION AND SECOND-LANGUAGE LEARNING

The discussion of the role played by L_1 in second-language learning leads inevitably to the question of *translation*. This question is particularly relevant during the initial learning stages since it is during these stages that learners tend to think in terms of the linguistic categories of their native language while attempting to decode and encode target language messages. In other words, the learner is translating mentally in attempting to decipher and produce utterances in the target language. The psychopedagogical question that is associated with this is whether it is possible to think directly in the target language without translating. Although there is experimental evidence that this is possible to some degree (e.g., Titone 1971b), the problem of mental translation is generally approached pedagogically by the use of translation techniques or exercises in the instructional process.

Historically, translation is one of the oldest pedagogical techniques. The Romans used it to teach Greek, and this practice was revived in the Middle Ages and in the Renaissance for the teaching of Latin. The use of translation was not challenged until early in the present century. But although the practice of using translation as an instructional technique has often been criticized, it continues to this day, probably because, as Mills (1977:744) quips, 'we cannot really stop second-language learners from translating.' In older learners translation seems to be a type of mental crutch that is used to facilitate the decipherment and production of target-language messages.

Before discussing the use of translation as a teaching methodology in Chapter 5, it is necessary to have a clear notion of what translation is. As already mentioned, translation implies the substitution or replacement of textual material in one language by equivalent textual material in another language (Catford 1965:20). The substitution process takes place by degrees of approximation. (1) *Free translation*: the highest degree of approximation. This is the substitution of a complete text in one language with an equivalent one in the other. For example,

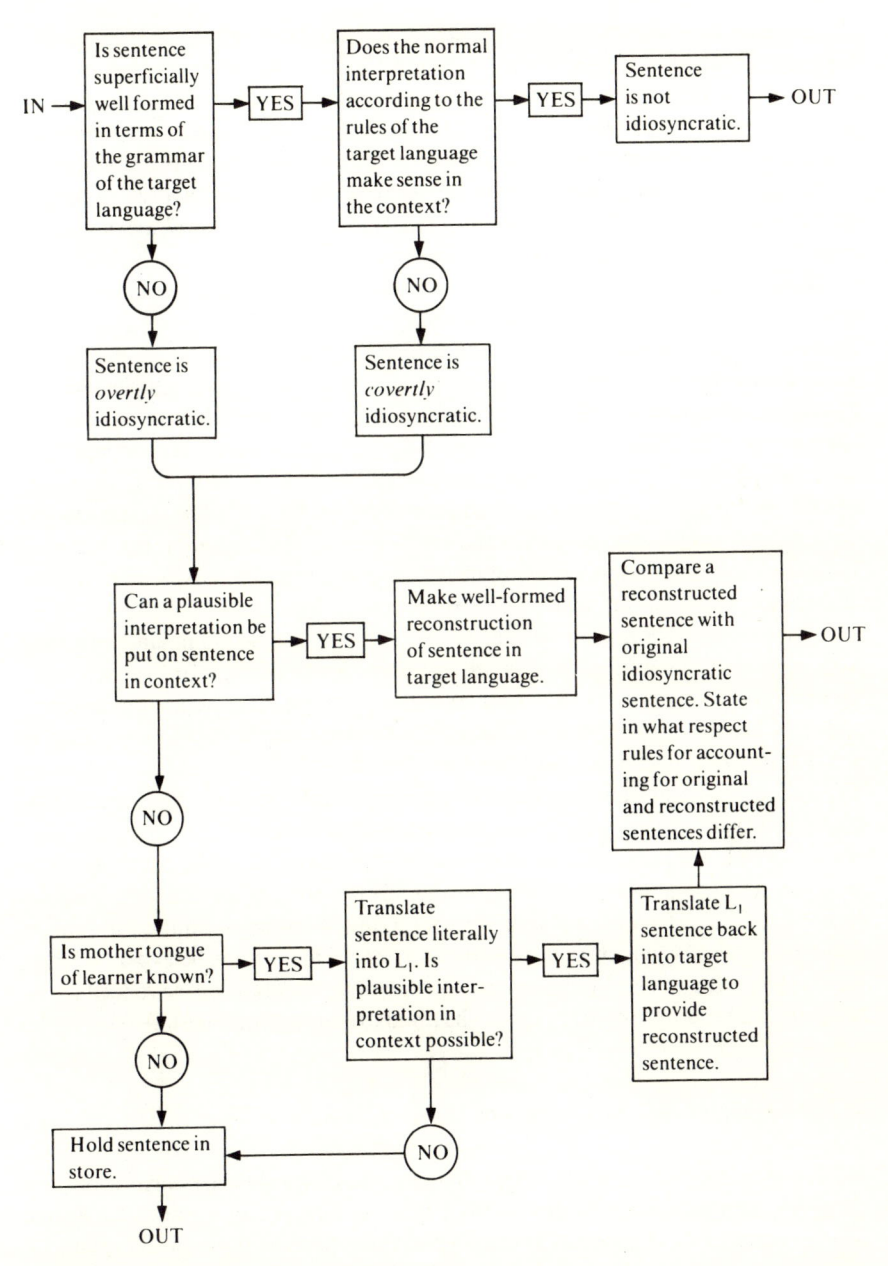

FIGURE 4.4 An algorithm for the recognition and correction of learner errors (from Corder 1973:276)

the English idiomatic utterance *It's raining cats and dogs* is replaced in French with *Il pleut à verse*. (2) *Literal translation*: the simple one-to-one replacement of lexical items with the necessary grammatical changes. Thus, for example, the English expression above would be translated literally as *Il pleut des chats et des chiens*, with the French partitive *des* inserted in its appropriate slots. (3) *Word-for-word translation*: the lowest degree of approximation. This involves a simple lexical substitution without any grammatical adjustments: *Il est pleuvant chats et chiens* (see Catford 1965:25-6).

Word-for-word and literal-translation processes characterize the learner's first attempts to understand and produce target-language utterances. Eventually, learners should be able to move back and forth between L_1 and L_2, expressing their thoughts in terms of the appropriate structural and lexical categories. However, advanced learners will occasionally run into difficulties in translation. Titone (1971a:272-8) found that even language teachers, university language students, and professional interpreters had difficulties in translation when presented with texts that could not be connected to a specific context or texts which contained rare and archaic words. The pedagogical implication of this finding is clear. Teachers should avoid using target-language utterances which are decontextualized or which are lexically esoteric.

In sum, translation probably cannot be avoided as a decoding and encoding strategy during the initial stages of second-language learning. However, it should be obvious that a desirable goal of second-language teaching is the elimination of the need for this crutch. As Moulton (1970:19) observes: 'Translation is precisely what he [the learner] must learn to overcome.' The teacher should also be aware of the fact that translation is bound to be imperfect (word-for-word or literal) during the early learning stages and can thus become an obstacle to the learning process. This suggests that the overt use of translation as an exercise should be avoided at the start of the learning process. However, there are some positive aspects to the use of translation. For one thing, translation equivalents might have to be used when certain structures or meanings cannot be explained adequately in other ways. Moreover, translation may be useful at advanced levels when it can be employed to evaluate the ability to move from one language to the other.

4.3 Bilingualism and Multilingualism

So far in this chapter we have looked at second-language learning as a process that occurs after the acquisition of a first language and in an educational environment. The ultimate goal of this process is proficiency in both L_1 and L_2. This mastery of two languages is called *bilingualism*. Generally, this is a very difficult linguistic state to reach when the learning of L_2 occurs after puberty for, as has been pointed out (sections 2.2.1, 3.2, 4.1.1), the most favorable period for the learning of sensorimotor and perceptual linguistic skills appears to be before puberty, particularly, as Penfield (1953) suggests, during the first eight years of life. This is, of course, the period during which the plasticity of the brain is at a maximum. However, as Stern and Weinrib (1978) caution, it is difficult to ascertain on the basis of neurological considerations alone what the optimal age is for learning a second language. Among other things, children are better learners of languages because they have more time than adults to accomplish the learning task, and because they are less inhibited about making errors. Clearly, then, the plasticity criterion is not, in itself, sufficient for determining the optimal age. Nevertheless, it does suggest that second-language learning should take place as early in life as possible. In fact the literature on this subject shows that when the second language is acquired simultaneously with the first, or learned at some time during childhood, then the child stands a very good chance of becoming a true bilingual. If more than two languages are involved, then the child can become a *multilingual*.

What does it mean to control two languages? Actually, psycholinguists distinguish between two kinds of bilingualism (e.g., Ervin and Osgood 1954). If the two languages are completely separate and the speaker is aware of their differences, then the bilingual is referred to as a *coordinate* bilingual. If, however, the differences are not perceived, then the bilingual is called a *compound* bilingual. The state of coordinate bilingualism is clearly the more desirable one. Another way of differentiating between the two types of bilingualism is in terms of conceptual systems (Kolers 1963). When bilinguals have two sets of concepts and meanings, one for each language, they have a *separated* conceptual system; if they have one set of concepts and ideas which they map onto each language they have a *shared* conceptual system. Figure 4.5 illustrates the difference between the two.

The coordinate (separated) form of bilingualism is, needless to say, the more desirable one for, in cases of compound (shared) bilingualism, the problem of interference always emerges. As mentioned earlier (Section 4.2.2), interference is the unconscious transfer of structural and/or lexical patterns from one language to the other. Many studies have been devoted to the investigation of interference mechanisms in bilinguals ever since the publication of Weinreich's (1953) classic work on language-contact phenomena.

From a sociolinguistic standpoint it is necessary to distinguish between bilingualism and *diglossia*. Ferguson (1959) used the term 'diglossia' to refer to the presence in a society of separate languages, each with a specific social function. But this presence does not imply that the members of that society necessarily speak or understand all the languages. On the other hand, neither does the

102 Applied Psycholinguistics

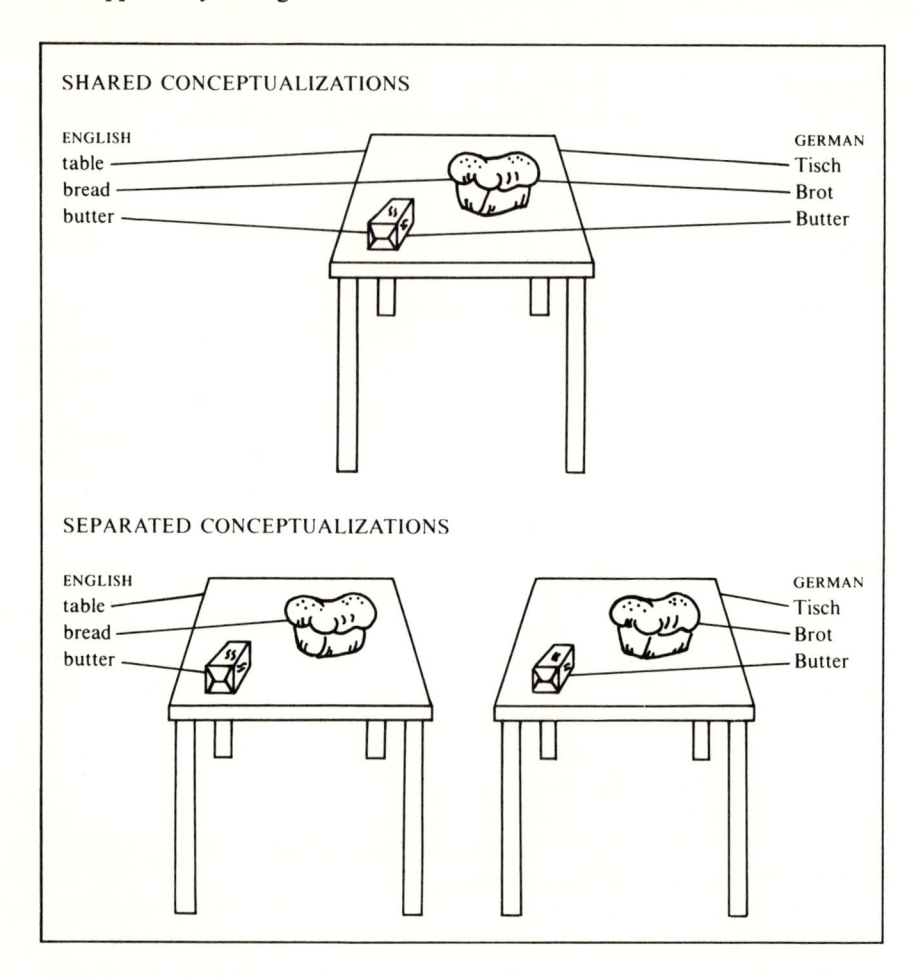

FIGURE 4.5 Shared and separated conceptual systems (from Glucksberg and Danks (1975:187)

presence of bilinguals in a society imply that the languages spoken by these individuals have any official status or social function. Thus a society may be characterized as monolingual (one official language), bilingual or multilingual (two or more official languages recognized and spoken), or diglottic (two or more languages recognized but not necessarily spoken by all members).

We now return to the question of what coordinate bilingualism implies from a psychological standpoint. Does the simultaneous acquisition of two or more languages in childhood mean that separate perceptual and cognitive mechanisms are developed, or that these mechanisms are expanded to process two types of language data? Are the two languages lateralized to the same hemisphere or to different hemispheres? Actually, there is very little research on this area of verbal development and there is consequently very little consensus on the psycholinguistic nature of bilingualism. As Brooks (1964:42) notes, bilingualism implies 'the presence in the nervous system of two parallel but distinct patterns of verbal behaviour.' How these patterns are separated, or coordinated, remains a mystery.

Research on the acquisitional effects of a bilingual upbringing is ambiguous. Some investigators claim that skills in one or both languages are retarded. For example, Morgan and King (1966:66) state: 'If two languages are spoken in the home, or if the child is forced to learn a foreign language while he is still learning his mother tongue, he gets confused and his skill in both languages is retarded.' Canale, Mougeon, and Beniak (1978:505) observe: 'Our data also suggest that bilinguals may lag behind monolinguals in their rate of acquisition of the grammatical elements in question and that a further lag exists for bilinguals in the rate of acquisition of these elements in their weaker, non-dominant language.' On the other hand, researchers such as Cummins (1978) have discovered that bilinguals possess a greater metalinguistic awareness than monolinguals, and that this, in turn, is beneficial to the acquisition of both languages. According to Fishman (1970:83), many of the so-called 'disadvantages' of bilingualism pointed out in the literature 'have been falsely generalized to the phenomenon at large rather than related to the absence or presence of social patterns which reach substantially beyond bilingualism.' Research on the broader issue of the effect of bilingualism on overall intelligence is likewise inconclusive. As Lambert (1978:537) cautions: 'Researchers in the early period expected to find all sorts of troubles, and they usually did: bilingual children, relative to monolinguals, were behind in school, retarded in measured intelligence and socially adrift.' But Lambert's own findings point in an opposite direction (1978:537): 'What surprised us, though, was that French-English bilingual children in the Montreal setting scored significantly ahead of carefully matched monolinguals on both verbal and non-verbal measures of intelligence. Furthermore, the pattern of test results suggested that the bilinguals had a more diversified structure of intelligence, as measured, and more flexibility in thought.'

A look at case studies also suggests that a bilingual upbringing is developmentally beneficial. Ronjat (1913), for example, described the simultaneous acquisition of French and German by his son Louis up to the age of 4 years 10 months. Louis learned German from his mother and French from his father, and the family lived in France. Ronjat's findings may be summarized as follows. (1) Louis's pronunciation was perfect in both languages from the very beginning. (2) Only a few isolated instances of interference were recorded. (3) There was a parallel development of the phonology, grammar, and lexicon of both languages.

(4) Louis became conscious at a very early age of his bilingualism, and he was able to translate messages from one language to the other. (5) Louis had also acquired abstract notions about language as a system.

Pavlovitch (1920) and Leopold (1953-4) found similar patterns of verbal development in their own bilingual children. The evidence of case studies such as these together with experimental findings such as those by Lambert show that a bilingual upbringing has a positive effect on verbal development. However, it should be noted that in most documented cases where a bilingual upbringing was beneficial a congenial learning environment and the proper motivational stimulus were present. The importance of motivation was shown dramatically in a case study by Kenyeres and Kenyeres (1938). When they arrived in Geneva, their daughter Eva was 6 years 10 months old. Eva knew Hungarian, her native language, and some German, but no French. In only ten months time she learned to speak French like a native speaker, even though Hungarian was spoken in the home. Although Eva attended a French school, her parents found that her greatest incentive for learning French was the desire to play with other children. This provided a strong motivational stimulus which led to a concentrated mental effort to learn French. The implication of case studies such as these for second-language teaching are obvious. An environment conducive to learning together with the proper motivational stimulation will inevitably increase the learner's chances of becoming bilingual.

4.4 A Pedagogical Summary

In this chapter we have looked at the ways in which second-language learning is different from, and similar to, first-language acquisition. The pedagogical inferences that can be derived from such a comparative study can be summarized as follows. (1) Whereas first-language acquisition occurs in childhood, second-language learning usually occurs after puberty (except in cases of childhood bilingualism). This means that the 'why' and the 'how' of second-language learning are different. Children learn their mother tongue in order to cope with their environment. Adults learn a second language for various motivational reasons. Children develop their native language unconsciously and automatically, whereas adults use conscious strategies during the learning process. These differences suggest that some aspects of the second-language-learning process should be approached more in accordance with the adult's increased cognitive capacities, i.e., explicit rules, exercises, etc. will invariably prove to be beneficial to adult language learners. Moreover, motor skills will probably lag behind cognitive ones for neurological reasons. The emphasis in second-language teaching should, therefore, be more on communicative and cognitive aspects. The teacher should expect pronunciation problems to persist for a very long time. (2) As in first-language acquisition, comprehension precedes production in second-language learning. This means that learners will require to do a lot more listening than speaking during the initial stages of language learning. (3) Pedagogical grammars can be of value to second-language learning because they are generally designed to reflect the chronology of language learning. (4) Teachers should expect and tolerate many errors (interlinguistic and intralinguistic) in the learning process. These result from the learner's attempts to construct hypotheses about the target language. They can therefore provide feedback as to the stage of learning. The ability to recognize and classify errors will provide the teacher with the information to pinpoint areas of difficulty. In addition, they can provide a basis on which to develop teaching strategies and materials. (5) Translation is used by second-language learners as both a decoding and encoding strategy during the initial learning stages. Since translation is bound to be imperfect, it should be avoided as a direct teaching strategy. However, it may have a practical value when certain structures or meanings cannot be explained in any other way. (6) Studies on personality variables and case studies on bilingualism show clearly that a congenial environment is conducive to successful language learning. The teacher should try to provide such an environment by adapting to the needs and personality traits of the learners. Above all else, the teacher should try to diminish or remove the inhibitions that can be generated by the classroom.

4.5 Signposts

Research into the psychology of second-language learning is relatively new. There is one promising line of investigation which may shed some light on the psychological mechanisms underlying this process, namely, the connection between errors and acquisition patterns. It seems that certain error types always characterize specific stages of the learning process. The questions currently being asked are concerned with discovering whether this correlation is due to neuropsychological factors or to the context of learning. However, as this area of research is quite new, it is not possible to draw any conclusions from it at the present time.

4.6 Suggestions for Further Reading

In addition to the various works cited in this chapter, the following can be consulted on second-language learning: Jakobovits (1968), Titone (1964a), Brown (1976), Eppert (1977), McDonough (1981), Dulay, Burt, and Krashen (1982), and Hatch (1983). Di Pietro (1972) provides an excellent introduction to CA. A good example of how to validate CA experimentally is outlined in the study by Arcaini, Py, and Pavretti (1979). Critical views of CA can be found in Wardhaugh (1974:173–86) and Jackson (1976). Critical views of EA can be found in Bell (1974) and Da Rocha (1975). A good survey of EA can be found in Richards (1974) and Powell (1975). Spolsky (1979) gives an overall view of CA and EA. An interesting discussion of errors can also be found in Burt and Kiparsky (1972). A good discussion of interlanguage can be found in Tarone, Frauenfelder, and Selinker (1976). James (1980) is perhaps the best current statement on the nature of interlinguistic interference. Titone (1974c) discusses the main psychological advantages of an early bilingual education. The personality advantages of bilingualism are discussed in Titone (1976, 1978) and Diebold (1966). A thorough discussion of bilingualism can be found in Mackey (1976). Titone (1979) is a recent anthology of studies on bilingualism. Excellent critical treatments of the optimal age issue can be found in Stern (1969, 1973, 1976).

5
The Language-Teaching Process

For too long, language teachers have searched for THE method rather than attempting to enhance the teacher's own particular capabilities, experience, preferences, and personality. More emphasis needs to be placed on the individual teacher's expression of teaching approaches rather than insisting upon profession-wide conformity. (Chastain 1971:2)

5.0 Introduction

In the previous three chapters we have focused on the psycholinguistic features which characterize language learning, and we have drawn some obvious pedagogical inferences. What emerges as clear from a study of learning theories is that no one theory or viewpoint can account adequately for the language-learning process. But, of what practical value is all this theorizing to the language teacher? In this chapter we will attempt to answer this question by looking at how some of the research and theories have been translated into teaching methodologies. Then we will discuss some practical applications of psycholinguistic learning theory to language teaching. And finally we will discuss teaching models in a general way.

It must always be kept in mind that there is no pedagogical panacea in language teaching: there is no *one* approach to the problem of facilitating the language-learning process. Teachers should be able to select for themselves those techniques that they have found to be effective either through direct experience or experimental confirmation. A knowledge of the theory and research related to language learning can, of course, be of help in making this selection more informed and intelligent. In Chapter 6 we will discuss how the teacher can go about testing the validity and effectiveness of teaching methods.

5.1 Language-Teaching Methods

It is in the area of foreign-language teaching that psycholinguistic and linguistic theories have found their most fruitful applications. The various theoretical paradigms of psychology and linguistics have always deeply influenced language-teaching methods and models. In this section we will draw a brief historical and descriptive sketch of the major language-teaching methods of the twentieth century. To facilitate the discussion, we will classify the various teaching methods in terms of four categories: *inductive*, *deductive*, *functional*, and *affective-based*. These categories will allow us to describe teaching methodologies both in terms of their pedagogical objectives and in terms of the psycholinguistic viewpoint which underlies them.

5.1.1 INDUCTIVE METHODS

At the turn of this century, the upsurge in interest in foreign languages brought about the construction of several teaching methods designed to impart the foreign language not by means of memorization and grammar rules, but in terms of the same strategies involved in first-language acquisition, namely, the induction of patterns through exposure to language data. The underlying psychological theory in such 'natural' or inductive approaches is, of course, behaviorism. These approaches stress the learning of patterns by induction until an automatic control of these patterns is attained. Thus, instrumental learning techniques form the pedagogical basis of most inductive methods.

One of the most popular of such methods is known as the *direct method*. The term 'direct' refers to the practice of using the foreign language directly without any reference to the native tongue. The earliest and most widely known example of the direct method is the so-called *Berlitz method* – a method which is still being widely used today in the many Berlitz schools of the world. The Berlitz method is based on several key inductive or behavioristic principles. First of all, only the foreign language is allowed in the classroom and the teacher must be a native speaker of the language. This creates a 'natural' linguistic environment similar to the one in which first-language acquisition occurs. Each lesson unit begins typically with the learner listening to, and then repeating, an oral example of the target language; it is believed that proper habit formation in the target language can be achieved primarily by osmosis and repetition. Words are explained by concrete associations (objects, pictures, etc.). These are the stimuli which should elicit the correct responses. Grammatical structure is also imparted inductively by the use of concrete examples or models which focus on one specific area of structure at a time. The oral lesson is followed by a series of questions which are designed to go over and practice matters of form and content pertaining to the lesson unit. Reading and writing skills are taught only after the student has attained proficiency in listening and speaking skills. Direct methods are, therefore, based on the chronological development of the four skills: (1) listening; (2) speaking; (3) reading; and (4) writing. Although this chronology does reflect the first-language acquisition process, it has often been pointed out that there is no reason to believe that it has any psychological validity in a second-language-learning context. Reading and writing skills can easily complement the audio-oral ones right from the very start. Moreover, a total ban on the use of the native language, or on explanations in the native language, may not be practicable. Certain items of structure or lexicon can be imparted more economically and effectively by a quick reference to what learners already know in their native language.

Another well-known inductive approach is the *intensive method*, an approach developed by the United States Army Specialized Training Program. This method brought together the 'natural' aspects of the Berlitz method and the descriptive procedures of structural linguistics. The teaching was therefore carried out by two instructors: a linguist who gave explanations of structure and an instructor who handled the drill and practice sessions. The drills were, of course, based on the behaviorist principles of imitation, repetition, and reinforcement although some translation was allowed for contrastive reasons.

In the 1950s and 1960s, another inductive methodology grew directly out of the techniques of contrastive analysis. After a detailed comparison of the structures and lexical features of L_1 and L_2, these *contrastive teaching methods* developed explanations and exercise materials that reflected the supposed hierarchies of difficulty (see Section 4.2.2). The idea was to go from the lowest level of difficulty (zero transfer) to the highest one. The theoretical shortcomings of such a viewpoint were outlined in Chapter 4. Once again, it was believed that the learning of a second language was simply a matter of learning new habits, and that the best way to do this was by transferring or realigning the old habits of the native language, as the situation warranted.

Perhaps the most influential inductive method of the 1940s, 1950s, and 1960s was the so-called *audio-lingual method*. In most versions of this method, only the foreign language was permitted and translation was forbidden. Moreover, the behavioristic techniques of imitation, rote memorization, pattern practice, and reinforcement formed its pedagogical nucleus. The idea was to start with the smallest units of language at the lower levels (phonetic, phonological) and to work up to the larger units in a chronological sequence. By memorizing patterns or structures, the student, it was believed, would inevitably extrapolate underlying structural principles inductively. Aural and visual stimuli (i.e., audio-oral and audio-visual devices such as language tapes and slides) came to be permanent features of this approach. Clearly, the behavioral emphasis on environmental conditioning and the formation of automatic verbal habits was at the root of such teaching strategies. The enthusiasm with which teachers embraced the audio-lingual method degenerated into disenchantment in the 1970s. As transformational linguistics and cognitive psychology came to the forefront in the late 1960s and 1970s, the audio-lingual method was seen to be inadequate and even counterproductive. It was discovered through classroom experience that verbal behaviors could not always be elicited or learned by S-R techniques. The major complaints against the audio-lingual approach have been summarized comprehensively by Chastain (1971:78): (1) The claim that the audio-lingual method would produce bilingual graduates was never realized. (2) Reliance on sensorial stimuli (audio-oral and audio-visual) may hinder those students who are not sensorially oriented. (3) It is impossible to eliminate the native language from the classroom. (4) It is time consuming to avoid any discussion of grammar. (5) The continuous mimetic and repetition tasks are monotonous for both teacher and learner.

5.1.2 DEDUCTIVE METHODS

What teachers began to realize after the audio-lingual experiment was that the psychological basis of second-language learning is not totally inductive. Nor is it totally deductive. The truth of the matter is that second-language learning is a process that probably lies midway between total induction and total deduction. Even so, deductively oriented teaching methods began to characterize second-language teaching in the late 1960s and came to the forefront in the 1970s because of the failure of behavioristically based inductive methods and because of the findings of cognitive psychology that deductive, or rule-based, strategies play a prominent role in second-language learning. Deductive teaching methods are therefore based on the learning principles of cognitive psychology and its linguistic counterpart, transformationalism, and they are generally known as *cognitive-code* procedures. A summary of the schools of psychology and linguistics associated with inductive and deductive teaching methods is given in Table 5.1.

But even long before the advent of transformational linguistics, perhaps the most extreme form of deductive teaching, the so-called *grammar-translation method*, came into prominence soon after the First World War and eventually became one of the major teaching methods on this continent. During this period it was believed that students did not have the time to master the four language skills (listening, speaking, reading, writing) with equal proficiency and consequently that high-school and university language curricula should concentrate on

TABLE 5.1

Parallels between inductive and deductive teaching methods

Method	School of psychology	School of linguistics
Inductive Direct (Berlitz) Intensive Contrastive Audio-lingual	Behaviorism (Neobehaviorism)	Structuralism
Deductive Cognitive-code	Cognitive	Transformationalism

reading the foreign language as the only really attainable goal. Thus, grammar-translation came to be the dominant approach to language teaching between 1920 and 1950 and is still used today in various disguises. Unlike recent deductive approaches, it is not based on any psychological or linguistic philosophy, but rather on the utilitarian view that time and resource limitations make it the only viable pedagogical approach.

The grammar-translation method is based, as its name implies, on two principles: (1) the learning of grammatical rules and vocabulary lists and (2) their subsequent application to translation tasks. Thus, students first learn the grammar of the target language by means of elaborate explanations together with vocabulary lists. Then, after having memorized the rules and vocabulary lists, they test their comprehension of the target language by translating texts either into the target language, or from the target into the native language. Comparisons with the native language are a constant feature of the teaching process, and instruction is generally conducted in the native language. There is little or no concern with the cultivation of audio-oral skills. Chastain (1971:60) gives a good overall characterization of this approach: 'The goal was to be able to convert each language into the other, and the process was one of problem-solving, the problem being that of puzzling out the correct forms assisted by the rules and the dictionary.'

Cognitive-code techniques, on the other hand, are not based on translation but rather on the cognitive principle that rule-learning must be meaningful. Moreover, since the framework for rule-learning is the one described by TG grammar (see Section 1.3), the sequencing of rules goes from deep to surface structures. Whereas inductive procedures focused on surface (phonological, morphological) differences in the initial teaching stages, cognitive-code techniques stress the learning of deep-structure relations first. To illustrate in a

112 Applied Psycholinguistics

simplified fashion the nature of cognitive-code procedures, we will use the example of simple question-formation in Italian. In TG theory, questions are transforms of corresponding deep-structure declarative sentences. In Italian, the transformational rule which converts deep structures to corresponding question surface structures states simply that the subject NP is transposed to sentence-final position and that a raised intonation contour is added (?).

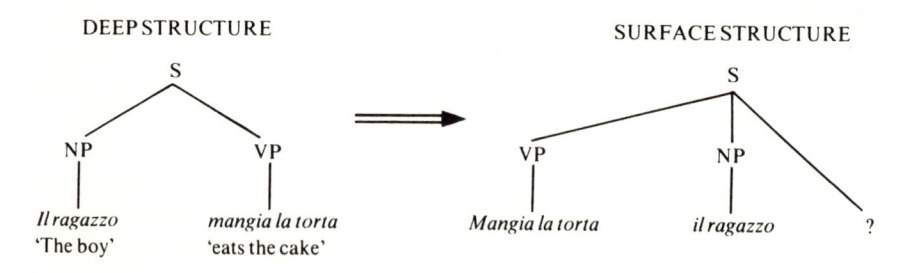

```
        DEEP STRUCTURE                              SURFACE STRUCTURE
              S                                            S
             / \                                          /|\
           NP   VP              ⟹                       VP NP \
           |     |                                      |    |    \
       Il ragazzo  mangia la torta              Mangia la torta  il ragazzo  ?
       'The boy'  'eats the cake'
```

Given this rule (with the appropriate grammatical symbols and tree diagrams to serve as mnemonic aids) the students then practice its applications with meaningful examples. These are utterances which are in line with the learner's cognitive structure (Ausubel 1963). Thus, the learner's intellectual capacities and background are assessed beforehand and the examples used in practice sessions relate directly to both. Both the form and content of the examples used in the classroom are important in cognitive-code teaching, whereas in inductive methodologies what counted above all else was the form.

The popularity of cognitive-code teaching strategies is due in part to the fact that after the age of puberty the formal operations become prominent in all learning tasks. Krashen (1976, 1977) has suggested that this cognitive maturity produces in second-language learners a 'monitor' which allows them to focus consciously on language forms. However, as Fischer (1979) has cogently argued, both induction and deduction play a role in second-language learning. It would seem logical to us that a teaching strategy which integrates both inductive and deductive techniques would be a more flexible and satisfactory one. More will be said about this in Chapter 7.

5.1.3 FUNCTIONAL APPROACHES

While both inductive and deductive methods focus primarily on language form, recently there has been a trend in language teaching which emphasizes language use. This trend is known as *functional* language teaching. The most widely used form of functional language teaching is called the *notional-functional syllabus* (e.g., Widdowson 1972; Wilkins 1973, 1976). This method relies on sociolinguistic typologies of speech acts such as the ones outlined by Austin (1962) and Halliday (1973) (see Section 1.4.1). The focus is on how to use the target language for such purposes as 'greeting,' 'inviting,' 'introducing,' 'agreeing,' 'insulting,' 'apologizing.' The appropriate structural and lexical patterns required for these communicative tasks are taught simultaneously, i.e., they are interwoven into the communicative settings.

In a recent study, Howard (1980) specifies what she considers to be the essential components of communicative situations which, in turn, should form the nucleus of a functional teaching strategy: (1) Communication is based on *interaction* and therefore involves at least two participants. (2) The form and content of the language used is *unpredictable*. This unpredictability is handled by means of appropriate verbal strategies (see also Di Pietro 1976, 1978, 1979). (3) An oral exchange involves a *time pressure* if communication is not to break down. (4) Communication takes place in a *context of situation* which involves such variables as the role, status, mood, and attitudes of the participants. These variables will influence grammatical and lexical choices. (5) Communication serves a *purpose* and is therefore meaningful. (6) Communication is colored by *sociolinguistic features* which determine the level of speech (e.g., formal vs. informal). (7) Communication involves *authentic language* which reveals the age, background, etc., of the participants. (8) Communication is *cohesive*; i.e., it involves the logical development of thought. (9) Communication involves *predisposition*. This refers to that feature of language use which affects both what the speakers say and how they say it in the light of how they perceive other speakers.

Inductive and deductive methods are aimed at building up linguistic competence and thus focus, at least initially, on the teaching of structure and vocabulary. Once these are mastered, the focus then shifts to language use. Functional approaches, on the other hand, are based on the development of communicative competence, as defined by such parameters as those outlined by Howard. But as McKay (1980) observes, there are some methodological problems associated with functional language teaching. For one thing, when a class is composed of students of diverse backgrounds, it is difficult to come up with communicational situations which will be relevant to all. Second, the social situation alone does not determine what will be said. Someone could have a variety of intentions unrelated to a social context (e.g., registering a complaint, cajoling). Third, it is difficult to decide on how to sequence the communicational situations because of their interconnection with matters of structure and vocabulary.

Despite such problems, functional approaches are becoming more and more popular. McKay (1980) illustrates the notional-functional approach in terms of seven strategies. (1) *Identifying the intention of an expression*. Students are asked to identify the intention of a language sample. For instance, in example 1 of Figure 5.1, students of English as a second language (ESL) are asked to match a specific

114 Applied Psycholinguistics

Example 1: Identifying the intention of an expression

INTENTION	LANGUAGE
1. Making a suggestion	A. What time's your train?
2. Showing enthusiasm	B. Why don't you go and see a doctor?
3. Greetings	C. Heh! That's marvelous!
4. Showing sympathy	D. Hello, Mike. Fancy seeing you here!
5. Asking for information	E. I think it was a very stupid thing to do.
6. Giving an opinion	F. Oh, I am sorry. I really am.

Example 2: Substitution

Receiving a call for someone who is away from the office:

EXPRESSIONS OF POLITENESS	EXPLANATION	OFFER TO TAKE A MESSAGE
I'm sorry	she's at a meeting.	Could I take a message?
I'm afraid	he's sick today.	Would you care to leave a message
Sorry but	she's out of town.	Is there any message?
	he's on holiday.	

Example 3: Fill-in dialogues

Roberto and Miguel are discussing where Roberto should go on his date with Maria.

Miguel: _____ go to a show or something?
Roberto: _____ I thought Maria might like to go to a concert.
Miguel: _____ have a look and see what's playing.
_____ Zellerback over in Berkeley?
Roberto: _____ That sounds good.
Miguel: _____ call up and see if you can still get tickets.

Example 4: Short rejoinders

Get together with another student and imagine yourselves in these situations: Get angry. You have just realized that a restaurant has overcharged you; get angry with the manager. You are fed up with the clothes your friend is wearing. You want to go to the beach but it is raining again.

Example 5: Selection of alternate forms

Choose the best answer:

Tom and Mary are students in the same class. Tom wants to borrow Mary's pen. He says: (a) Will you lend me a pen? (b) May I ask to borrow your pen? (c) Would you be so kind as to lend me your pen?

Example 6: Role playing

Imagine you want to start a conversation with the girl sitting next to you after class and want to take her out to dinner. What would you say?

Example 7: Fieldwork

Tell a native speaker something incredible and report the response.

FIGURE 5.1 Notional-functional teaching strategies for ESL (adapted from McKay 1980:183–5)

intention with its appropriate language form. (2) *Substitution*. Students are asked to select the possible expressions of a certain function (example 2 of Figure 5.1). (3) *Fill-in dialogues*. Students are required to fill in the missing parts of dialogue samples (example 3 of Figure 5.1). (4) *Short rejoinders*. These are intended to provide students with short statements which correspond to certain emotional states (example 4 of Figure 5.1). (5) *Selection of alternate forms*. Students are presented with a social context and then asked to select the most appropriate form of an intention (example 5 of Figure 5.1). (6) *Role playing*. This allows the students the opportunity to interact in actual communicative settings (example 6 of Figure 5.1). (7) *Field work*. Advanced students can be asked to try to elicit a particular function from native speakers and record what they hear (example 7 of Figure 5.1).

It should be clear from the foregoing discussion that functional teaching methods are not based on any specific psychological theory of language learning. They are based, rather, on the belief that languages are best taught and learned in ways that approximate normal human verbal interaction.

5.1.4 AFFECTIVE-BASED METHODS

The history of language-teaching methodology shows quite clearly that no one approach (inductive, deductive, functional) constitutes a pedagogical panacea. This is simply because there are too many variables involved in the language-learning process. As Yorio (1976) points out, and as has been discussed in previous chapters, there are at least six interacting variables which influence language learning: age, cognition, the native language, the instructional input, affective factors, educational background (see Figure 5.2). Teaching experience has repeatedly shown that no single approach can account for all these complex variables. Mainly for this reason, language teachers and applied linguists and psycholinguists are beginning to propose eclectic or 'integrated' methods more and more. These invariably attempt to blend together some of the more salient features of specific approaches (inductive, deductive, functional). The main psycholinguistic principle underlying integrated methodologies is that language teaching should be *affective-based*; i.e., it should be adapted to the student's needs, motivations, and learning style. The selection of a specific heuristic technique will depend on how it will promote learning for a specific learner or group of learners. This view of language teaching has been influenced to some extent by the findings and views of humanistic psychology (see Section 2.3.3).

Several affective-based methodologies have sprung up in the last two decades. Of these, there are four that have received considerable attention and which merit a brief discussion here: Asher's *total physical response* (e.g., Asher 1965, 1969, 1972, 1977); Terrell's *natural approach* (e.g., Terrell 1977, 1980); Curran's

1. Age

Children	{ 1–5 5–10 }	Biological and cognitive factors Social factors (parental influence, schooling, peer group pressure)
Adolescents	{ 11–15 }	Biological factors (critical period) Social factors (parental influence, etc.)
Adults	{ 16 on }	Biological factors (critical period) Social factors (peer-group pressure, context of second-language learning/teaching)

2. Cognition

General intelligence
Language aptitude (learning strategies)

3. Native language

Transfer (phonological, grammatical, semantic)

4. Input

Free learner	{ context of learning }	Place of learning (foreign-language environment, second-language environment, bilingual environment) Type of language contact Family-language environment Peer-language environment
Instructed learner	{ context of teaching }	Type of instruction (formal, informal) Length of instruction Place of instruction (foreign language environment, etc.) Material of instruction Source of instruction (teacher attitude and training)

5. Affective domain

Socio-cultural factors (attitude towards native- and second-language cultures and people)
Egocentric factors (depression, anxiety, self-consciousness, etc.)
Motivation (integrative, instrumental)

6. Educational background

Illiterate
Literate (professional, nonprofessional)

FIGURE 5.2 Language-learning variables (adapted from Yorio 1976:61)

community counseling (e.g., Curran 1976); and Lozanov's *suggestopedia* (e.g., Bancroft 1972, 1978; Mignault 1978; Bélanger-Popvassileva 1979).

Asher's method is based on two psychological principles: (1) receptive skills are prior to productive ones; (2) both learners and teacher should be involved in a close relationship which is intended to minimize, or remove, inhibitions and fears. Asher has produced a guidebook (1977) which shows how a series of up to 150 lessons based on listening comprehension can be developed. The method uses physical responses to command stimuli: e.g., 'When Jack has written that word on the board, Jill will erase it.' Students thus participate directly in meaningful tasks. Visual and auditory stimuli are reinforced by motor responses. It is believed that by an active participation of this type, learning, especially mnemonic, will be enhanced greatly. In other words, the total physical response method connects physical activity with meaningful language use.

A method which also puts comprehension before production is Terrell's natural approach. Terrell incorporates Krashen's acquisition-learning dichotomy into the *modus operandi* of language teaching by focusing on acquisition in the classroom, while learning exercises are restricted to outside the classroom. According to this method, acquisition will result from a focus on communication, whereas learning will result from cognitively oriented exercises which focus on rules and their applications. In addition, it is claimed that both acquisition and learning will be activated only if the teacher-learner relationship is one that makes the learner feel comfortable; and this can be achieved if the teacher does most of the talking in the target language during the initial stages. This will apparently not only make the student feel less intimidated by removing the pressure to produce correct responses right from the very beginning, but will also take advantage of the psychological reality of comprehension over production. Students are therefore allowed to ask questions and make responses in their native language until their self-image and ease in the classroom 'is such that a response in the second language will not produce anxiety' (Terrell 1977:333).

Curran's community counseling is based on Rogers' humanistic view of education (see Section 2.3.3) that the teacher-learner relationship ought to be similar to the one between a counselor and a client. This approach consists of five stages. (1) The students are grouped together in the classroom. Initially they will be totally dependent on the teacher-counselor. The students are encouraged to establish an interpersonal relationship with the teacher-counselor and among themselves in their native language. Ideas and structural matters are discussed in the native language and the teacher-counselor provides the appropriate target-language words and structures in a slow and 'sensitive' manner. (2) As the students start to gain courage and to know each other better, they will make some attempts to speak in the target language. During this stage the teacher-counselor continues to provide information and direct translation. (3) As the students progress further, they will become less dependent on the translations of the teacher-counselor who now becomes a source for error-correction. (4) When the students become very familiar with the target language, they will need the teacher-counselor only for subtle points of grammar and vocabulary. (5) During the last stage of the learning process, the students become totally independent, and free communication in the target language emerges. The teacher-counselor's 'silent' presence simply reinforces grammatical and lexical correctness. Thus, through careful attention to the student's needs, the teacher-counselor aids the student in moving from total dependence to independence and self-assurance (see Figure 5.3).

Lozanov's suggestopedia also stresses the importance of creating an interpersonal learning environment. This method is quite interesting because it relies on subthreshold learning techniques, i.e., learning that occurs without the subjects realizing it. This method was first developed by the Bulgarian physician and psychotherapist Dr Georgi Lozanov, and it is used extensively in Bulgaria, the Soviet Union, East Germany, and Hungary. A typical class in suggestopedic teaching is four hours long and consists of three separate components within a 'suggestopedic cycle'. (1) There is a review of the previous day's material through conversations, skits, games, etc. Some exercises are also used. (2) New material is presented in a traditional way with the necessary grammatical and lexical explanations, as well as the needed translation. The new material consists mainly of dialogues based on real-life situations. (3) Then the *séance*, which lasts approximately one hour, follows. This involves subthreshold teaching techniques. The students relax and sit comfortably in reclining chairs. They use yoga breathing techniques and listen to background music (e.g., the slow movements of the concerto music of such Baroque composers as Bach, Vivaldi, Handel, Corelli, and Telemann) while the new language materials are read in the target language and in translation. It is claimed that the *séance* accelerates the learning process by unlocking the subconscious reserves of the mind. The value of the musical component is explained by Mignault (1978:700): 'first, it is very effective in reaching the unconscious levels of awareness and, second, it strengthens long-term memorization.' Since this method has not been used extensively in the West, it is difficult at present to ascertain its effectiveness. Some initial research, however, is quite positive (Bancroft 1978).

5.2 Language Teaching and Applied Psycholinguistics

Faced with complex psychological learning variables and with many teaching methodologies to choose from, what criteria should guide the teacher in choosing teaching strategies and materials? As we have argued in previous chapters, a

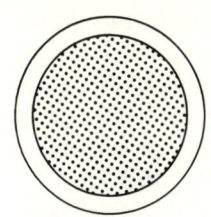

1. Total dependence on teacher-counselor who is translator and source of information. Target-language words and structures taught slowly.

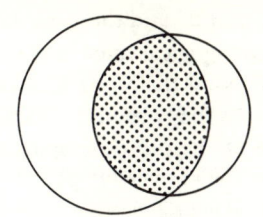

2. Students beginning to gain courage to speak. Teacher-counselor continues to be source of translation and information.

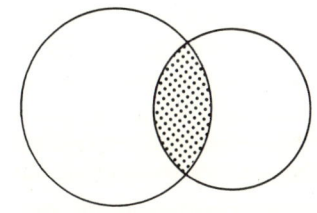

3. Growing independence. Teacher-counselor corrects errors.

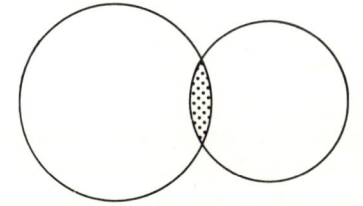

4. Teacher-counselor now needed only for subtle points of grammar and vocabulary.

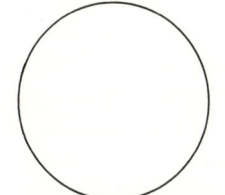

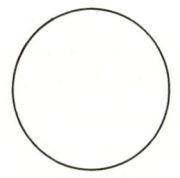

5. Total independence and free communication. Teacher-counselor reinforces language correctness by 'silent' presence.

FIGURE 5.3 The community counseling method (adapted from Curran 1976:53)

knowledge of the psycholinguistic mechanisms underlying the learning process can be of help in aiding the teacher select some strategy or prepare instructional materials. In this section, we will summarize briefly some of the salient implications that applied 'educational' psycholinguistics (APL) has for language teaching. We wish to reiterate here what was said in the preface that our intention is not to provide a list of details on the *how* and *what* of language teaching. Rather, our purpose is to familiarize teachers with some of the findings of the psychology of language learning which can aid them in making instructional techniques 'psychologically valid,' and thus, one hopes, to maximize their efficiency. Therefore, the main pedagogical value of APL is as an *assessment* instrument. It will prepare teachers to assess their instructional procedures and materials on the basis of the learning results they produce. The assessment process consists of three stages. (1) *Pre-assessment*. Before developing an instructional strategy or curriculum, teachers can use the knowledge gleaned from the investigations into the psychology of language learning in order to make selections from available instructional materials and methodologies or to develop teaching procedures when necessary. (2) *Instruction-feedback-assessment*. During the actual teaching process, APL can help teachers adjust and adapt their materials and procedures according to the results they actually produce. (3) *Post-assessment*. After the teaching process, teachers can evaluate student performance in order to determine the efficiency of the instructional procedures and materials used and ultimately to develop an overall pedagogical plan based on APL. The first stage is a *selective* one; the second an *adaptive* one; and the third an *evaluative* one (see Figure 5.4).

In previous chapters we have looked at some of the neurological, perceptual, cognitive, and affective aspects of language learning. Needless to say, these should influence the choice of instructional techniques and materials at the pre-assessment stage. We will now summarize the pre-assessment implications that APL has for language teaching.

It is to be expected that motor skills will lag behind other language skills since after puberty the brain has all but lost its plasticity and it becomes more difficult to adjust one's articulatory habits to the phonological system of the target language. This implies that instruction should not emphasize native-like pronunciation at the beginning of the teaching process for this can lead to unnecessary frustration. An appreciation of the difficulty involved in developing new motor habits on the part of both teachers and learners can, in itself, enhance the learning of pronunciation. Since articulation involves habit formation, it would seem appropriate to use strategies and materials which are instrumental in nature (e.g., imitation, pattern practice, repetition). Nevertheless, it should always be kept in mind that if habit-formation is to become permanent, then the instrumental techniques should be contextualized in a meaningful way by relating the samples of the target language used to the backgrounds and interests of the learners. Moreover, since it will normally take a while to develop the target-language phonology, the teaching and practice of phonological structure should probably be interspersed throughout the teaching process, even at the intermediate and advanced stages when learners will feel comfortable enough to focus more consciously on forming articulatory habits.

In the area of grammatical and vocabulary teaching, the psychological research into second-language learning shows quite conspicuously that cognitively oriented instruction is more suitable. Unlike children who develop their

The Language-Teaching Process 121

| APL
Information on the neurological, perceptual, cognitive, affective mechanisms underlying the language learning process | PRE-ASSESSMENT or SELECTIVE STAGE
Selection of instructional procedures and materials | INSTRUCTION-FEEDBACK-ASSESSMENT or ADAPTIVE STAGE
Adjustment and adaptation of instructional materials and procedures | POST-ASSESSMENT or EVALUATIVE STAGE
Student performance evaluated and instructional procedures and materials assessed accordingly |

OVERALL TEACHING PLAN BASED ON APL

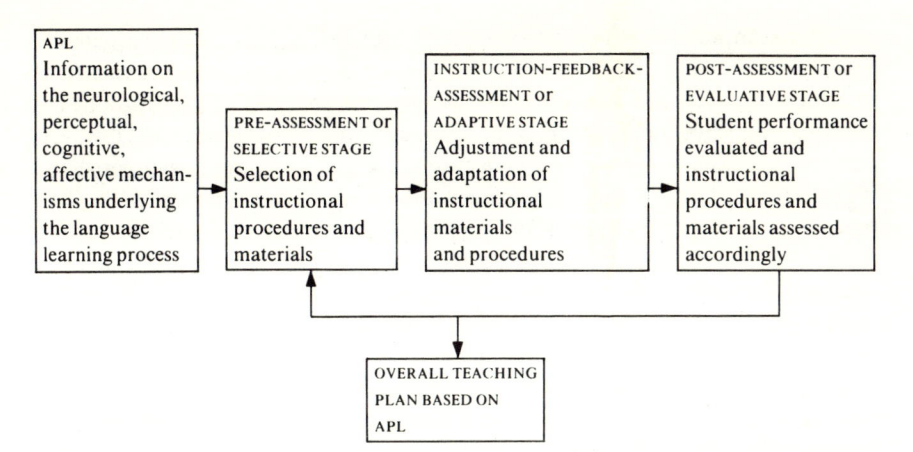

FIGURE 5.4 Applied psycholiguistics as a pedagogical assessment instrument

native-language morphology, syntax, and semantics unconsciously and automatically, adult learners use conscious strategies such as monitoring and comparisons with the native language. In accordance with this increased cognitive capacity, the use of rules, exercises, etc., as in cognitive-code approaches, seems to be an appropriate instructional strategy. Comparisons with native-language structure and meanings can often facilitate the learning process and help to obviate interlinguistic errors. It is difficult to decide the order in which structures and lexical items should be taught. This generally depends on the language being taught and its structural and lexical peculiarities. Applied linguistics, rather than APL, can contribute to the sequencing of grammatical and lexical topics. Normally, it will be found that learners will be able to understand more complex syntactic constructions than they are able to produce. Production patterns in second-language grammar often follow the pattern of first-language acquisition – from one- or two-word utterances to simple declarative sentences. Complex utterances with embedded clauses come much later on. In general, those target-language syntactic and lexical patterns which correspond to native-language ones are produced much more easily and readily than those which do not correspond. This suggests that totally new grammatical and syntactic patterns will require much more teaching time than familiar ones.

Teachers should expect, and consequently tolerate, many errors in a second-language-learning context. These result from the student's attempts to construct hypotheses about the target language. The ability to diagnose errors by means of CA and EA will help the teacher formulate an appropriate course of correction and identify more accurately *what* to focus on and *when* to teach it.

Since comprehension is superior to production in language learning in general, learners will need to do a lot more listening (and reading) than speaking (and writing) during the initial stages of the learning process when they are forming the ability to perceive the meaningful, or emic, cues in the flow of speech. However, since perception involves control over structure (e.g., analysis by synthesis), the teacher should make sure that explicit directions or instructions on how to identify structural units such as words, phrases, etc., are given right from the very start. The use of written speech can be of help in this instance for it helps to identify such important cues as word and sentence boundaries. If there is any key pedagogical principle that can be derived from APL, it is that the teaching process should put reception before production, as in Terrell's natural approach or Curran's community counseling. The teacher's direct input is required mostly during the initial learning stages when students are learning to perceive the target language correctly. This input should decrease gradually as the learner's productive abilities increase. Thus, students should be exposed to as much of the target language as possible from the very beginning, not simply to bits and pieces of it. This does not mean that there should be no sequencing but simply that those structures which for some reason must be taught before others should always be contextualized in a broad linguistic framework. This also does not imply that productive skills need to be excluded from the initial learning stages. It means, rather, that the *degree* to which receptive skills are emphasized should be greater at the beginning. As Davies (1980) found in an experimental study, putting receptive skills first led to the establishment of a sound base for the development of productive skills and to an increase in motivation.

A second equally important pedagogical principle that can be derived from APL is that affective and personality variables (the learners' aptitude for languages, style, motivations, etc.) always play a crucial role in determining success at language learning. Teachers should therefore always make an effort to *know* their students. Above all else, teachers should strive to create a congenial and stimulating learning environment in which students' needs are met and in which inhibitions and fears are minimized or removed. When selecting a language manual, the teacher should make sure that it is suitable to the cognitive style of the learners. A manual which is based, say, solely on behavioristic learning principles may not be appropriate for students whose language background includes an emphasis on the formal study of language. On the other hand, a manual which stresses only the learning of rules may prove to be useless because language is communication and should be taught in communicative settings.

In sum, together with applied linguistics (AL) – which helps the teacher translate models of linguistic structure into pedagogical media (manuals, exercises, etc.) – APL can help the teacher make informed choices and decisions on such

The Language-Teaching Process

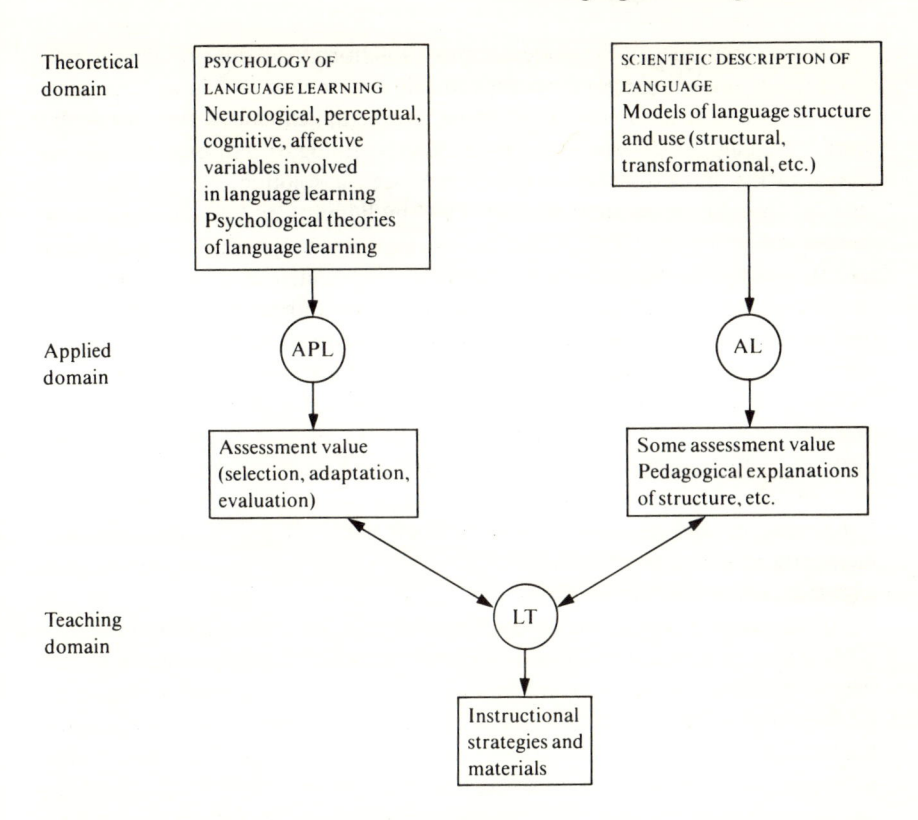

```
Theoretical    PSYCHOLOGY OF                    SCIENTIFIC DESCRIPTION OF
domain         LANGUAGE LEARNING                LANGUAGE
               Neurological, perceptual,        Models of language structure
               cognitive, affective             and use (structural,
               variables involved               transformational, etc.)
               in language learning
               Psychological theories
               of language learning

Applied             (APL)                              (AL)
domain

               Assessment value                 Some assessment value
               (selection, adaptation,          Pedagogical explanations
               evaluation)                      of structure, etc.

Teaching                           (LT)
domain
                            Instructional
                            strategies and
                            materials
```

FIGURE 5.5 The relationship among APL, AL, and LT

practical matters as: (1) in which order teaching points should come; (2) how much should be taught at any specific point; (3) what to expect from a learner at any given time; (4) what methods and materials are suitable to specific learning tasks. The locus of APL with respect to AL and language teaching (LT) is shown in Figure 5.5.

5.3 Language-Teaching Models

The discussion on the value of APL as a pedagogical assessment instrument leads to the question of LT models in general. Stern (1978) distinguishes among four main categories of LT models. (1) *Separation* or *hands-off models*. These are not based on any of the findings of AL or APL (e.g., the grammar-translation method). They are perhaps the weakest type because, as Stern (1978:682) notes, even if 'research does not provide definitive solutions to all our problems it may still produce some findings of interest and value to language teaching. Moreover, researchers and teachers live in the same intellectual climate: if they speak the same "language" they can share and exchange thoughts and experiences and jointly tackle the problems to which they seek a solution.' (2) *Applicational models*. These are suggested or constructed by linguists and psycholinguists by themselves on the basis of their findings and theories. They are usually based on a specific theoretical viewpoint (e.g., behaviorism, cognitive learning theory) and, as teachers have found out all too often, linguists and psycholinguists change their views and come forward with conflicting recommendations. (3) *Resource models*. These view AL and APL as pre-assessment instruments, i.e., as resources on which teachers can draw, selecting from the offerings of AL and APL those theories and findings which they discover to be useful. In order to develop their own applications, however, teachers must know the right questions to ask, where to find the appropriate information, how to translate theory into practice, etc. (4) *Convergent* or *common-ground models*. These take resource models one step further by putting researchers and teachers on an equal footing. Researchers who wish to translate their findings into teaching practice must acquire an understanding of language pedagogy. Teachers, for their part, need to understand AL and APL at least to the extent that they can formulate appropriate questions and that they know where to go for information.

The theme of this book has been that convergent-type models are the most desirable ones. In terms of the assessment nature of AL and APL, these models have not only a pre-assessment value, but also instruction-feedback-assessment and post-assessment values. During the teaching process, practitioners can adapt, modify, revise, or reject certain pre-assessment choices on the basis of their efficacy in specific classroom situations. After the teaching process is completed, practitioners can evaluate, or measure, the actual efficacy of the pedagogical decisions made during the pre-assessment and instruction-feedback-assessment stages. Post-assessment techniques will be discussed in Chapter 6. Ideally, the language teacher should also be a linguist and psycholinguist. However, this is rarely the case, so that researchers and practitioners will have to work together for the common goal of constantly improving language-teaching technology. Figure 5.6 summarizes the various types of LT models.

5.4 A Pedagogical Summary

Sections 5.2 and 5.3 have been concerned with the relationship between AL/ALP and language teaching. This part of the chapter has, therefore, constituted a

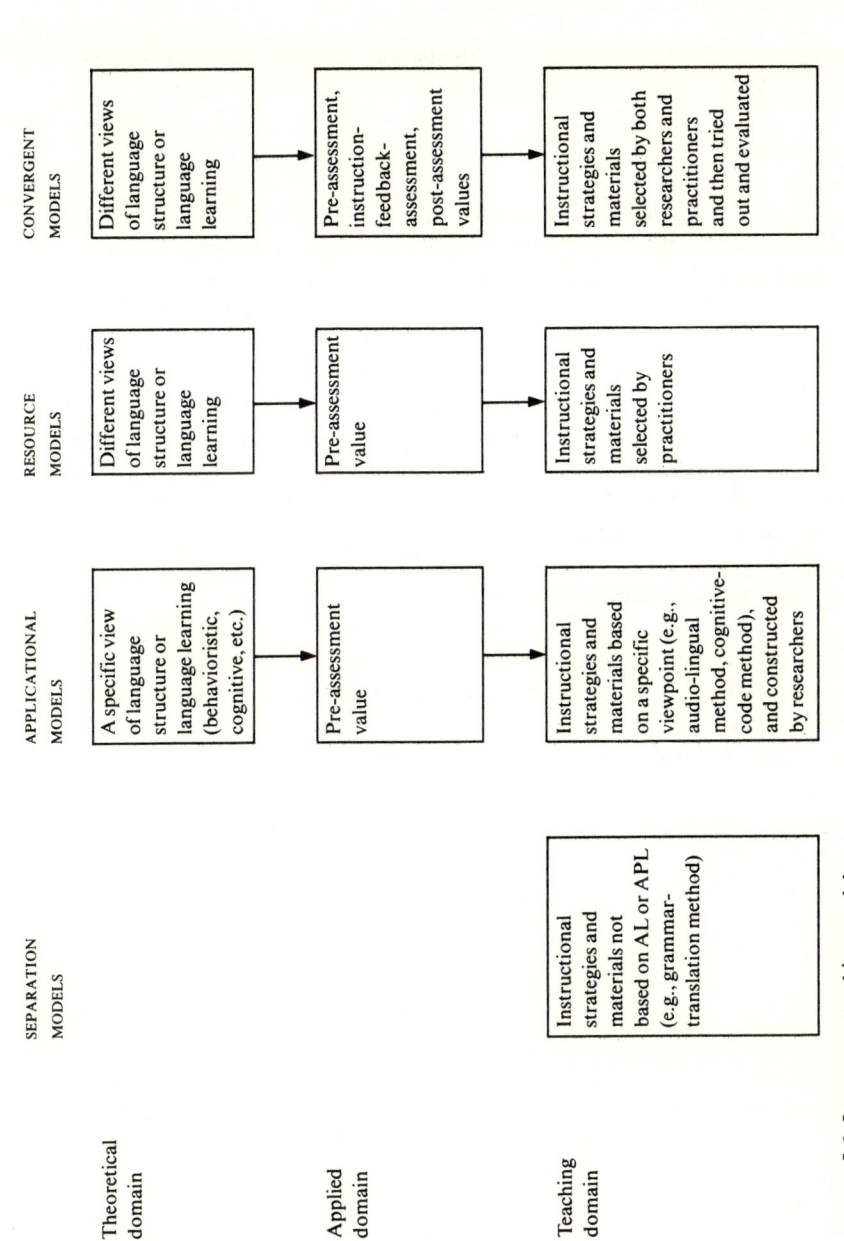

	SEPARATION MODELS	APPLICATIONAL MODELS	RESOURCE MODELS	CONVERGENT MODELS
Theoretical domain		A specific view of language structure or language learning (behavioristic, cognitive, etc.)	Different views of language structure or language learning	Different views of language structure or language learning
Applied domain		Pre-assessment value	Pre-assessment value	Pre-assessment, instruction-feedback-assessment, post-assessment values
Teaching domain	Instructional strategies and materials not based on AL or APL (e.g., grammar-translation method)	Instructional strategies and materials based on a specific viewpoint (e.g., audio-lingual method, cognitive-code method), and constructed by researchers	Instructional strategies and materials selected by practitioners	Instructional strategies and materials selected by both researchers and practitioners and then tried out and evaluated

FIGURE 5.6 Language-teaching models

pedagogical summary in itself. The theme that we wish to emphasize here once again is that truly effective teaching is not tied to any one method.

5.5 Signposts

If there is one salient trend in language teaching today it is flexibility and adaptiveness to the ever-changing conditions of the classroom. In the area of methodology, there is one development that merits the attention of all teachers; namely, so-called 'immersion' students in some or all of their regular school subjects. Thus, for example, in Canadian French immersion programs (e.g., Swain and Lapkin 1977, Swain 1980) English-speaking students are taught many of their school subjects in French. The initial results from this experimental teaching program have shown quite convincingly that immersion teaching has helped the students develop high levels of proficiency in the target language without any detrimental effects on first-language proficiency, cognitive development, and academic achievement.

5.6 Suggestions for Further Reading

For a historical survey of LT methods see Titone (1968, 1975), Stevick (1976), and Grabe (1979). For a description of LT models see, for example, Papalia (1975, 1976), Strevens (1978), and Bialystock (1979). Wardhaugh and Brown (1976) is an informative survey of AL in various disciplines.

6
Measurement, Testing, and Research

Although tests and experiments are most often used for giving information to the external world about what school or university leavers are supposed to be able to do, tests play a central part – or should play a central part – in any experiment on language learning processes or instructional practices. (Ingram 1977:32)

6.0 Introduction

As discussed in sections 5.2 and 5.3, the evaluation of instructional practices based on APL constitutes the post-assessment stage of the language-teaching process. In this chapter, we will outline briefly the main concepts associated with evaluation. First, we will describe some elementary, but essential, statistical concepts. Then, we will look at testing, relating it to the psychological and linguistic principles discussed in earlier chapters. Finally, we will discuss experimentation and research procedures on language-learning processes and teaching practices.

6.1 Some Elementary Statistical Concepts

Statistics can be defined as that branch of applied mathematics which allows us to extract any general pattern from a mass of data; and it permits us to determine whether there exists any relationship between two or more factors present in a situation. In this section, it is our purpose to introduce some basic statistical notions and formulas which are relevant to testing and experimentation in APL, AL, and LT. A familiarity with these notions will be indispensable for those teachers who may wish to evaluate their instructional practices at the post-assessment stage. Even for those teachers who do not wish to evaluate their instructional techniques, the ability to understand what a formula implies will

TABLE 6.1

Hypothetical raw scores received on a listening-comprehension test in ESL

12	54	63	70	75
21	55	64	70	75
29	56	65	70	75
32	57	68	70	76
32	58	68	70	76
32	59	68	71	76
37	60	68	71	76
38	61	68	71	77
45	61	68	71	77
45	61	68	72	78
45	61	68	72	79
46	61	68	72	79
46	61	68	72	80
47	61	69	72	80
48	61	69	72	83
49	61	69	73	84
50	61	69	73	85
52	61	69	74	90
52	61	69	74	91
53	61	69	74	96

help make the technical research literature in AL and APL much more intelligible. Specifically, we will look at: (1) the statistical presentation and organization of data; (2) measures of central tendency and dispersion; (3) significance measures; and (4) correlation techniques. Our discussion will, of course, be kept at a non-technical level, i.e., we will not discuss the mathematical reasons behind formulas and techniques. The interested reader can consult any standard textbook on statistics for these reasons.

6.1.1 THE PRESENTATION AND ORGANIZATION OF DATA

If the data gathered from a test, an experiment, etc., are not organized in some fashion, it will be hard, if not impossible, to detect any general pattern or trend that may be present in the data. Consider the hypothetical data given in Table 6.1. These are the hypothetical test scores received by 100 subjects on a listening-comprehension test in ESL (English as a second language). The scores are listed in numerical order, and each score is calculated out of 100, i.e., from 0 to 100. Obviously, it is very difficult to make anything out of a set of raw scores such as

TABLE 6.2

Frequency distribution of hypothetical listening-comprehension test in ESL

Score	Number of testees
0–10	0
11–20	1
21–30	2
31–40	5
41–50	9
51–60	10
61–70	38
71–80	29
81–90	4
91–100	2

these. Is there any one score that characterizes the group of subjects as a whole? The best way to examine this question is to organize the scores into some system. The technique most often used in the statistical presentation of data is called a *frequency distribution*. This is a chart of data (e.g., test scores) arranged in logical steps or categories. For our group of hypothetical subjects, the test categories are arranged conveniently into the categories 0–10, 11–20, 21–30, etc. (Table 6.2). This type of arrangement is not only more compact and systematic, but it reveals at a glance that most of the testees received scores in the 61–70 and 71–80 categories. In other words, a frequency distribution allows us to detect any general pattern or trend immediately. In addition, it allows us to avoid the unnecessary repetition of scores. The categories selected for our frequency distribution are known as *class intervals*, and the number of testees in each category is called the *class frequency*. The spread of scores from the lowest to the highest is called the *range (R)*. Here, since the lowest score is 12 and the highest 96 (see Table 6.1), the range is $R = 96 - 12 = 84$.

We may also wish to display the same data in a pictorial way. If we take the class intervals of our frequency distribution (0–10, 10–20, 20–30, etc.) and plot them against the class frequencies on a graph consisting of two intersecting axes at right angles, we get a *histogram* of the data (Figure 6.1). This is simply a graphical version of our frequency distribution (Table 6.2). The height of each block in the histogram shows the class frequency, i.e., the number of testees in each category or class interval. The tallest block is called the *modal group*. In our example, the modal group is the 61–70 category. The pictorial representation of data in the form of a histogram is a highly desirable technique in statistics because it allows

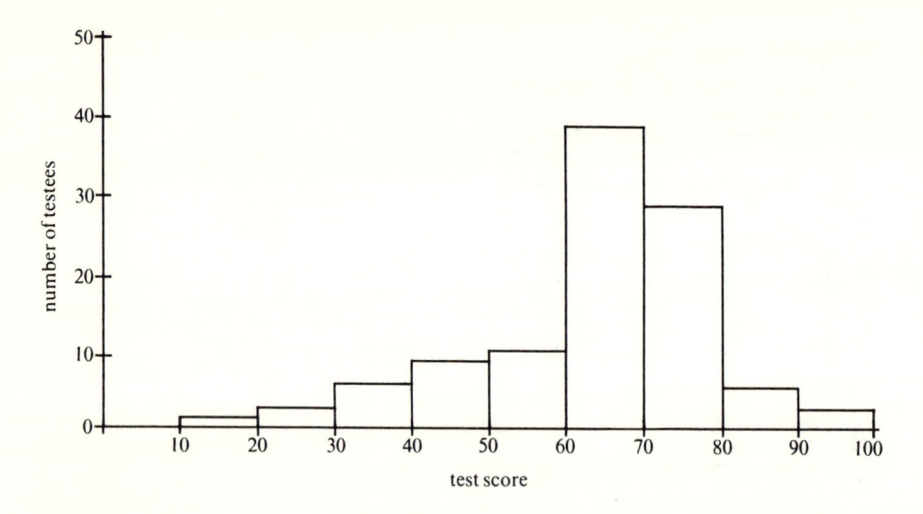

FIGURE 6.1 Histogram of hypothetical listening-comprehension test scores in ESL

the eye to take in a trend at a glance. As Franzblau (1958:16) states: 'This is especially useful when we desire to convey information to others who have neither the time nor the inclination to examine lists of figures.'

If we wish to display our data with a smooth curve, we can do so by assuming that all the scores fall exactly at the midpoint of the rectangle representing each category. When we join these points by straight lines we get a *frequency polygon*, which then can be transformed by approximation into a smooth curve as shown in Figure 6.2. For mathematical reasons which are beyond the scope of the present discussion, smooth curves are very useful for statistical inference. If the curve is symmetrical – i.e., if it resembles a bell – then it is called a *normal curve*. If, however, the curve tails off, then it is called a *skewed curve*. If the left-hand side drags out into a tail, it is designated a *left-handed skew*; if the right-hand side drags out into a tail, then it is called a *right-handed skew* (see Figure 6.3). The curve of our hypothetical test scores (Figure 6.2) is an example of a left-handed skew.

Sometimes, we may wish to present our data in a cumulative fashion. If we arrange the hypothetical scores of our group in terms of categories such as 10 and below, 20 and below, etc. (Table 6.3), we are then able to display the same data in a cumulative arrangement. This method is often used with test or examination results where the cut-off point between passing and failing is to be illustrated or determined. If we now plot the cumulative test scores of Table 6.3 against the

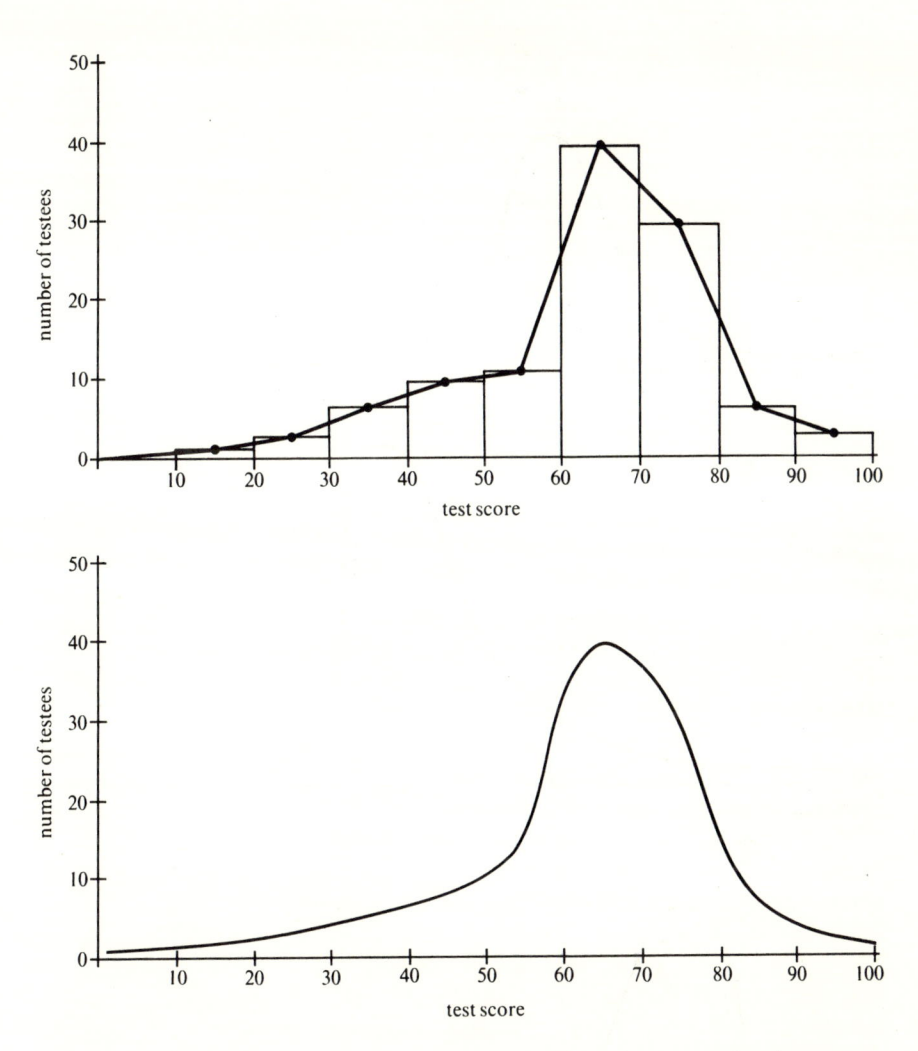

FIGURE 6.2 Frequency polygon and curve of hypothetical listening-comprehension test scores in ESL

number of testees, we get an S-curve known as a *cumulative frequency distribution*, or *ogive*. The ogive for our hypothetical data is shown in Figure 6.4.

The specific type of display arrangement used (frequency distribution, ogive, etc.) will depend on the researcher and on the nature of the test or experiment. But

132 Applied Psycholinguistics

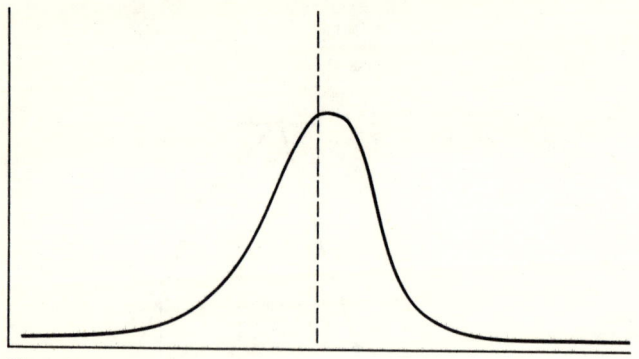

Normal curve

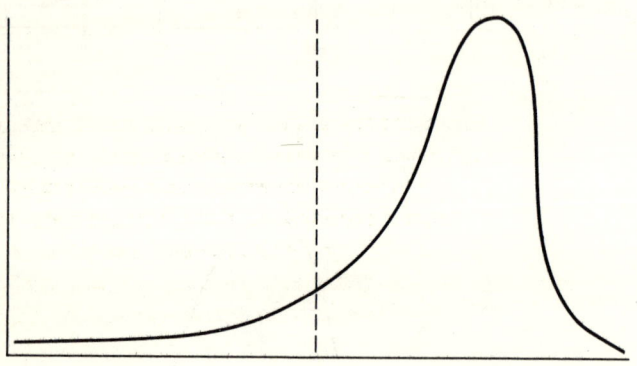

Left-handed skew

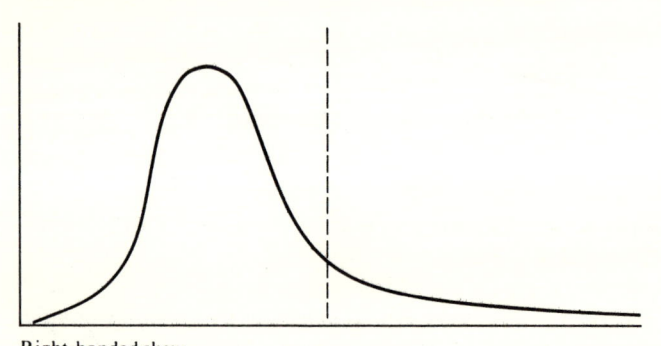

Right-handed skew

FIGURE 6.3 Types of curves

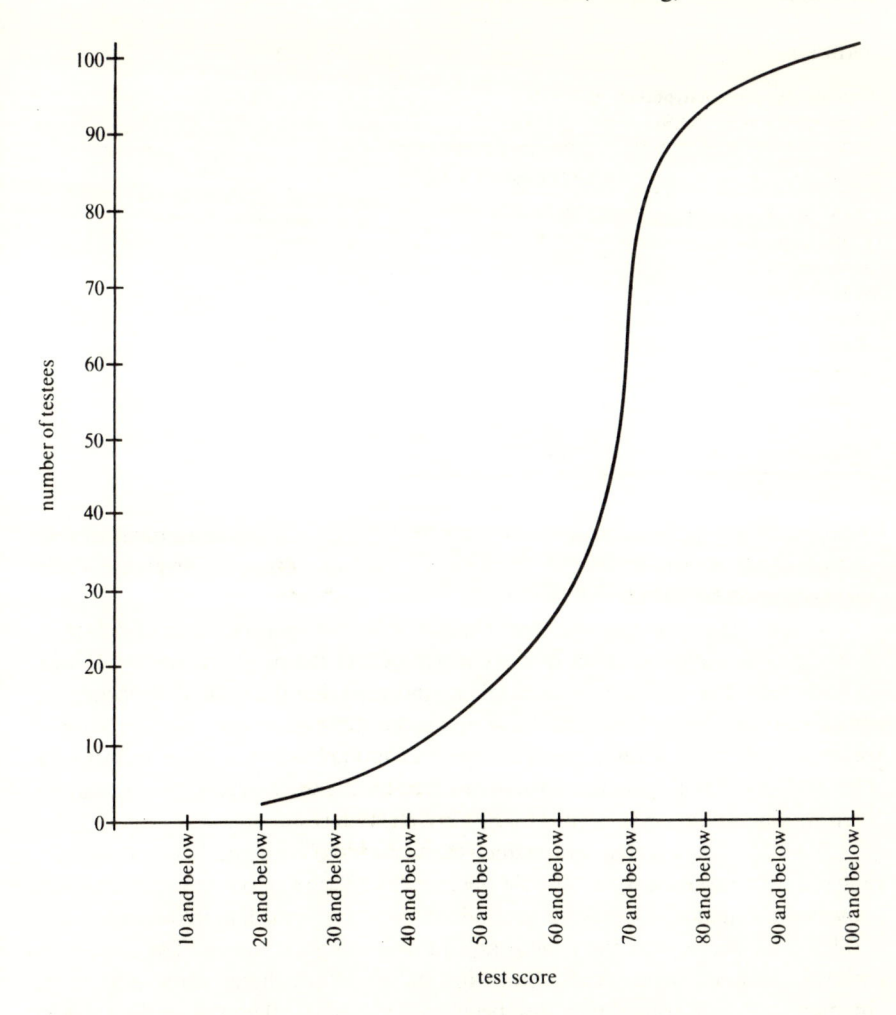

FIGURE 6.4 Ogive of hypothetical listening-comprehension test scores in ESL

regardless of the type used, the systematic organization and presentation of data is a necessary first step in statistical practice.

6.1.2 CENTRAL TENDENCY AND DISPERSION

Although the judgments that can be made based on the general inspection of frequency distributions or graphs can be very useful, we need a more precise

TABLE 6.3

Cumulative scores of hypothetical listening-comprehension test in ESL

Score	Number of testees
10 and below	0
20 and below	1
30 and below	3
40 and below	8
50 and below	17
60 and below	27
70 and below	65
80 and below	94
90 and below	98
100 and below	100

measure of any pattern or trend present in the data. The measurement of any overall trend is known as the location of *central tendency*. There are three methods used by statisticians to locate central tendency.

(1) *Mode*. This is simply the modal group of the histogram for a set of data; i.e., it is the observation in a set of data which occurs the most frequently. In our hypothetical data (Table 6.1), it can be readily seen that the score that occurs the most is 61, as thirteen testees received that score. This is the least-used measure of central tendency because its significance is limited when a large number of observations is not available. Moreover, if none of the observations is repeated, then the mode does not exist.

(2) *Median*. This is that score which divides a set of data into halves of exactly equal numbers; i.e., it is the middle observation in a set of data that arranges its observations from the lowest to the highest. To find the median in our set of data (Table 6.1), we look at the fiftieth and fifty-first highest scores. The median is midway between these scores. Since in our data both these scores are 68, the median is also 68. But if they had been, say, 67 and 68, then the median would have been 67.5. The number of observations in our data is even (100); when the number is odd, the median is easier to find. Suppose there are seven scores in a set of data. Then the median is simply the fourth highest score because there are exactly three scores below it and three scores above it (e.g., in the set of scores 35, 58, 62, 68, 69, 70, 88, the median score is 68). The median can also be estimated directly from the ogive of a set of data. From the ogive for our set of data (Figure 6.4) we can approximate the median by drawing a line from the midpoint on the vertical axis, which corresponds to the midpoint in the number of testees, to the

ogive and then down to the horizontal axis, which corresponds to the median score (Figure 6.5).

(3) *Mean*. This is the most commonly used measure of central tendency. It is the arithmetic average of the observations in a set of data. Therefore, to find the mean, we simply add up all the observations and divide by the number of observations:

$$\text{Mean} = \frac{\text{Sum of observations}}{\text{Number of observations}}$$

In our data, we add up the one hundred scores in Table 6.1 (12 + 21 + ... + 96) and then divide by 100, the number of scores. The resulting number, 64, is the mean for our data. Statisticians normally use *summation notation* to calculate the mean:

$$\bar{x} = \frac{\Sigma x}{N}$$

In this formula: (1) $\bar{x}$ is the mean; (2) x represents any observation (e.g., $x = 12, 21, ..., 96$); (3) Σx ('sigma x') stands for the sum of all the observations (e.g., $\Sigma x = 12 + 21 + ... + 96 = 6400$); (4) N indicates the total number of observations (e.g., $N = 100$). Thus, for our data:

$$\bar{x} = \frac{\Sigma x}{N} = \frac{12 + 21 + ... + 96}{100} = \frac{6400}{100} = 64$$

It is obviously desirable to facilitate the calculation of the mean by reducing the computations involved in arriving at Σx. This can be done by the use of classified data such as a frequency distribution. There are several ways to calculate means from classified data, but these are beyond the scope of the present discussion. The interested reader can consult, for example, Arkin and Colton (1970:14–18).

Each situation requires its own best method of calculating central tendency. The mean generally gives the most reliable measure because it 'balances' the observations; i.e., it locates a point in a set of data which is truly central. Unlike the mode and median, it uses all the observations present in the data. Moreover, as we will soon see, it has many more uses in statistical inference. If there is any disadvantage associated with the mean, it is that it may be distorted by extreme values.

The measures of central tendency do not tell us all we need to know about a set of data. In our data, for example, what does a score of 69 indicate when compared to one of 29? One quick way to relate scores is to consider the ogive of our data

136 Applied Psycholinguistics

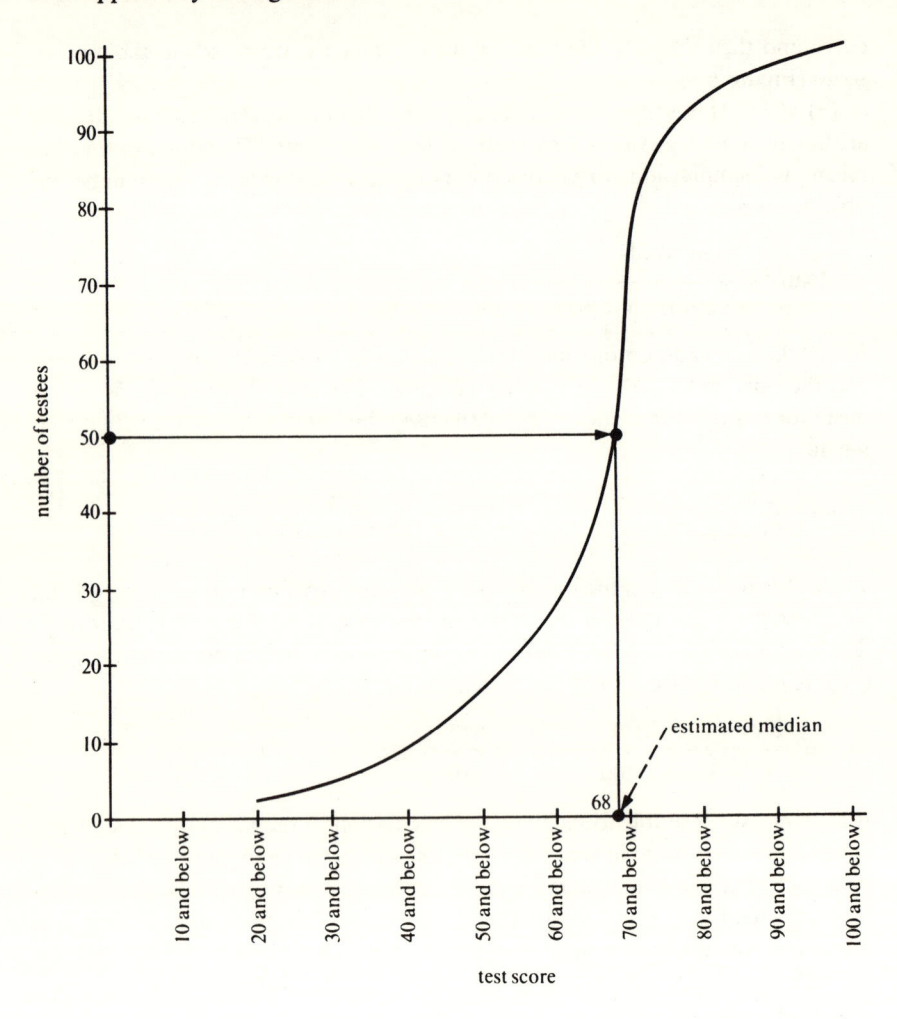

FIGURE 6.5 Estimation of the median from the ogive of our hypothetical data

(Figure 6.4). It can be seen at a glance that the score of 69 is slightly above the midpoint of the number of testees; while the score of 29 is only the third from the bottom. Thus, the testee who receives a score of 69 is said to fall just above the 50-percent point of the group or to be near the fiftieth percentile; whereas, the testee with a score of 29 is said to be at the third percentile (see Figure 6.6). In

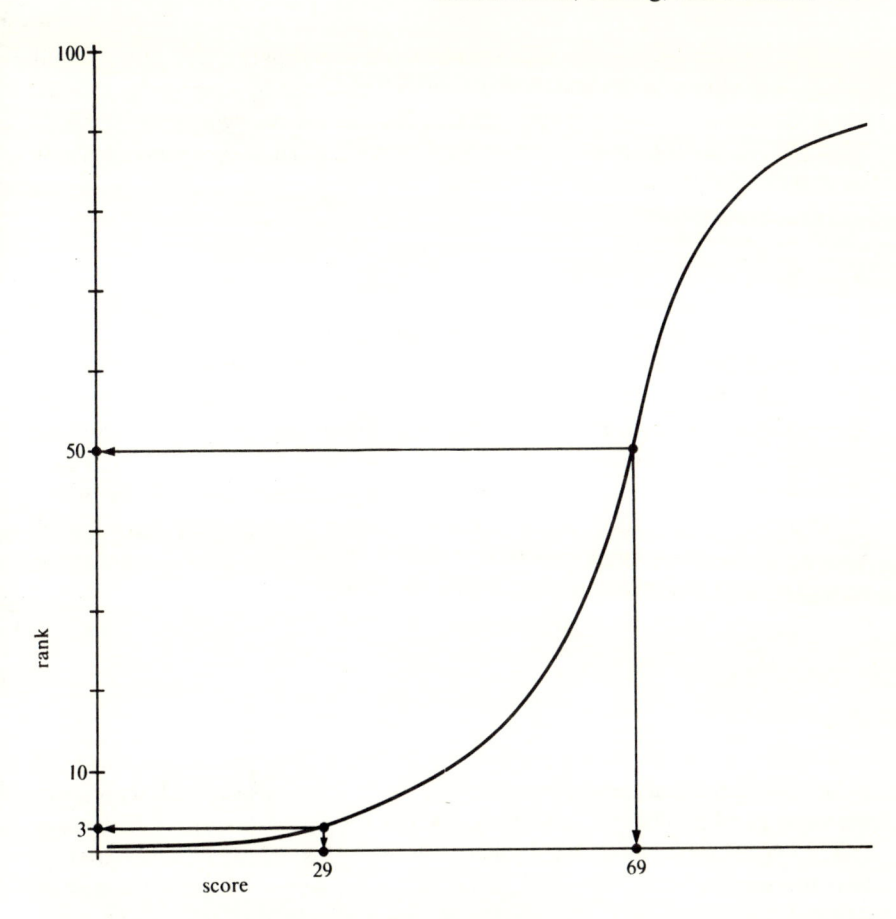

FIGURE 6.6 Percentile ranking of 29 and 69 from our data

statistics, this quick method of relating scores is known as *ranking*; it is used often in educational testing.

What if we want to know more specifically how any individual observation relates to the mean? We will obviously need to calculate for this purpose the degree of *dispersion* present in the data, i.e., the degree to which observations deviate from the mean. The most useful measure of dispersion is the one that will tell us what the *average* deviation of scores from the mean is, i.e., how far each individual observation departs, on the average, from the mean. This measure is called *standard deviation (s)*. In our data, the deviation of the score 68 from the mean of 64 is a positive number: 68 − 64 = +4. But the deviation of 32 is a negative number: 32 − 64 = −32. Since positive and negative deviations would cancel each other out, the standard deviation is obtained by squaring all individual deviations to remove negatives, adding them all up, averaging them, and then taking the square root to compensate for the squaring. These procedures can now be translated into the following formula:

$$s = \sqrt{\frac{\Sigma d^2}{N}}$$

where d^2 represents the individual deviations squared.

For mathematical reasons beyond the scope of our discussion, the divisor $N - 1$, rather than N, is used for statistical inference. This is because, as Kalton (1966:8) notes, the divisor $N - 1$ is the correct one when estimating the standard deviation of the population from the standard deviation of a sample. In statistics, a *sample* is a group selected at random from a *population*, which is the whole group under consideration. More will be said about this important distinction in Section 6.1.3. Therefore, if we use $N - 1$ as the divisor and substitute the more explicit form $(x - \bar{x})^2$ for d^2 (i.e., the squared difference between any observation x and the mean $\bar{x}$), the formula becomes:

$$s = \sqrt{\frac{\Sigma(x - \bar{x})^2}{N - 1}}$$

To find the standard deviation of our example, we proceed as follows. (1) To obtain the individual deviations squared, $(x - \bar{x})^2$, we subtract each score from the mean of 64 and then square the result. For example, the score of 32 deviates from 64 by 32 − 64 = −32. The squared value of −32 is $-32^2 = 1024$. (2) After we have found each individual deviation squared in this way, we then add them all up to give us $\Sigma(x - \bar{x})^2 = 21474$. (3) We then divide this sum by $N - 1 = 100 - 1 = 99$: $[\Sigma(x - \bar{x})^2]/(N - 1) = 21474/99 = 216.909$. (4) Finally, we take the square root of this number: $\sqrt{[\Sigma(x - \bar{x})^2]/(N - 1)} = \sqrt{216.909} = 14.73$ (rounded off). The standard deviation for our data is $s = 14.73$. For the sake of facilitating future computations, we will round off the standard deviation to $s = 15$.

We can now say that any score which is exactly 15 above the mean is exactly *one positive* standard deviation from the mean, or $+1s$. In our data that score is 79. Any score which is exactly 15 below the mean is exactly *one negative* standard deviation from the mean, or $-1s$. In our data that score is 49. Any score falling in between 49 and 79 falls within $-1s$ and $+1s$, or $\pm 1s$. It has been found, moreover, that observations will tend to fall within $\pm 1s$, $\pm 2s$, or $\pm 3s$ but almost never beyond these limits. Thus, for example, the score of 71 of our data falls within $+1s$ of the mean; 58 within $-1s$; 91 within $+2s$; 42 within $-2s$; 96 within $+3s$; and 21 within $-3s$

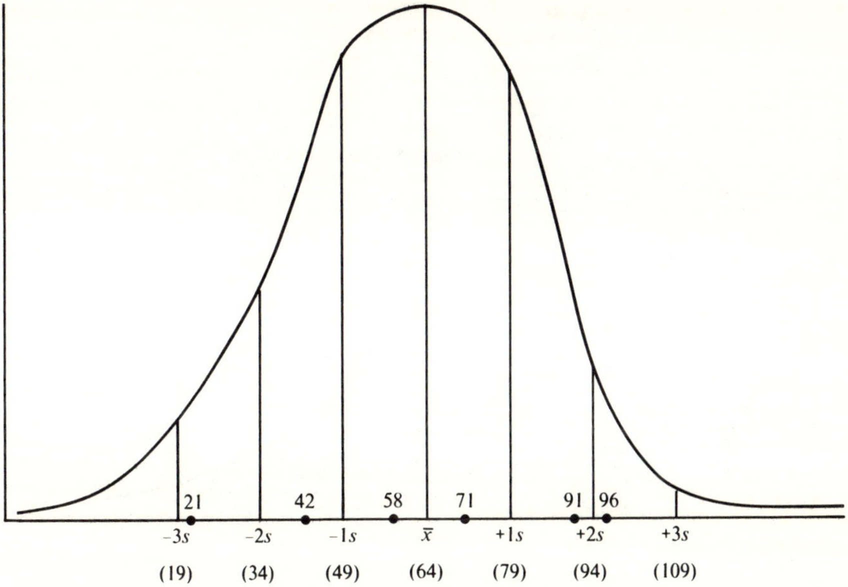
21
42
58
71
91
96
-3s
-2s
-1s
$\bar{x}$
+1s
+2s
+3s
(19)
(34)
(49)
(64)
(79)
(94)
(109)

FIGURE 6.7 The mean and standard deviations for our data

(see Figure 6.7). Only the score of 12 falls beyond the limit of three standard deviations. In fact, one of the most important statistical discoveries of all time is that practically all traits measured at random distribute in the shape of the normal curve. This curve has the following mathematical characteristics: (1) 99.78 percent of all cases fall within $\pm 3s$; (2) 95.46 percent of all cases fall within $\pm 2s$; and (3) 68.26 percent of all cases fall within $\pm 1s$ (see Figure 6.8). This means that on a reliable test, for example, we can expect to find that approximately 68 percent of our testees will get scores ranging from $-1s$ to $+1s$ of the mean for the set of scores actually obtained, approximately 95 percent of our testees will get scores ranging from $-2s$ to $+2s$, and only a few will get scores beyond these limits. All depends on the reliability and validity of the testing procedures and on the selection of the sample of testees. More will be said about sampling later in this chapter.

Relating scores in terms of the standard deviation has an obvious comparative value. For example, the scores of 21 and 72 in our data mean almost nothing in isolation. However, in terms of the mean and standard deviation they take on a specific significance. Since 21 lies below $-2s$, it is a comparatively low score because we know that 95 percent of all scores will fall above $-2s$. On the other hand, 72 lies above the mean and below $+1s$, and is thus a score that is slightly

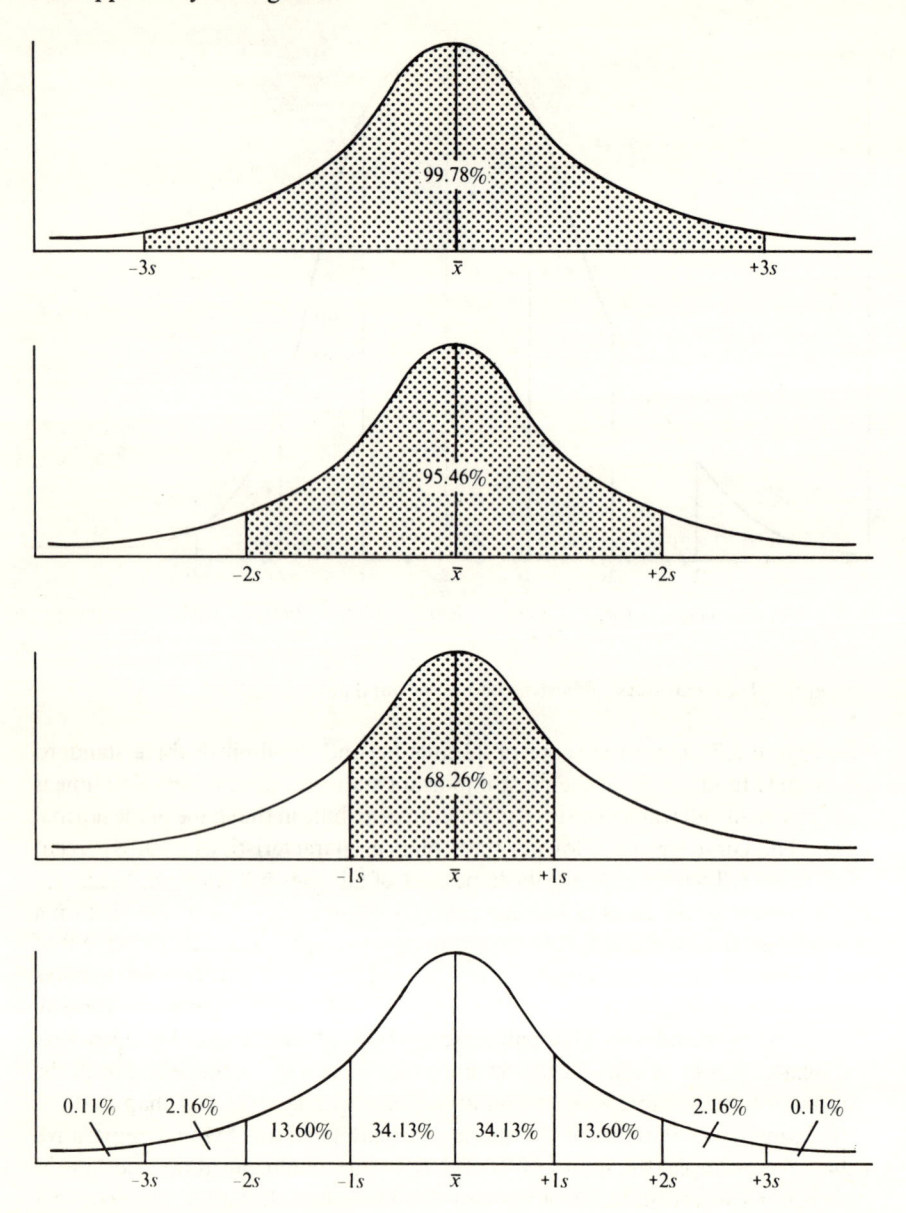

FIGURE 6.8 The normal curve and the standard deviation

Measurement, Testing, and Research 141

above average. Scores reported in this way are known as z-scores. With such scores it is possible to deduce the proportion of cases above or below any individual score.

6.1.3 STATISTICAL SIGNIFICANCE AND INFERENCE

As mentioned above, a sample is a randomly made selection from a population. Is it possible to infer anything about the population from the sample? In other words, when we pick a sample from a population how likely is the mean of that sample to be the population, or 'true' mean? To answer this question we need to find out what the difference is between the population mean and any sample mean. The statistical method used for this purpose is called the *standard error of the mean* (SEM). It is based on the statistical fact that, if the sampling procedures are carried out correctly, the means of all samples will cluster around the population mean. The mathematical translation of this fact is that the standard deviation of a particular sample, s, decreases as the square root of the number of observations, N. Therefore, the formula for the SEM is

$$\text{SEM} = s/\sqrt{N}$$

Readers interested in the technical derivation of this formula can consult Arkin and Colton (1970:268-70).

For our example, let us assume that the population consists of all first-year foreign university students enrolled in ESL and that our sample of 100 was selected at random. In Section 6.1.2 we found s to be equal to 15. The SEM for our data is as follows:

$$\text{SEM} = s/\sqrt{N} = 15/\sqrt{100} = 1.5$$

What can we infer from this SEM? Statisticians have found once again that SEMs also distribute in the shape of the normal curve. Thus, approximately 68 percent of all future sample means will fall within −1SEM and +1SEM, 95 percent of all future sample means will fall within −2SEM and +2SEM, and 99 percent of all future sample means will fall within −3SEM and +3SEM. For our data, we can now say that we are 99 percent sure that the mean of 64 lies within the limits of −3SEM and +3SEM, which are as follows: since 3SEM = 3 × 1.5 = 4.5, therefore, −3SEM = 64 − 4.5 = 59.5 and +3SEM = 64 + 4.5 = 68.5. Thus, we would expect the population mean of all first-year foreign university students enrolled in ESL to lie between 59.5 and 68.5 for our specific listening-comprehension test. The difference between the standard deviation and the standard error of the mean is explained clearly by Franzblau (1958:53). One should think 'of the standard deviation as a *measure of the dispersion of cases about the mean of a distribution*

TABLE 6.4

Hypothetical means, standard deviations, and standard errors of the means for three groups

Samples of 100 testees each	Mean score	Standard deviation	Standard error of the means
GROUP A (original group of sections 6.1.1 and 6.1.2): trained by the grammar-translation method	64	15	1.5
GROUP B: also trained by the grammar-translation method	67	16	1.6
GROUP C: trained by the audio-lingual method	88	12	1.2

and of the standard error of the mean as a *measure of the probable extent to which a mean is apt to vary on future samplings.*'

We will now look at the concept of statistical *significance*. If we draw two or more samples from a population we would expect the means of these samples to distribute in the form of the normal curve around the population mean. However, what if we get a mean that lies *beyond* −3SEM or +3SEM? If we do, then it can be said that the difference is significant and not due to mere chance. To illustrate this, let us assume that the same hypothetical listening-comprehension test was administered to two other samples of equal size (100 testees each). We now have compiled the test scores for these three groups and have calculated their respective means, standard deviations, and standard errors of their means. Let us assume further that the original group and a second group were both trained with a grammar-translation method, while the third group was trained with an audio-lingual approach. The hypothetical calculations are shown in Table 6.4. Notice that the means of groups A and B are very close, whereas the mean of group C is considerably above that of group A. Does this mean that group C is significantly better at listening comprehension? To answer a question such as this, statisticians use a method known as the *standard error of the difference* (SED). The appropriate formula is as follows (see Arkin and Colton 1970:152):

$$SED = \sqrt{SEM_1^2 + SEM_2^2}$$

where SEM_1 is the standard error of the mean of one group and SEM_2 is the standard error of the mean of the second group being compared to the first one. If the SED is greater than the difference between the two means of the groups being compared, then we can say that the difference is *significant*. This is so because statisticians have again found that we can be 68 percent sure that the difference between two sample means will lie between −1SED and +1SED, 95 percent sure that it will lie between −2SED and +2SED, and over 99 percent sure that it will lie between −3SED and +3SED.

For our three hypothetical groups the following results emerge. (1) *Groups A and B*. SED = $\sqrt{1.5^2 + 1.6^2}$ = $\sqrt{4.81}$ = 2.19. The difference between the mean of group A and that of group B is 67 − 64 = 3. Since the SED does not exceed the difference of the means, we can say that the results of 64 and 67 are not significantly different. (2) *Groups A and C*. SED = $\sqrt{1.5^2 + 1.2^2}$ = $\sqrt{3.69}$ = 1.92. The difference between the mean of group A and that of group C is 88 − 64 = 24. This is well beyond +3SED. We can now be over 99 percent sure that this difference is significant. Another way of putting this is to say that the probability, p, that such a difference is due to chance alone is *less than 1 out of 100*. Statisticians call this a *confidence limit* and represent it as $p < 0.01$. If we wish to refer to the 95 percent confidence level (beyond −2SED and +2SED but within −3SED and +3SED), then we represent it as $p < 0.05$.

What conclusion can we draw from this statistical analysis? It appears that group C did indeed perform significantly better than group A on the listening-comprehension test. Does this mean that the audio-lingual method is superior to the grammar-translation one for the cultivation of listening-comprehension skills? Although one is tempted to answer this in the positive, one can never be completely sure that a statistically significant difference is always reliable. The difference could be due to other factors such as diverse language aptitudes, motivations, etc. The conscientious researcher should always follow such studies up with a *controlled* experiment where such interfering variables can be eliminated. This will be discussed in Section 6.3.1.

In order to find the confidence limit we are actually dividing the difference of the two sample means by the SED. This is known as the *critical ratio* (CR) and is expressed by the formula:

$$CR = \frac{\text{Difference of sample means}}{\text{Standard error of the difference}} = \frac{\bar{x}_1 - \bar{x}_2}{\text{SED}}$$

$$= \frac{\bar{x}_1 - \bar{x}_2}{\sqrt{\text{SEM}_1^2 + \text{SEM}_2^2}}$$

When the two samples being compared are small (below 30), then the CR must be used together with a table of values (Appendix D). Statisticians refer to this method as the *t-test*. To illustrate the *t*-test we will use the hypothetical data of

144 Applied Psycholinguistics

TABLE 6.5

Hypothetical data for the *t*-test

GROUP A

Test score	$\bar{x}_1$	s_1	SEM_1	SEM_1^2
6	8.2	1.14	0.36	0.13
7				
8				
8				
8				
8				
9				
9				
9				
10				

GROUP B

Test score	$\bar{x}_2$	s_2	SEM_2	SEM_2^2
2	5.4	2.17	0.69	0.48
3				
4				
5				
5				
5				
6				
7				
8				
9				

Table 6.5. These are the scores out of 10 (0–10) received on a spelling test by two groups of ESL students consisting of 10 testees each. Table 6.5 also contains the values of the means and SEMs squared for both groups. To determine if the difference between the means of these two groups is significant we substitute these values into the critical-ratio formula and we will then obtain a value for *t*:

$$CR = t = \frac{\bar{x}_1 - \bar{x}_2}{\sqrt{SEM_1^2 + SEM_2^2}} = \frac{8.2 - 5.4}{\sqrt{0.13 + 0.48}} = 3.59$$

We now consult a table which contains values for *t*. One such table is given in Appendix D. In order to look up a value for *t*, the concept of *degrees of freedom* (df) must be understood. In brief, this is a numerical constraint that exists in a set of observations. For example, if we have three numbers which must add up to 10, then the first two numbers can be chosen relatively freely (i.e., as long as they do not add up to 10). But choice of the third number is restricted by the requirement that the total must be 10. This means that two numbers are free and one fixed. There are, therefore, two degrees of freedom. In the *t*-test there are always $N - 1$ degrees of freedom for each of the two samples, i.e., one less than the sample size. For our data the degrees of freedom equal 18 since each sample contains 10 observations and, therefore, $10 - 1 = 9$ degrees of freedom. We now look up 18 degrees of freedom in the table contained in Appendix D and we find that at the $p < 0.05$ confidence level the value is 2.101 and at the $p < 0.01$ confidence level it is 2.878. Since our value for t ($t = 3.59$) is larger than either one, we can now say that the difference in results between group A and group B is significant at the $p < 0.01$ confidence level.

If we wish to compare more than two groups at once to see if there exists any significant difference, we use a technique known as the *F-ratio*. If any significant level is detected, then the *t*-test is applied successively to two samples at a time in order to locate where the significant difference lies.

For mathematical reasons we need not go into here, the *F*-ratio is computed as follows. (1) We obtain the squared deviations of each sample mean from the overall mean, i.e., the mean for all the samples combined. Each of these squared deviations is multiplied by the number of cases in each sample and then they are all added together. This number is then divided by the number of degrees of freedom for the total group, i.e., the number of samples minus 1. The resulting figure is called the *between variance*. (2) We then obtain the squared deviations of each observation from its own sample mean and add them all up. This number is then divided by the degrees of freedom for the samples, i.e., the total number of observations minus the number of samples. The resulting figure is called the *within variance*. (3) The *F*-ratio is defined by the formula:

$$F = \frac{\text{between variance}}{\text{within variance}}$$

(4) Finally, we look up the confidence level of *F* in a statistical table such as the one reproduced in Appendix E.

For example, suppose that our hypothetical listening-comprehension test in ESL is administered to four homogeneous groups consisting of 6 testees each. The results are compiled in Table 6.6 which also shows the means of each group and the squared deviations of the scores from their own group means.

To calculate the between variance we proceed as follows. The overall mean of the combined four groups is 73.75. The deviations of the group means from the overall mean are as follows: $76 - 73.75 = +2.25$ for group A; $85 - 73.75 = +11.25$ for group B; $72 - 73.75 = -1.75$ for group C; and $62 - 73.75 = -11.75$ for group D. We now square these deviations ($+2.25^2 = 5.06$; $+11.25^2 = 126.56$; $-1.75^2 = 3.06$; $-11.75^2 = 138.06$), multiply them by the number of scores in each group ($6 \times 138.06 = 828.36$), and then add them up: $30.36 + 759.36 + 18.36 + 828.36 +$

TABLE 6.6

Hypothetical data for the F-ratio

Score (0–100)	Mean	Deviation from mean	Squared deviation from the mean
GROUP A			
63	76	−13	169
71		−5	25
75		−1	1
76		0	0
78		+3	9
93		+17	289
			493
GROUP B			
77	85	−8	64
78		−7	49
82		−3	9
85		0	0
91		+6	36
97		+12	144
			302
GROUP C			
56	72	−16	256
64		−8	64
68		−4	16
72		0	0
77		+5	25
95		+23	529
			890
GROUP D			
49	62	−13	169
55		−7	49
64		+2	4
66		+4	16
68		+6	36
70		+8	64
			338

1636.44. This number is then divided by the degrees of freedom for the between variance which is the number of groups minus 1, or 4 − 1 = 3: 1636.44/3 = 545.48. This figure is, then, the between variance.

To obtain the within variance, we first calculate the sum of the squared deviations of the scores from their respective group means (which are given in Table 6.6): 493 + 302 + 890 + 338 = 2023. This number is then divided by the degrees of freedom for the within variance which is the number of scores minus the number of groups, or 24 - 4 = 20: 2023/20 = 101.15.

The F-ratio is now calculated as follows:

$$F = \frac{\text{between variance}}{\text{within variance}} = \frac{545.48}{101.15} = 5.39$$

Finally, we look up this figure in the table contained in Appendix E. Since the degrees of freedom for the within variance were found to be 20 and those for the between variance 3, we look up 20 across and 3 down in the table and find F to be 4.94. Since our figure of 5.39 is larger than this, we can now say that a significant difference at the $p < 0.01$ confidence level exists somewhere in the test results. If we now wish to locate exactly where this difference lies, we must apply the t-test to two groups at a time. This is left as an exercise for the reader.

There is one other widely used measure of significance, the *Chi square* (χ^2) test, that can be of use as a post-assessment technique. This test compares *expected* values *(E)* with actual ones *(A)*. The formula for this test is as follows:

$$\chi^2 = \Sigma \left[\frac{(A - E)^2}{E} \right]$$

Once again we need not go into the mathematical reasons behind this formula (see, for example, Edwards 1980:258–74). Suffice it to say that it allows us to test for a significantly different result from the expected one. The value obtained from this formula is then looked up in a table such as the one given in Appendix F in order to obtain a confidence level, if any.

To illustrate this test we will use the example given by Marrone and Rasor (1972:50-2). Suppose that at the start of a school year a teacher tells the students that letter grades (A, B, C, D, F) will be assigned on the basis of the normal curve. With 100 students the teacher tells them that they can expect 7As, 24Bs, 38Cs, 24Ds and 7Fs. The actual outcomes at the end of the year are shown in Table 6.7. Are these outcomes significantly different from the expected ones? In order to obtain a value for χ^2, we take each value of $(A - E)^2$, as given in Table 6.7, and divide it by the corresponding value of E in the chart: 4/7 = 0.57; 196/24 = 8.17; 0/38 = 0; 81/24 = 3.38; 49/7 = 7. When we add all these up we get a value for χ^2:

$$\chi^2 = \Sigma \left[\frac{(A - E)^2}{E} \right] = 0.57 + 8.17 + 0 + 3.38 + 7.00 = 19.12$$

148 Applied Psycholinguistics

TABLE 6.7

Hypothetical data for the χ^2 test (adapted from Marrone and Rasor 1972:51)

Grade	A	E	(A - E)	(A - E)²
A	5	7	-2	4
B	10	24	-14	196
C	38	38	0	0
D	33	24	+9	81
F	14	7	+7	49
	100	100		

The number of degrees of freedom for our example is the number of categories (A, B, C, D, F) minus 1: 5 - 1 = 4. For a complete discussion on how to compute the degrees of freedom for the χ^2 test see Franzblau (1958:119–20). We now look up the value of χ^2 against 4 degrees of freedom in the table given in Appendix F and we find that at the $p < 0.01$ confidence level the value is 13.28. Since our value for χ^2 (19.12) is larger than this, we can now say that there is indeed a significant difference between what the teacher says and what the teacher does.

6.1.4 CORRELATION

Suppose that, as a post-assessment strategy, we wish to determine if any relationship exists between any two sets of observations. In statistics the degree of relationship between any two sets of variables is given by a measure of relationship known as the *coefficient of correlation*. This is a number ranging from -1.0 (a perfect negative correlation) through 0 (no correlation) to +1.0 (a perfect positive correlation) which expresses the degree of association between any two sets of variables. A positive correlation indicates that an increase in one variable coincides with the increase in another variable. A negative correlation indicates that an increase in one variable coincides with the decrease in another variable.

Correlations can be illustrated graphically and the coefficient of correlation can be estimated from a graph. As an example, consider the data in Table 6.8. This contains the simple ranking of five subjects in French and Spanish. As the graph of this data shows (Figure 6.9) there is a perfect positive correlation between the position in French and the position in Spanish; i.e., the subject who scored highest in French also scored highest in Spanish; the subject who scored second highest in French also scored second highest in Spanish; and so on. For a perfect negative correlation consider the data in Table 6.9. This contains a simple ranking of five subjects in mathematics and biology. As the graph of these data shows (Figure 6.10), there is a perfect negative correlation between the position in

TABLE 6.8

Hypothetical ranks of subjects in French and Spanish

Subject	French position	Spanish position
A	1	1
B	2	2
C	3	3
D	4	4
E	5	5

TABLE 6.9

Hypothetical ranks of subjects in mathematics and biology

Subject	Mathematics position	Biology position
A	1	5
B	2	4
C	3	3
D	4	2
E	5	1

mathematics and the position in biology; i.e., the subject who scored highest in mathematics scored lowest in biology; the subject who scored second highest in mathematics scored second lowest in biology; and so on.

In most tests or experiments such perfect correlations are rarely found. Scores tend to be scattered as shown in Figure 6.11. A positive correlation slopes from left to right and a negative one from right to left. A zero correlation has no direction whatsoever.

Statisticians employ two commonly used methods for calculating correlations of the scattered variety. These are *Spearman's rank order correlation* (ρ) and *Pearson's product moment correlation (r)*. The formula for the former method is

$$\rho = 1 - \frac{6\Sigma d^2}{N(N^2 - 1)}$$

Again, the mathematical reasons behind this formula will not be discussed here (see Arkin and Colton 1970:82–111). In this formula, d^2 stands for the squared deviations in rank position and N is the sample size. To illustrate this method we will use the hypothetical example used by Allen and Davies (1977:189–90).

150 Applied Psycholinguistics

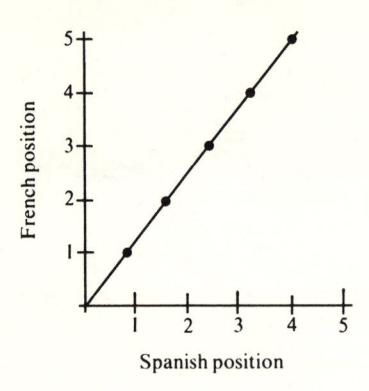

FIGURE 6.9 Graph of hypothetical ranks of subjects in French and Spanish

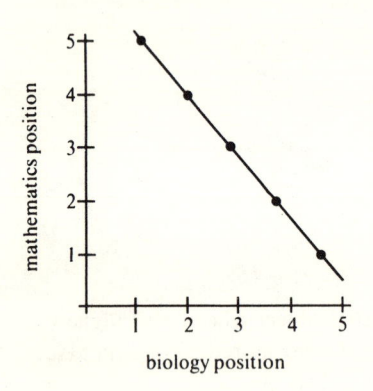

FIGURE 6.10 Graph of hypothetical ranks of subjects in mathematics and biology

Suppose five subjects took a French test consisting of 100 items and were ranked by their teacher in advance according to the teacher's estimate of their command of French. Table 6.10 contains the teacher's ranking, the test scores and ranks, as well as the necessary calculations for d^2. The sum of the squared deviations, or Σd^2, is therefore $0 + 4 + 0 + 4 + 0 = 8$, and the sample size is $N = 5$. Substituting these figures into the formula we get the following correlation coefficient:

$$\rho = 1 - \frac{6\Sigma d^2}{N(N^2 - 1)} = 1 - \frac{(6 \times 8)}{(5 \times 24)} = +0.60$$

This figure indicates that there is a moderate degree of positive correlation between the test ranks and the teacher's expectations. Spearman's method is used to relate a test result with a criterion such as a teacher's ranking and is, therefore, used frequently in education and psychology.

Measurement, Testing, and Research 151

High degree of positive correlation

Moderate degree of positive correlation

High degree of negative correlation

Moderate degree of negative correlation

Zero correlation

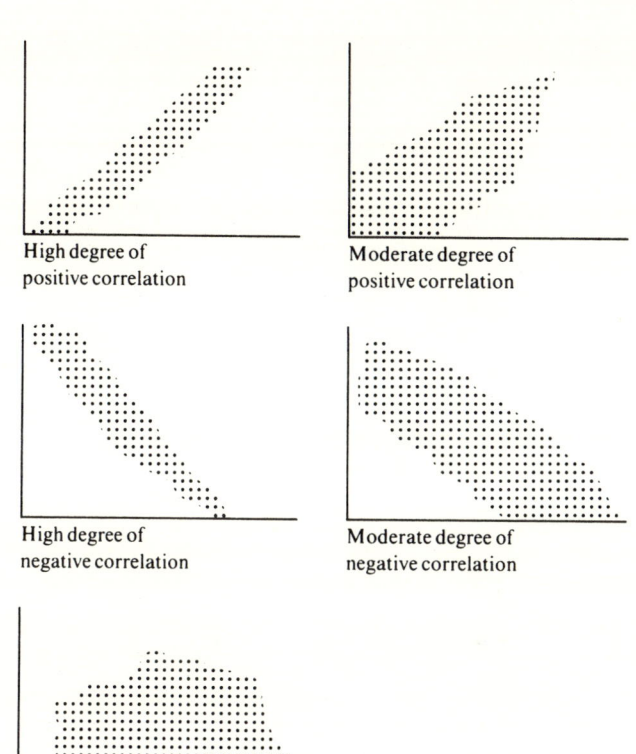

FIGURE 6.11 Scatter diagrams exemplifying different types of correlation

TABLE 6.10

Hypothetical data for Spearman's rank-order correlation (adapted from Allen and Davies 1977:190)

Subject	Test score	Test rank	Teacher's ranking	d	d^2
A	76	1	1	0	0
B	63	2	4	−2	4
C	62	3	3	0	0
D	59	4	2	+2	4
E	38	5	5	0	0

152 Applied Psycholinguistics

TABLE 6.11

Hypothetical data for Pearson's product-moment correlation (adapted from Allen and Davies 1977:191)

Subject	Score on test X (0–10)	Score on test Y (0–10)
A	7	8
B	6	7
C	6	5
D	5	6
E	3	6
F	3	4

Without going into the mathematical reasons behind the formula, Pearson's product moment correlation is given as follows:

$$r = \frac{\Sigma xy - \frac{(\Sigma x)(\Sigma y)}{N}}{\sqrt{\left[\Sigma x^2 - \frac{(\Sigma x)^2}{N}\right]\left[\Sigma y^2 - \frac{(\Sigma y)^2}{N}\right]}}$$

In this formula x and y stand for the scores obtained on separate tests. To illustrate this method we will once again use the hypothetical example provided by Allen and Davies (1977:190–4). Suppose that six people take two French tests. Their results are tabulated in Table 6.11. We want to know the degree to which the two sets of scores correspond. For test X, the sum of the scores is $\Sigma x = 7 + 6 + 6 + 5 + 3 + 3 = 30$; this quantity squared is $(\Sigma x)^2 = 30^2 = 900$; and the sum of the squared scores is $\Sigma x^2 = 49 + 36 + 36 + 25 + 9 + 9 = 164$. For test Y, the sum of the scores is $\Sigma y = 8 + 7 + 5 + 6 + 6 + 4 = 36$; this quantity squared is $(\Sigma y)^2 = 36^2 = 1296$; and the sum of the squared scores is $\Sigma y^2 = 64 + 49 + 25 + 36 + 36 + 16 = 226$. The sum of the product of two corresponding scores is $\Sigma xy = 7 \times 8$ or $56 + 6 \times 7$ or $42 + 6 \times 5$ or $30 + 5 \times 6$ or $30 + 3 \times 6$ or $18 + 3 \times 4$ or $12 = 188$. The sample size is $N = 6$. We now substitute these figures into the formula and we get the following correlation coefficient:

$$r = \frac{\Sigma xy - \frac{(\Sigma x)(\Sigma y)}{N}}{\sqrt{\left[\Sigma x^2 - \frac{(\Sigma x)^2}{N}\right]\left[\Sigma y^2 - \frac{(\Sigma y)^2}{N}\right]}}$$

$$= \frac{188 - \frac{(30 \times 36)}{6}}{\sqrt{\left(164 - \frac{900}{6}\right)\left(226 - \frac{1296}{6}\right)}}$$

$$= +0.676$$

Once again we find that there is a moderately high positive correlation between the scores received on test X and those on test Y.

In essence, what does the correlation coefficient tell us? In the area of testing, which is perhaps the most relevant one as a post-assessment strategy, a high correlation coefficient (above +0.80) probably indicates that we are measuring the same things. But when the correlation coefficient is very low (below +0.20), then we should either give the two tests again or search for a reason to explain why it is so low. Furthermore, if we use a test to predict future performance, then we should make sure that the results correlate highly with the future performance.

The correlation coefficient r has also a use as a significance measure. Because every measurement has some unreliability, we can never be sure that one administration of a test will yield the 'true' score for a subject. Although the true score cannot be determined directly, it is possible to know how far off we might be. This is done by employing the formula for the *standard error of measurement* (SEMeas.):

SEMeas. $= s\sqrt{(1 - r)}$

The s of the formula stands for the standard deviation of the sample group and r is the correlation coefficient, or reliability figure for the test. Suppose we want to find out how close the score of 80 is to the true score for the subject who took the hypothetical listening comprehension test in Section 6.1.1. Let us assume that r is very high, or $r = +0.9$. In Section 6.1.2 we found s to be 15. By substituting these figures into the formula we get:

SEMeas. $- s\sqrt{(1 - r)} = 15\sqrt{(1 - 0.9)} = 4.74$

As pointed out in Section 6.1.3, statisticians have found that errors tend to produce the pattern of the normal curve. Therefore, in this case as well we can be 68 percent sure that the true score lies within −1SEMeas. and +1SEMeas., or 75.26 (80 − 4.74) and 84.74 (80 + 4.74); 95 percent sure that it lies within −2SEMeas. and +2SEMeas., or 70.52 (80 − 2 × 4.74) and 89.48 (80 + 2 × 4.74); and over 99 percent sure that it lies within −3SEMeas. and +3SEMeas., or 65.78 (80 − 3 × 4.74) and 94.22 (80 + 3 × 4.74).

6.2 Testing

Statistical techniques aid the researcher and practitioner in the analysis of data. The statistical methods described above, which are summarized in Appendix G, provide quantitative information about the significance of certain results, or the relationship among sets of results, obtained from tests and experiments. They are, in sum, measuring instruments. A word of caution is necessary here. Only if the test or experiment is designed properly will the quantitative methods of statistics tell us something about the validity of, say, a particular instructional practice.

In general, it can be said that correlation techniques (Section 6.1.4) are indispensable measuring tools in the area of language testing where they allow us to determine how reliable or valid tests actually are. Significance measures (Section 6.1.3), on the other hand, are indispensable quantitative devices in the area of experimental research. In this section we will look briefly at language testing in Section 6.3, at experimentation.

6.2.1 RELIABILITY AND VALIDITY

What is a test? In general, a test can be defined as a method of measuring an individual's ability, skill, or knowledge in some area. A test can be either formal or informal. The former involves some form of quantification (e.g., 80 percent), whereas the latter is a qualitative assessment of observed behavior (e.g., 'good,' 'poor,' 'excellent'). To a student a test usually constitutes a learning or achievement goal; to a teacher it can become a valuable empirical indicator of teaching effectiveness. As a post-assessment strategy, testing is perhaps the most effective evaluative tool at the disposal of teachers. It allows them to measure whether certain learning behaviors have been attained by means of statistical correlation techniques. As a corollary, if these behaviors have not been attained testing will indicate that something is wrong; however, it will not identify what is wrong. This can only be done under controlled experimental conditions.

In order for it to be of any pedagogical use, a test must be both reliable and valid. Test *reliability* is the consistency or accuracy with which a test measures whatever it is supposed to measure; i.e., a test should give the same results every time it is administered to the same subjects, regardless of who the scorer is. More precisely, test reliability can be defined as 'the extent to which an evaluative instrument will produce the same pattern of scores with the same population on two different occasions' (Stones 1970:53).

There are several ways to check for test reliability, which is expressed as a correlation coefficient. (1) *Test-retest*. A test is administered twice to the same subjects at different times. The two sets of scores obtained in this way are compared by a product moment correlation technique, such as the one described in Section 6.1.4. A correlation coefficient of +0.9 and above is considered to show test reliability, while a coefficient of +0.5 and below indicates that the test is probably unreliable. Coefficients in between are difficult to interpret. (2) *Parallel*, or *equivalent*, *tests*. Two similar versions of a test are given at the same time or at different times and the results are compared by a product moment correlation technique. (3) *Split-half method*. The test is split into two halves in which the items of one half correspond to the items in the other half. Once again, the results obtained in the two halves are compared statistically by means of a product moment correlation technique. In addition to correlation techniques, test reliability can be determined by calculating the standard error of the mean for a test (Section 6.1.3). This allows us to determine the probable margin of error.

The second important requirement of tests is *validity*. This is the extent to which a test measures what it is intended or expected to measure. There are four types of validity (Table 6.12). (1) *Content validity*. This refers to the extent to which a test measures achievement on the existing knowledge to be tested. (2) *Predictive validity*. This refers to the association between scores on a given test and future behavior. Is the test a good indicator of how the testee will perform in the future? Predictive validity can be determined statistically by comparing the two sets of scores with a product moment correlation technique. (3) *Concurrent validity*. This refers to the association between test scores and some other measure, known as a *criterion*, taken at the same time. For example, the concurrent validity of a test of listening comprehension might be determined by comparing the test scores to a teacher's judgments of student ability. The most common type of statistical correlation technique used to determine concurrent validity is Spearman's rank order correlation method (Section 6.1.4). (4) *Construct validity*. This refers to the extent to which certain theoretical or explanatory constructs account for the performance on a test. In other words, a test has construct validity if it is based on information from existing research and theory.

For both predictive and concurrent validity, a correlation coefficient of +0.60 and above is said to be high, and one of +0.30 and below is considered low. These ranges are thus lower than those set for reliability coefficients.

6.2.2 TYPES OF TESTS

We can classify tests according to their format and purpose. As to format, tests can be either *standardized* or *teacher-made*. The former are *objective*; the latter can be either objective or *subjective (essay-type)*. As to purpose, there are four main types of test: *aptitude*, *diagnostic*, *achievement*, and *proficiency*. Moreover, a key issue in language testing revolves around both the format and purpose of tests,

TABLE 6.12

Types of validity (from Davies 1977:59; based on Cronbach 1961:106)

	Question asked	Procedure	Principal use	Examples
Predictive	Do test scores predict a certain important future performance?	Give test and use it to predict the outcome. Sometime later obtain a measure of the outcome. Compare predictive with outcome.	Selection and classification	Admission test for medical students compared with later marks
Concurrent	Do test scores permit an estimate of a certain present performance?	Give test. Obtain a direct measure of the other performance. Compare the two.	Tests intended as a substitute for a less convenient procedure	Group mental test compared to individual test
Content	Does this test give a fair measure of performance on some important set of tasks?	Compare the items logically to the content supposed to be measured.	Achievement tests	A test of shorthand ability is examined to see whether the content is typical of office correspondence.
Construct	How can the scores on this test be explained psychologically?	Set up hypotheses. Test them experimentally by any suitable procedure.	Tests used for description or in scientific research	A test of art aptitude is studied to determine how largely scores depend on art training, experience in Western culture, etc.

namely, whether language proficiency should be tested in terms of the 'bits and pieces' of language (*discrete-point* testing) or in terms of its communicative nature (*integrative*, or *global*, testing). Although the discussion of any one of these types overlaps with any one of the others, we will describe each type separately for the sake of convenience.

It is often desirable to have language tests which have been already checked for reliability and validity by statistical means. These tests are known as *standardized*. *Teacher-made* tests, on the other hand, have to be checked for both reliability and validity in the statistical ways discussed in Section 6.2.1. All standardized tests are objective in format so that there is only one way to score them. A manual normally accompanies the test to insure that it is always administered in the same manner. A series of standardized tests designed to measure a specific area of knowledge administered within a certain period of time is known as a *test battery*. Some existing published standardized tests are the following ones. In the 1960s, the Modern Language Association developed test batteries in five languages. In these batteries there was a test for each of the four language skills: listening, speaking, reading, writing (Woodford 1980:97). The two most commonly used standardized language-aptitude tests are the Modern Language Aptitude Test (Carroll and Sapon 1958) and the Pimsleur Language Aptitude Battery (Pimsleur 1966). These tests require subjects to perform such tasks as listening, spelling, identifying grammatical patterns, memorizing, and learning numbers. Recently, the Bilingual Syntax Measure (Dulay, Burt, and Hernández 1975) and the Ilyin Oral Interview (Ilyin 1973) have attempted to standardize the testing of oral production.

Both standardized and teacher-made tests have four general purposes. (1) *Aptitude tests*. These tests measure the capacity to learn a language and to be successful in that venture. These tests must obviously have predictive validity, and they are independent of any particular language. The Modern Language Aptitude Test and the Pimsleur Language Aptitude Battery mentioned previously are examples of standardized language-aptitude tests. (2) *Diagnostic tests*. These tests are concerned with diagnosing a presence or absence of some skill in the learner's interlanguage. A diagnostic test aims primarily to determine which aspects of a given language will pose difficulties. (3) *Achievement tests*. These tests aim to measure how much a learner has learned from a given curriculum. An achievement test is therefore related directly to classroom experience. It should have content validity; i.e., the content of the test should reflect what is expected from the learning experience. (4) *Proficiency tests*. These tests aim to measure what has been learned without reference to any given curriculum. They aim to measure the learner's knowledge of the 'whole' language.

The format of tests can be either *objective* or *subjective (essay-type)*. Objective formats are used in standardized tests because scoring procedures constitute a major source of test unreliability. An objective test aims to minimize or eliminate any differences in results there might be due to variations among different scorers. An objective test can be marked in one way only. There are two main kinds of objective tests: *multiple choice* and *open ended*. In multiple-choice formats, a series of answers is provided from which the testee must choose the correct one. Sometimes, it is required simply to choose between 'true' and 'false.' Extended versions of multiple-choice testing consist in underlining or rearranging items. In the open-ended format, the testees must write their own answers, usually a word or phrase, in the space provided. Examples of both types of objective language questions are given in Figure 6.12. The first question aims to determine the testee's knowledge of semantic appropriateness in a poetic setting. The second one seeks to determine the testee's knowledge of intonation patterns. The third and fourth questions test for morphological and syntactic competence. The fifth question tests for lexical knowledge and the sixth for transformational syntactic ability. Notice that multiple-choice questions test receptive skills whereas open-ended ones test productive skills.

It is, however, almost impossible to eliminate the subjective element in testing completely. For one thing, the construction of a test is in itself based on some theoretical position in AL or APL and is therefore inevitably subjective. It can be said, none the less, that a test is objective if a scorer does not have to express a judgment on the score. In language testing it is not always possible to use objective testing. If one wishes to determine the student's ability to express ideas in writing, then the essay-type test, which is maximally subjective, is probably the most appropriate type.

In objective achievement tests, the statistical correlation procedures used can be either *criterion-referenced* or *norm-referenced*. These can be explained as follows. If we wish to correlate the competence of a subject to a set of norms drawn from a population, then the measure is norm-referenced. This means that the ability being tested is distributed in the pattern of the normal curve. If, however, we wish to correlate the subject's score to an objective standard of attainment, or criterion, then the measure is *criterion-referenced*. As Stones (1970:456) puts it: 'Do we give a test, score it, arrange the students in rank order and then decide on pass, credit, distinction and so on? Or do we decide beforehand on certain skills and concepts which we expect the students to have, devise a test to test these attributes and then score students' performance according to the extent to which they demonstrate their grasp of those skills and concepts?' The difference between the two correlation techniques is fundamental. In norm-referencing, grading and rank order of testees is emphasized, whereas in criterion-referencing the achievement of predetermined standards is emphasized.

We come now to one of the most important questions of all in language testing: *What* should we test? In the history of language testing, the answer to this question has been formulated, predictably, in terms of the particular psychological-linguistic theory in vogue at the time in AL or APL. In the 1920s, when the grammar-translation method dominated language teaching (see Section 5.1.2), tests consisted mainly of translation and composition tasks. With the advent of inductive teaching methods (see Section 5.1.1), testing became more objective and based on the statistical methods required to determine reliability and validity. Moreover, testing was influenced by the behaviorist-structuralist

Multiple-choice questions (from Pilliner 1974:30 and 45-7)

(1) Some words are missing in the following lines of poetry. Select the word that fits each space best.

1. Their song was soft and ... (shrill/clear/sharp/low/sweet)
2. The blossoms in the gentle ... (wind/breeze/trees/hands/glows)
3. Were ... like the snow (falling/freezing/soft/white/not).

(2) In the sentences below underline the one word you would *stress* to make clear (without actually saying) what is in the brackets.

1. Please close your desk lids gently now (do not make a loud noise).
2. Please close your desk lids gently now (do it immediately).

(3) In the following sentences choose the verbal expression that fits each space best.

1. What ... to do tomorrow? (would you like/do you like/could you like)
2. This new building ... since Christmas. (went up/has been going up/goes up)

(4) Complete the following sentences by putting the words in their proper order.

1. I've called for _____ (us/promised/you/books/the new)
2. Would you be so kind as _____ (this letter/the reason/explain/for/to).

Open-ended questions (from Ingram 1974:320)

(5) Complete the following sentence by filling in the blank.

... do you live? I live on High Street.

(6) Change the following sentences into negative sentences.

1. She sings well.
2. Does he own a car?

FIGURE 6.12 Objective test questions

view that language is a system of levels consisting of discrete 'parts' or 'points.' The assumption in testing was, therefore, that each point should be tested separately. The points are, of course, the units of language (phonemes, morphemes, etc.), and the four skills (listening, speaking, reading, writing). This type of testing has come to be known as *discrete-point*. The discrete points are illustrated by Oller (1976:150) (see Figure 6.13). The underlying question that a discrete-point test seeks to answer is: Does the student know the grammar and vocabulary? In other words, discrete-point testing is concerned with evaluating linguistic, rather than communicative, competence.

Recently, with the advent of functional teaching methods (see Section 5.1.3), there has been a concomitant shift in emphasis in language testing (see, for example, Savignon 1972, Oller 1976, Chastain 1977, Howard 1980, Wesche 1981).

160 Applied Psycholinguistics

	RECEPTIVE MODE	PRODUCTIVE MODE
Auditory/ articulatory modality	Listening (phonology/structure/vocabulary)	Speaking (phonology/structure/vocabulary)
Visual/ manual modality	Reading (graphology/structure/vocabulary)	Writing (graphology/structure/vocabulary)

FIGURE 6.13 The discrete points of language testing (from Oller 1976:150)

A wide variety o__ crops i__ now known t__ t__ West African farmer. T__ a__ a few peoples, mostly o__ t__ Jos plateau, w__ still plant only a__ inferior small grain. B__ most o__ t__ savana peoples h__ long depended o__ varieties o__ millet o__ guinea crop. T__ origin o__ rice cultivation i__ t__ Mande areas o__ t__ upper Niger remains a mystery.

FIGURE 6.14 Modified cloze test (from Davies 1977:82)

The slant now seems to be on testing *global*, or *integrative*, competence, which is defined as the mastery of language use in the total social context of the target language. In the discrete-point approach, testing was concerned primarily with measuring particular language skills. But the ability to inflect adjectives or conjugate verbs does not, in itself, constitute global language proficiency. The type of testing used to measure such global proficiency has come to be known as *integrative* testing. Typical integrative tests include dictations, interviews, reading and listening passages, and written essays. But perhaps the most commonly used integrative test is the so-called *cloze* test. This test was first introduced by William Taylor (1953), and it consists of a reading, or listening, passage which has been mutilated by the deletion of every nth word (usually every fifth, sixth, or seventh word). The testee is then required to supply either the exact, or an appropriate, word. Because Taylor intended the cloze test as a measure of silent reading ability, it first fell into the category of discrete-point tests. However, recently some (e.g., Oller 1973, 1976; Caulfield and Smith 1981) have claimed that cloze tests are excellent indicators of global proficiency because they require knowledge of vocabulary, grammatical structure, and discourse expectancy or anticipation. An example of a modified cloze test in which structure words are indicated only by their initial letter and a dash is given in Figure 6.14. There are, none the less, some questions pointed out by Brière et al. (1978) connected with cloze testing. (1) How will the scoring procedure affect the decisions which can be made? (2) To what extent do such variables as type of writing system used in the test, level of reading difficulty, different types of texts, test formats, and time limit influence scores? (3)

What effect will the different deleted morphosyntactic categories have on test scores? (4) Can cloze tests be used diagnostically? (5) Given a linguistic analysis of the categories of the deleted words, what are the implications of this information for the improvement of teaching and learning? (6) Can and should cloze tests be used as teaching devices?

In an important study, Savignon (1972) pointed out that global tests measure both receptive and productive skills simultaneously. Moreover, they measure the student's overall processing of the target language. However, as we have maintained throughout this book, language learning is a multidimensional process. It involves acquiring both linguistic and communicative competence. It would, therefore, seem more appropriate to use both discrete-point and integrative tests according to the specific pedagogical purpose. As Upshur (1976) has cautioned, communicative competence is only a single factor in the learning process, independent of the input-output mode and the sensory-motor modality. As Wesche (1981:555) has suggested, discrete-point testing may be more appropriate at the lower levels of language (phonology, morphology), if our viewpoint is that some control over these skills is essential to the learning task at hand. The higher the level of language, the more 'integrative' it is. Integrative testing is more appropriate in evaluating discourse ability.

We come now to one final question connected with language testing. *Why should we test?* There are, of course, practical reasons for testing students. The results obtained from tests can be used to grade and promote students. This is done normally at the end of a unit, term, or course. Rather than test, the term *examination* is often used in this context. This type of testing is known as *summative*. Tests can also have value as post-assessment devices; i.e., the results of tests can be used to assess the degree of learning in order to infer whether the instructional practices being used are effective or not. This type of testing is called *formative*. It is the formative function of testing which is germane to the evaluation of a teaching methodology based on the insights of APL. Tests that have been checked for reliability and validity can therefore be used as experimental tools which can assess the effect of certain instructional practices on a specific learning situation. However, tests can only indicate or detect that something is effective or ineffective. They cannot locate or identify the factor or factors which are responsible. This is left to experimentation which therefore constitutes the second and final stage of pedagogical post-assessment.

6.3 Research

Experimental research is at the core of the scientific method. So too with APL. As mentioned in Section 6.2.2, once a reliable and valid test produces very low results, it is an indication that something is wrong. The students may be poorly motivated or low in general language aptitude. On the other hand, the instructional practice used, and the theory on which it is based, may be ineffective. To determine, in fact, if it is the instructional practice which is at fault, the researcher or practitioner should proceed to test it experimentally.

The value of experimental research for language teaching was saliently demonstrated by the well-known Pennsylvania project (see Smith 1970). This experiment was a large-scale study which compared the grammar-translation method to the audio-lingual one and found, much to everyone's surprise, that the grammar-translation method produced better listening-comprehension results than the audio-lingual one which was, of course, supposed to pay more attention to the spoken language. Although, as Ingram (1977:34) notes, the comprehension test used in the experiment may have demanded a lot of vocabulary that only the grammar-translation subjects would have encountered through their reading program, this experiment left an indelible mark on language teaching – it led to the large-scale abandonment of language curricula based exclusively on the audio-lingual method.

6.3.1 CONTROLLED EXPERIMENTS

There are two main types of experiments which are relevant to APL. The first is concerned with investigating the language-learning process itself. Although this falls into the domain of general psycholinguistics, the findings are of obvious importance for APL. In previous chapters we have alluded to experimental studies of such phenomena as perception, inductive generalization, etc., which have shed some light on the psychological mechanisms involved in learning or acquiring a language. The second type of experimental research involves evaluating the efficacy of instructional practices under given experimental conditions. It is this type which concerns us here.

When evaluating instruction the experimental conditions should be *controlled*; i.e., the experiment should be designed in such a way that interfering variables are controlled in order to minimize or eliminate their influence on the outcome. Those variables which we wish to control are called the *independent variables*. The uncontrolled variable, which is the one we wish to evaluate experimentally, is known as the *dependent variable*. Controlled experiments can be classified as either *weakly* or *strongly controlled*. If we simply vary certain conditions and then observe the effects, we are maintaining only a weak control over the experimental conditions. But if we hold certain variables constant while the effects of some other variable on behavior are observed, then we are exercising a strong control over the experimental conditions.

We will illustrate these concepts with a hypothetical example. Suppose we wish to determine if the use of the language laboratory as a 'feedback' device has any significant influence on the learning of phonemic discriminations. The experiment which aims to discover if this is so may be conducted in the following ways.

The experimenter might, for example, use the laboratory to teach only vowel discriminations. The subjects listen to stimuli in the form of minimal pairs; repeat them and record their responses simultaneously on tapes; listen to their responses and compare them to the models used as stimuli (feedback component); and finally repeat them a second time. For consonant discriminations, however, the experimenter might use simple explanations and comparisons to L_1 to the same group of subjects in a classroom situation. Here the subjects repeat the experimenter's examples, but they do not have the opportunity afforded by the laboratory of listening to, and self-correcting, their responses. This procedure lacks, in other words, the feedback component of the laboratory. At the end of the training period, during which equal amounts of time are devoted to the teaching of vowel and consonant discriminations, the experimenter might administer a standardized test – or any one found to be reliable and valid – on phonological discrimination in the target language. The scores obtained for vowel discriminations are then compared to those obtained for consonant discriminations by using a significance measure such as the SED (Section 6.1.3). If a statistically significant difference in favor of vowel discriminations is found, then the experimenter may wish to say that this difference is due to the feedback component of language laboratories. However, in this experiment not all the independent variables have been controlled. For one thing, vowel discriminations might be 'easier' to learn than consonant ones for interlinguistic reasons. Perhaps the experimenter's explanations used in teaching consonant discriminations were not well formulated. In sum, the experiment was a weakly controlled one.

The experimenter uses instead two different groups, an *experimental group* and a *control group*. The two groups are, of course, chosen in such a way that they are homogeneous; i.e., independent variables such as age, sex, scholastic level, aptitude, intelligence, etc., are controlled and held constant. Now, the experimenter will use the laboratory on the experimental group to teach all phonemic discriminations, vocalic and consonantal. With the control group, the experimenter will now use the exact procedures that the experimental group is exposed to, only in a classroom setting. The classroom subjects are given the same minimal pair stimuli by the teacher. These are repeated by the subjects. The only difference is that the subjects in the experimental group can listen to their responses and compare them to the models. Thus, only the feedback component is lacking from the training procedures used with the control group. At the end of the training period, the same test on phonological discriminations in the target language is administered to both groups and the results compared statistically. If it is found that there is a statistically significant difference in favor of the experimental group, the experimenter can conclude, within the confidence limits associated with the significance measure used, that the influencing variable was the feedback component of the language laboratory.

Even with the use of control groups, one can never be completely sure that all interfering variables have been eliminated. In the above experiment, the experimenter may have had an initial bias towards the language laboratory and may therefore have unwittingly influenced the result by the procedures used *(experimenter bias)*. Or, since they may have known that they were being manipulated experimentally, the subjects of the experimental group might have put an unusual effort into the experiment (the *Hawthorne effect*). Therefore, when drawing conclusions from an experiment, one should always be careful to check for the presence of such *extraneous variables*. For this reason, it is always better to conduct a *pilot experiment* on a small group of subjects and analyze the results for possible extraneous variables before conducting the actual experiment.

6.3.2 EXPERIMENTAL DESIGN

The design of an experiment obviously depends on the nature of the dependent variable. Once this has been established, there are four main features of design that are connected with experimentation. (1) *Sample selection.* Needless to say, the selection of subjects is a very important component of design. Crocker (1969:109) gives several good suggestions for sample selection. The experimental group should be randomly selected from the population. The control group should either be randomly selected from the same population or matched with the experimental group on the selection criteria. Pseudo-large samples should be avoided. (2) *Control of extraneous variables.* Extraneous variables should always be controlled. To avoid experimenter bias, the one who conducts the experiment should be someone other than the experimenter, if possible. (3) *Materials and procedures.* Once the subjects have been chosen and extraneous variables eliminated, the actual materials and procedures to be used in the experiment should be prepared or selected. These depend obviously on the purpose and nature of the experiment. The experimenter should ask the following questions (Marrone and Rasor 1972:9): What is the problem? What is the hypothesis? What are the dependent and independent variables? What controls are needed? What apparatus is needed? What is the exact sequence of procedures to be followed? One of the more important aspects of experimental design is *replicability*; i.e., some other researcher should be able to repeat the experiment exactly. The experimenter should thus take special steps to insure that the materials and procedures are carefully prepared or chosen. When possible standardized materials (curricula, tests, etc.) should be used because these are available to other researchers. And when reporting the findings, the experimenter should always state all aspects of the experiment in detail. (4) *Analysis of the results*. After the experiment has been conducted, the experimenter must analyze the data statistically; i.e., the experimenter must determine if the findings are statistically significant or not.

If the findings of the experiment are statistically significant, then the experimenter may wish to examine their pedagogical implications. For example, in the hypothetical experiment mentioned above, the experimenter may wish to state that because of its feedback component, the language laboratory is an effective teaching device for the learning of phonemic discriminations.

There is one final point to be made about experimental research. The reporting of an experiment in the technical journals is an important part of APL. The findings of any experiment should always be shared with the other members of the research and teaching professions. The exchange of ideas is crucial to the well-being of any science. When reporting an experiment in a professional journal, the experimenter should try to follow the common format that is used in such journals. In short, the format generally consists of seven components. (1) First, there is an introduction to the purpose of the experiment together with a brief survey of the salient features of the experimental and theoretical work previously conducted in the area under investigation. (2) Then there is a description of the subjects and sampling criteria used. (3) This is followed by a description of the materials and procedures used which may also be appended to the study. (4) Then the data are presented in the form of tables, charts, graphs, etc. (see Section 6.1.1). (5) The data are then analyzed statistically (see sections 6.1.2, 6.1.3, and 6.1.4). (6) The findings are then discussed. (7) And finally a summary and conclusion are given. The conclusion may also contain practical implications and/or suggestions for further research.

6.4 A Pedagogical Summary

In our view, the statistical concepts discussed in the first part of this chapter (Section 6.1) and the experimental design notions described in the latter part (Section 6.3) might prove to be useful to the teacher on at least two counts. First of all, they may help the teacher understand the technical research literature in AL and APL. Second, they might provide a starting point for teachers to develop their own scientifically valid methods of evaluating the efficacy of their classroom procedures. The description of tests (Section 6.2) will, we hope, give teachers an overall view of the kinds and uses of tests so that they can apply them to their own situations.

6.5 Signposts

In the past testing research was directed towards the development of language tests for the evaluation of linguistic competence. But in the last decade or so, the emphasis has shifted towards the construction of tests designed to assess communicative skills. Cloze tests, for instance, have been receiving particular attention. In our view, testing procedures should be in line with teaching practices. And since we believe that such practices should be as eclectic as possible, our view is that testing should attempt to evaluate both the student's discrete-point and global capabilities.

6.6 Suggestions for Further Reading

For very good explanations of statistical concepts, see, for example, Franzblau (1958), Crocker (1969), or Arkin and Colton (1970). R. Clark (1977a and 1977b) provides good descriptions of statistical techniques as they apply to language testing and research.

Some very good treatments of language testing are: Lado (1961), Valette (1968), Savignon (1972), Davies (1974, 1977), Pilliner (1974), and Ingram (1977). Cloze tests and integrative testing techniques are discussed at length in Oller (1973, 1976), Chastain (1977), Howard (1980), Wesche (1981).

Experiments are discussed in Lathrop (1969), Marrone and Rasor (1972), Plutchik (1974), and R. Clark (1977c).

7
A Glossodynamic Model of Language Learning and Language Teaching

No single method suffices to answer all the needs of all learners at all times. We are wary of jumping onto bandwagons. But there is no magic about eclecticism. It is easy to claim to be an eclectic, and dip haphazardly into every attractive aspect of every conceivable method or approach, and then jumble everything together. It is quite another task to practice 'enlightened' eclecticism – that is, to engage in an intelligent use of selected approaches built upon and guided by an integrated and broadly based theory of second language acquisition.

(Brown 1980:243)

7.0 Introduction

In previous chapters we have discussed the more widely known theories and experimental findings connected with language learning, as well as their pedagogical implications. We have also described the major teaching methodologies which have translated the theories and findings into instructional practices. Our point of view has been that no one theory can possibly account for the whole language-learning process. The pedagogical value of familiarizing oneself with the various theories and their methodological translations lies in developing a flexible approach that will respond to each learning situation in as effective a manner as possible. In our opinion, therefore, such an approach is bound to be 'eclectic,' 'interdisciplinary,' or 'integrated.' An integrated approach can perhaps be characterized by the following five verbs: *familiarize* (yourself), *adapt*, *try out*, *adjust*, and *evaluate*. The practitioner should be familiar with as many of the theories and research on the linguistic, psychological, and pedagogical aspects of language learning and teaching as possible. These should then be selected according to a given situation, translated into teaching practice, and adapted accordingly. Then they should be tried out in the actual situation and adjusted in the course of the teaching process if so required. Finally, they should be evaluated by the scientific methods of measurement and experimentation. The integrated approach to language teaching can perhaps be best summarized by an algorithm such as the one given in Figure 7.1.

An integrated point of view does not imply in any way that no theory can ever be formulated to account for language learning. It does suggest, however, that any theory which attempts to explain such a complex process will have to be an integrated one; i.e., the framework for a theory of language learning will have to be one which blends together the behavioral, cognitive, and personality components of language learning. In this chapter we will describe briefly one such integrated theory that has been proposed by one of the authors (e.g., Titone 1977a), known as the *glossodynamic model* (GDM) of language learning. We will also look at a suggested teaching model based on the GDM.

7.1 The Glossodynamic Model of Language Learning

The term *glossodynamics* was used for the first time by Roback (1955) who utilized it to designate motivational variables in language learning. Here it is used instead to indicate that language learning is a stratified and dynamic process. Basically, the GDM proposes that operant conditioning, cognitive structuring, and personality dynamics all interact during the learning of language. This does not imply a mere mixture of theories, but rather a synthesis of three substantially complementary viewpoints.

The GDM proposes two basic dimensions involved in the language-learning process: a *deep structure* and a *surface structure*. These two terms are not used in the same way as they are in TG grammar. The deep structure of language learning in the GDM consists of three interconnected levels. (1) *Tactics*. At this level, the formation of encoding and decoding processes is accomplished by means of experiential learning; i.e., through the coordination and integration of the cortical and peripheral centers of the brain, the speaker-hearer establishes perceptual schemata (auditory/visual) and motor habits (articulatory/graphic) by arranging and organizing the input stimuli and output responses. The tactics correspond, therefore, to operations that are behavioral in nature. Since language learning is a feedback phenomenon, the development of the tactic operations is coordinated by self-regulatory, or monitoring, mechanisms. Like all experiential learning, the tactics are learned in some environment or context. The tactics constitute, therefore, the *act* of communicating. (2) *Strategy*. At this level, conceptualization and cognitive structuring interact with the experiential processes of the tactics to produce in the speaker-hearer the ability to recognize the meaningfulness and grammaticality of utterances. Strategic operations are cognitive in nature and they include: the ability to organize language into phonological, morphological,

A Glossodynamic Model 169

```
IN →  What linguistic, psychological, → No such theory      → Use any method or
      or pedagogical theory seems to   currently available.   approach deemed
      be applicable to situation?                             applicable.
              ↓
      Select the theory and translate
      it into a teaching approach.
      Adapt it accordingly.
              ↓
              Try out the approach  → Seems to be
              in actual situation.    appropriate.
                      ↓                       ↓
              Seems to be             Evaluate the efficacy  → Found to be
              inappropriate.          of the approach at the    effective.
                                      end of the teaching
                                      session with the
                                      scientific techniques
                                      of measurement and
                                      experimentation.
                      ↓                       ↓                       ↓
              Go back to the start ← Found to be            Keep in store
              and reassess the       ineffective.           for possible
              theoretical aspects                           future use.
              of the approach.
              Check for other
              factors as well.
                                                                      ↓
                                                                     OUT
```

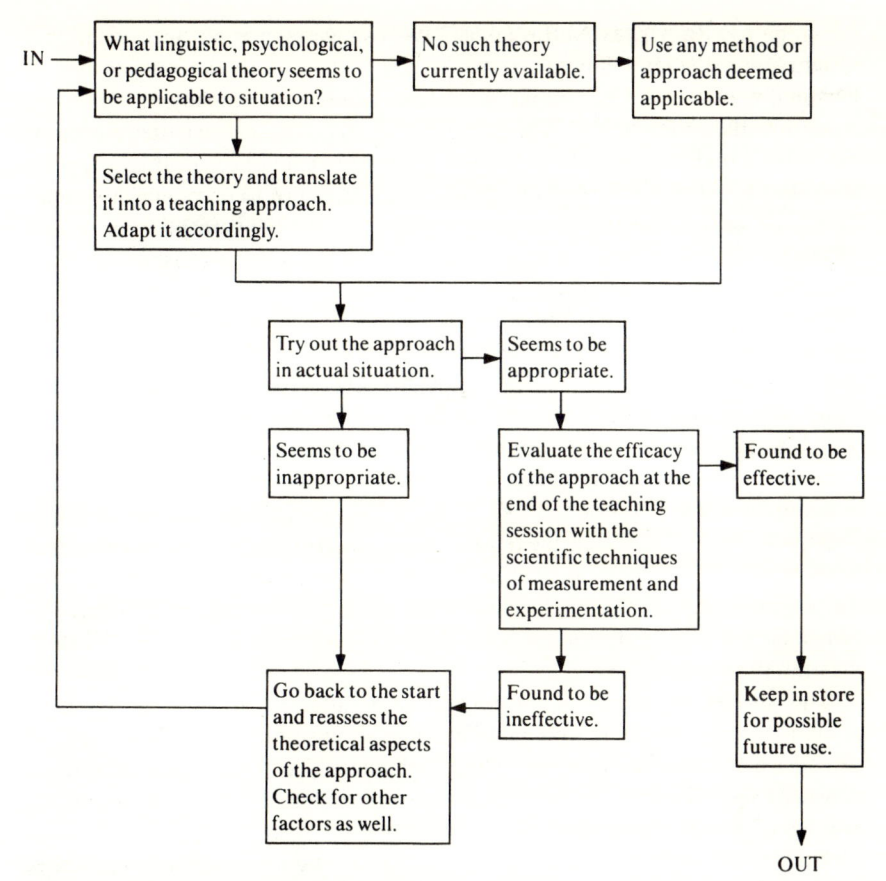

FIGURE 7.1 An integrated teaching algorithm

syntactic, and lexico-semantic rules (rule-making process); the ability to select from raw speech data the constant, or emic, cues (selection process); the ability to contextualize speech, i.e., to 'program' a message to fit a communicative situation (programming process); the ability to regulate the flow of speech due to the presence of cognitive feedback mechanisms (conscious self-regulatory process). This level constitutes, therefore, the *ability* to communicate. (3) *Ego-Dynamic Level.* This is the level which coordinates the tactic and strategic levels. This is the personality level. The view of personality adopted here is a *dynamic* one in the sense used by Allport (1965:28), namely that personality is 'the dynamic organization within the individual of those psychophysical systems that determine his characteristic behavior and thought.' Dynamic personality is not identical to individuality. Rather, as Nuttin (1968:205-6) suggests, it is an open, relational system; i.e., it allows human beings to relate directly to the outside world. Personality may therefore be conceived of as an ego-dynamic relational structure. It controls the ability to 'talk' about experience, to adjust speech patterns according to life situations (including the knowledge of when not to speak), to express attitudes, to retrieve information about oneself verbally, to communicate intentions, and to use language for self-awareness (i.e., for the perception of oneself through communicative interaction). The ego-dynamic level constitutes, therefore, the *will* to communicate.

These three levels are stratified in the deep structure in such a way that the ego-dynamic level forms the lowest layer, followed by the strategic one, and finally by the tactical level which connects the other two to the surface structure. In usual linguistic terminology, the strategic level corresponds to both linguistic and communicative competence and the tactical one to performance. The surface structure dimension refers to the actual use of verbal symbols (oral/visual) to communicate one's experiences or intentions. This dimension of verbal behavior is directly observable, hence the term 'surface' structure. Here the tactical operations manifest themselves as a set of abilities to 'symbolize' and 'communicate.' The surface manifestations of verbal behavior can thus indicate the degree of functioning of the deep structure levels during the learning process. The GDM is illustrated in Figure 7.2.

This model is general in the sense that it attempts to account for both second-language learning and first-language acquisition. In the latter case, it provides a framework again for viewing language development as an integrated process which depends on the simultaneous development of tactical, strategic, and ego-dynamic operations. At the tactical level, both perceptual and motor verbal development depend on the formation of linguistic habits. This implies that conditioning is always involved in the development of the tactics. It also assumes the proper functioning of the neural endings and the cerebral centers which control perception and articulation. Tactical development is controlled by verbal feedback mechanisms which continually monitor the inflow and outflow of speech. As Dingwall (1975:52) observes: 'Both production and recognition are linked by a complex feedback system involving at least tactile, proprioceptive, and acoustic feedback loops. This feedback system appears to play a particularly important role in the early stages of speech acquisition during which what we have termed the automatization of speech production is taking place.' At the strategic level, the mentalistic aspects of language development are formed. Here cognitive mechanisms (rule-making processes, programming processes, etc.) interact with the tactics in organizing linguistic data. At the ego-dynamic level, the child, who is born with the will to communicate, initiates the tactical and strategic

SURFACE STRUCTURE

```
                                    ┌─────────────────────────┐
                                    │ The actual use of verbal│
                                    │ symbols for communication│
                                    └─────────────────────────┘
                                              ▲
              DEEP STRUCTURE                  │
                                    ┌─────────────────────────┐
                                    │ TACTICS                 │
                                    │ Formation of motor      │
The *act* of communicating ─────────│ ability and perceptual  │
                                    │ schemata by means of    │
                                    │ self-regulatory         │
                                    │ mechanisms              │
                                    └─────────────────────────┘
                                              ▲
                                    ┌─────────────────────────┐
                                    │ STRATEGY                │
                                    │ Rule-making, selection, │
The *ability* to communicate ───────│ programming, conscious  │
                                    │ self-regulation         │
                                    └─────────────────────────┘
                                              ▲
                                    ┌─────────────────────────┐
                                    │ EGO-DYNAMICS            │
                                    │ Control over the ability│
                                    │ to talk about experience│
                                    │ to adjust speech        │
The *will* to communicate ──────────│ patterns according to   │
                                    │ life situations,        │
                                    │ to express attitudes, to│
                                    │ retrieve information    │
                                    │ about oneself, to use   │
                                    │ language for            │
                                    │ self-awareness          │
                                    └─────────────────────────┘
```

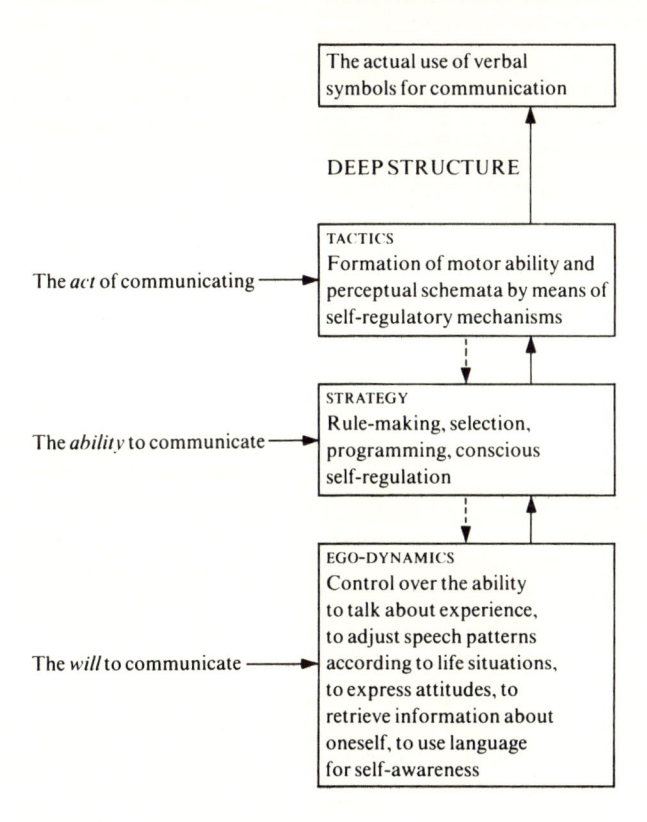

FIGURE 7.2 The glossodynamic model of language learning

operations; i.e., the experiences, perceptions, emotions, needs, etc., of the child converge to form the 'trigger' mechanism of language development. It is interesting to note that the view that first-language acquisition and second-language learning can be accounted for in terms of a single learning process has recently been expressed by Carroll (1981).

Although it may be beyond the scope of this book, it is nevertheless interesting to note that the GDM has been used as a convenient framework for explaining verbal malfunctioning or aphasia. In a recent article, Tanzarella (1978) adopts this framework and concludes, after having studied typical aphasic symptoms (see Section 2.2.1), that aphasic speech is defective in the cognitive strategic domain. Aphasic individuals are aware of their communicative intentions and of their need to communicate because their ego-dynamic operations are intact, but they cannot carry out their intentions at the strategic level. In other words, they skip this level and go directly to the tactics producing 'strategically deviant' utterances in the phonology, grammar, and lexicon of the language. However, despite aberrant utterances, the personality and language awareness of aphasic individuals remain intact. Thus, in terms of the GDM, aphasia can be defined as a dysfunction of the strategic operations which manifests itself at the tactic level in the form of phonologically, grammatically, and lexically deviant utterances. There is, in other words, an ensuing disruption of the inherent interactional processes that exist among the tactical, strategic, and ego-dynamic levels.

But what does this mean from a neurological viewpoint? As Tanzarella observes, various researchers have tried to relate aphasic disorders to particular areas of cortical damage, but generally to no avail. It is turning out to be very difficult to pinpoint the neurological causes of aphasia. Consequently, Tanzarella suggests that a psychologically oriented approach in terms of the GDM, instead of a neurological one, will be beneficial from a therapeutic standpoint. According to the glossodynamic interpretation, there exists in the central nervous system a mechanism which controls the tactical, or automatic, speech operations. This mechanism is dysfunctional in the adult aphasic, inhibiting the successful programming of such operations at the strategic level. This is why aphasic speech is so laborious and distorted. Moreover, the jump from the ego-dynamic to the tactic level makes aphasic speech sound more 'affective' or 'emotional' because the egodynamic operations are not processed strategically and are carried over directly to the tactics. Thus, according to Tanzarella, if aphasia is viewed from a glossodynamic perspective, it becomes clear that personality, as well as other, variables should play a part in determining the therapeutic *modus operandi*.

7.2 A Glossodynamic View of Language Teaching

The GDM of language learning posits interacting behavioral, cognitive, communicative, and personality components. From a teaching standpoint, the following three broad implications can be drawn from this model. (1) The teaching of the tactical operations of the target language will inevitably require conditioning techniques (imitation, repetition, pattern practice, etc.). This is because the tactics involve perceptual and motor operations. (2) The learning of strategic operations such as grammatical rules or the proper use of the target language in communicative settings will require both deductive and functional teaching techniques. (3) Since the ego-dynamic level of language learning is crucial to the proper functioning of the tactical and strategic levels, the teacher should always be aware of personality variables and adapt any teaching technique to these variables. Above all else, the teacher should strive to create as congenial a learning environment as possible so that inhibitions can be minimized or eliminated and the ego-dynamic functions allowed to operate freely.

Therefore, a teaching model based on the GDM of language learning is necessarily an integrated one, synthesizing inductive, deductive, functional, and humanistic instructional practices in a complementary fashion. One such model has been developed and subjected to experimental verification with positive results (e.g., Titone 1973, 1977b:99–140). In this model, a *matheme* is a *learning* unit which is covered by a *macromatheme*, or complete *teaching* unit. Each macromatheme is composed of various teaching stages known as *micromathemes*. These stages are *inchoation*, *practice*, and *control*.

The inchoation stage aims to develop perceptual and cognitive skills in both the tactical and strategic components. This stage consists of three sequential phases. (1) *Global perception*. Since it is a known fact that reception precedes production, learners should first be exposed to the target language by means of dialogues, narratives, or other samples of the target language. (2) *Operational analysis*. Then by the use of comprehension exercises based on the discourse material of the first phase, the learner's understanding of the form and content of the discourse unit is tested and improved. (3) *Operational synthesis*. By means of activities and exercises the student then reconstructs the discourse unit.

The practice stage consists of reinforcement techniques. Here, the term 'reinforcement' is used to mean both the mechanical practice of verbal skills through pattern drills (as in inductive approaches) and the practice of communicative functions through meaningful situational exercises (as in functional approaches). Throughout this stage a feedback component should be present; i.e., both teacher and student should monitor what is going on (as in cognitive-based approaches). Thus, during the practice stage, both the tactical and strategic operations are activated.

The control stage is an evaluation and correction stage. The evaluation and correction procedures can be produced externally by the teacher, or by the students themselves. And they can be either occasional or programmed (i.e., incorporated into the instructional process and materials). Figure 7.3 schematizes the macromathetic teaching process.

In this teaching model, elements of various pedagogical approaches are brought together. The reinforcement procedures of inductive approaches together with the situational techniques of functional approaches constitute the reinforcement micromatheme. Meaningful learning techniques, as in cognitive-code approaches, are used during the operational analysis and synthesis parts of the inchoation micromatheme. And reception is put before production since the whole process starts off with global perception. In addition, it provides for a

```
                              ┌ Global perception ──────→ Exposure to target-language
                              │                            data (discourse unit)
                              │         ↓
INCHOATION      ──────────→   ┤ Operational analysis ───→ Understanding of form and
MICROMATHEME                  │                            content
    ↑                         │         ↓
    │                         └ Operational synthesis ──→ Reconstruction of discourse
    │                                                      unit
    ↓
REINFORCEMENT  ──────→ Practice ──────→ ┤ Pattern drills
MICROMATHEME                              Situational exercises
    ↑
    │                         ┌ Evaluation ──→ ┤ Self
    ↓                         │                  External          Occasional
CONTROL        ──────────→    ┤                                       ↕
MICROMATHEME                  │       ↓                            Programmed
                              └ Correction ──→ ┤ Self
                                                 External
```

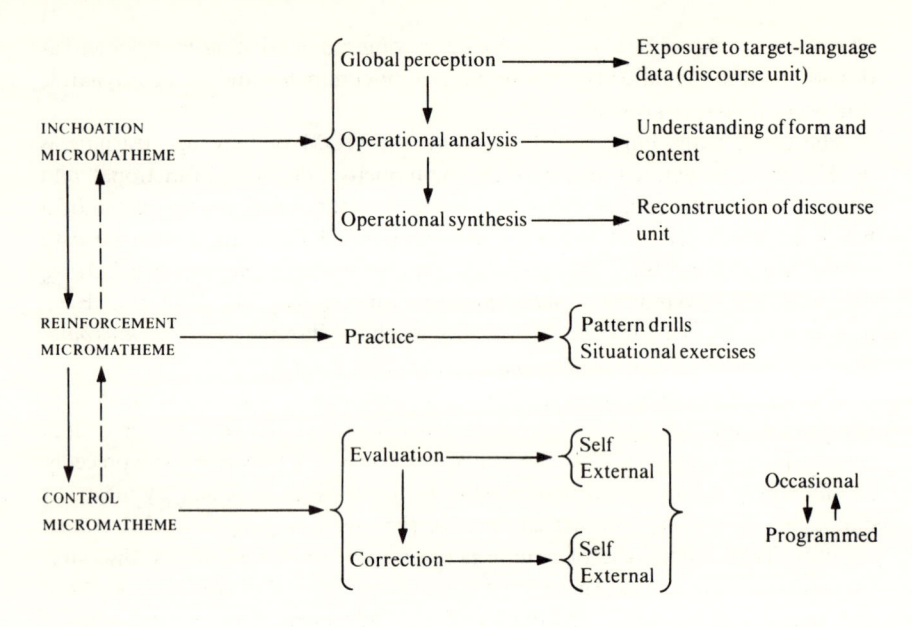

FIGURE 7.3 A macromatheme or complete teaching unit

control stage in the teaching process. Since the process is cyclical rather than linear, the teacher can move back and forth among micromathemes, adapting them to the learning style and personality of the learner.

In sum, a model based on the glossodynamic view of language learning should synthesize the insights and findings of various schools of linguistics, psychology, and language-teaching methodology in some logical fashion. The GDM suggests very strongly that, since language learning is an integrated process, the most suitable teaching approach is an integrated one as well.

7.3 A Concluding Pedagogical Summary

It should be abundantly clear by now that it is our belief that only through a convergence of theoretical perspectives can a truly effective approach to language teaching be developed. It is interesting to note that evidence in favor of integrated approaches has recently come from specialized language teaching. Boari (1978), for example, discovered that with an integrated teaching method mentally retarded children seemed to learn language much better. Similarly, Cipolla, Mosca, and Titone (1978) found that an integrated approach was particularly effective with socially disadvantaged children.

A Glossodynamic Model 175

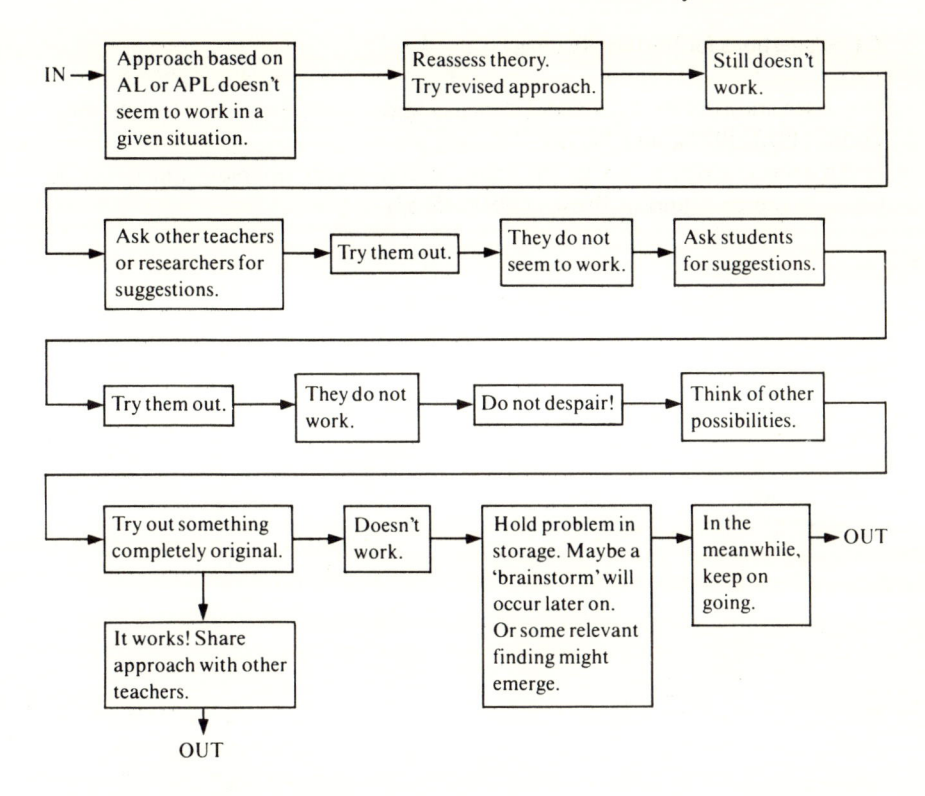

```
IN → [Approach based on      ] → [Reassess theory.    ] → [Still doesn't]
     [AL or APL doesn't       ]   [Try revised approach.]   [work.        ]
     [seem to work in a       ]
     [given situation.        ]

     → [Ask other teachers   ] → [Try them out.] → [They do not ] → [Ask students  ]
       [or researchers for   ]                     [seem to work.]   [for suggestions.]
       [suggestions.         ]

     → [Try them out.] → [They do not] → [Do not despair!] → [Think of other]
                         [work.      ]                       [possibilities.]

     → [Try out something   ] → [Doesn't] → [Hold problem in    ] → [In the      ] → OUT
       [completely original.]   [work.  ]   [storage. Maybe a   ]   [meanwhile,  ]
            ↓                               ['brainstorm' will  ]   [keep on     ]
       [It works! Share     ]               [occur later on.    ]   [going.      ]
       [approach with other ]               [Or some relevant   ]
       [teachers.           ]               [finding might      ]
            ↓                               [emerge.            ]
           OUT
```

FIGURE 7.4 'If Nothing Works' algorithm

In conclusion, we wish to state once again that language teachers can benefit from a knowledge of the psychology of language learning. By understanding better what is going on in the minds of their students, they will be able to identify typical patterns as they emerge during the learning process and thus be better prepared to devise appropriate teaching strategies. But *caveat emptor*! A knowledge of APL should be only one of the many components that make up good language teaching. Among other things, the language teacher should also be as proficient as possible in the language being taught. Moreover, the teacher should know as much as possible about the people who speak it and about their culture, history, achievements, etc.

Finally, we wish to end on a humorous note which none the less expresses our viewpoint that effective language teaching should be as flexible as possible. What if no approach based on AL or APL seems to work? The answer to this question is answered anecdotally in Figure 7.4.

7.4 Suggestions for Further Reading

For descriptions of the GDM and its pedagogical applications, see, for example, Titone (1973, 1977a, and 1977b).

An excellent discussion of the value of convergent techniques in language teaching can be found in Brown (1980:245-53).

APPENDICES

APPENDIX A
The Major Symbols of the IPA (from Robins 1971:86–7)

Consonants	Bila-bial	Labio-dental	Dental & alveolar	Retro-flex	Palato-alveolar	Alveolo-palatal	Palatal	Velar	Uvular	Pha-ryngal	Glottal
Plosives (stops)	[p] [b]		[t] [d]	[ʈ] [ɖ]			[c] [ɟ]	[k] [g]	[q] [G]		[ʔ]
Nasals	[m]	[ɱ]	[n]	[ɳ]			[ɲ]	[ŋ]	[N]		
Lateral fricatives			[ɬ] [ɮ]								
Lateral non-fricatives			[l]	[ɭ]			[ʎ]				
Rolled vibrants			[r]						[R]		
Flapped vibrants			[ɾ]	[ɽ]					[R]		
Fricatives	[ɸ] [β]	[f] [v]	[θ] [s] [ð] [z]	[ʂ] [ʐ]	[ʃ] [ʒ]	[ɕ] [ʑ]	[ç] [j]	[x] [ɣ]	[χ] [ʁ]	[ħ] [ʕ]	[h] [h]
Frictionless continuants and semi-vowels	[w]	[ɥ]	[ɹ]				[j]		[ʁ]		

Vowels	Front	Central	Back
Close	[i] [y]	[ɨ] [ʉ]	[ɯ] [u]
Half-close	[e] [ø]		[ɤ] [o]
Half-open	[ɛ] [œ]	[ə]	[ʌ] [ɔ]
Open	[æ]	[a]	[ɐ] [a] [ɑ]

APPENDIX B
Lenneberg's Description of Language Development with Respect to Motor Development (from Lenneberg 1967)

At the completion of:	Motor development	Vocalization and language
12 weeks	Supports head when in prone position; weight is on elbows; hands mostly open; no grasp reflex	Markedly less crying than at 8 weeks; when talked to and nodded at, smiles, followed by squealing-gurgling sounds usually called *cooing*, which is vowel-like in character and pitch-modulated; sustains cooing for 15-20 seconds
16 weeks	Plays with a rattle placed in his hands (by shaking it and staring at it), head self-supported; tonic neck reflex subsiding	Responds to human sounds more definitely; turns head; eyes seem to search for speaker; occasionally some chuckling sounds
20 weeks	Sits with props	The vowel-like cooing sounds begin to be interspersed with more consonantal sounds; labial fricatives, spirants, and nasals are common; acoustically, all vocalizations are very different from the sounds of the mature language of the environment
6 months	Sits; bends forward and uses hands for support; can bear weight when put into standing position, but cannot stand yet without holding on; reaching: unilateral; grasp: no thumb apposition yet; releases cube when given another	Cooing changes into babbling resembling one-syllable utterances; neither vowels nor consonants have very fixed recurrences; most common utterances sound somewhat like *ma, mu, da,* or *di.*
8 months	Stands holding on; grasps with thumb apposition; picks up pellet with thumb and fingertips	Reduplication (or more continuous repetitions) becomes frequent; intonation patterns become distinct; utterances can signal emphasis and emotions.
10 months	Creeps efficiently; takes side-steps, holding on; pulls to standing position	Vocalizations are mixed with sound-play such as gurgling or bubble-blowing; appears to wish to imitate sounds, but the imitations are never quite successful; begins to differentiate between words heard by making differential adjustment.

APPENDIX B continued

At the completion of:	Motor development	Vocalization and language
12 months	Walks when held by one hand; walks on feet and hands – knees in air; mouthing of objects almost stopped; seats self on floor	Identical sound sequences are replicated with higher relative frequency of occurrence and words *(mamma* or *dada)* are emerging; definite signs of understanding some words and simple commands ('show me your eyes')
18 months	Grasp, prehension, and release fully developed; gait: stiff, propulsive, and precipitated; sits on child's chair with only fair aim; creeps downstairs backward; has difficulty building tower of three cubes	Has a definite repertoire of words—more than three, but fewer than fifty; still much babbling but now of several syllables with intricate intonation pattern; no attempt at communicating information and no frustration at not being understood; words may include such items as 'thank you' or 'come here,' but there is little ability to join any of the lexical items into spontaneous two-item phrases; understanding is progressing rapidly
24 months	Runs, but falls in sudden turns; can quickly alternate between sitting and standing; walks up or down stairs, one foot forward only	Vocabulary of more than fifty items (some children seem to be able to name everything in environment); begins spontaneously to join vocabulary items into two-word phrases; all phrases appear to be own creations; definite increase in communicative behavior and interest in language
30 months	Jumps up into air with both feet; stands on one foot for about two seconds; takes few steps on tiptoe; jumps from chair; good hand and finger coordination; can move digits independently; manipulation of objects much improved; builds tower of six cubes	Fastest increase in vocabulary with many new additions every day; no babbling at all; utterances have communicative intent; frustrated if not understood by adults; utterances consist of at least two words, many of three or even five words; sentences and phrases have characteristic child grammar, that is, they are rarely verbatim repetitions of adult utterances; intelligibility is not very good yet, though there is great variation among children; seems to understand everything that is said to him

APPENDIX B continued

At the completion of:	Motor development	Vocalization and language
3 years	Tiptoes three yards; runs smoothly with acceleration and deceleration; negotiates sharp and fast curves without difficulty; walks stairs by alternating feet; jumps 12 inches; can operate tricycle	Vocabulary of some 1000 words; about 80 percent of utterances are intelligible even to strangers; grammatical complexity of utterances is roughly that of colloquial adult language, although mistakes still occur
4 years	Jumps over rope; hops on right foot; catches ball in arms; walks line	Language is well-established; deviations from adult norm tend to be more in style than in grammar

APPENDIX C
Summary of the Biological and Maturational Factors in Language Acquisition
(from Lenneberg 1967:180–1)

Age	Usual language development	Effects of acquired, lateralized lesions	Physical maturation of central nervous system
0–3 months	Emergence of cooing	No effect on onset of language in half of all cases; other half has delayed onset but normal development.	About 60 to 70 percent of developmental course accomplished
4–20 months	From babbling to words		
21–36 months	Acquisition of language	All language accomplishments disappear; language is re-acquired with repetition of all stages.	Rate of maturation slowed down
3–10 years	Some grammatical refinement; expansion of vocabulary	Emergence of aphasic symptoms; disorders tend to recover without residual language deficits (except in reading or writing). During recovery period, two processes active: diminishing aphasic interference and further acquisition of language.	Very slow completion of maturational processes
11–14 years	Foreign accents emerge	Some aphasic symptoms become irreversible (particularly when acquired lesion was traumatic).	An asymptote is reached on almost all parameters. Exceptions are myelinization and electroencephalogram spectrum.
Midteens to old age	Acquisition of second language becomes increasingly difficult.	Symptoms present after 3 to 5 months after injury are irreversible.	None

Lateralization of function	Developmental potential	Explanation
None; symptoms and prognosis identical for either hemisphere	Perfect equipotentiality	Neuro-anatomical and physiological prerequisites become established.
Hand preference emerges.	Right hemisphere can easily adopt sole responsibility for language.	Language appears to involve entire brain; little cortical specialization with regard to language though left hemisphere beginning to become dominant towards end of this period.
Cerebral dominance established between 3 and 5 years but evidence that right hemisphere may often still be involved in speech and language functions. About 25 percent of early childhood aphasias due to right hemisphere lesions.	In cases where language already localized in left hemisphere and aphasia ensues with left lesion, it is possible to re-establish language presumably by reactivating language functions in right hemisphere.	A process of physiological organization takes place in which functional lateralization of language to left is prominent. 'Physical redundancy' is gradually reduced and polarization of activities between right and left hemispheres is established. As long as maturational processes have not stopped, reorganization is still possible.
Apparently firmly established but definitive statistics not available.	Marked signs of reduction in equipotentiality	Language markedly lateralized and internal organization established irreversibly for life. Language-free parts of brain cannot take over except where lateralization is incomplete or had been blocked by pathology during childhood.
In about 97 percent of the entire population language is definitely lateralized to the left.	None for language	

APPENDIX D
Values of t (from Crocker 1969:122)

Degrees of freedom	$p < 0.05$	$p < 0.01$
1	12.706	63.657
2	4.303	9.925
3	3.182	5.841
4	2.776	4.604
5	2.571	4.032
6	2.447	3.707
7	2.365	3.499
8	2.306	3.355
9	2.262	3.250
10	2.228	3.169
11	2.201	3.106
12	2.179	3.055
13	2.160	3.012
14	2.145	2.977
15	2.131	2.947
16	2.120	2.921
17	2.110	2.898
18	2.101	2.878
19	2.093	2.861
20	2.086	2.845
21	2.080	2.831
22	2.074	2.819
23	2.069	2.807
24	2.064	2.797
25	2.060	2.787
26	2.056	2.779
27	2.052	2.771
28	2.048	2.763
29	2.045	2.756
30	2.042	2.750
	1.960	2.576

APPENDIX E
Values of F at the p < 0.01 Confidence Level (from Crocker 1969:124)

Degrees of freedom of the within variance	Degrees of freedom of the between variance				
	1	2	3	4	5
1	4052.20	4999.50	5403.40	5624.60	5763.60
2	98.50	99.00	99.17	99.25	99.30
3	34.12	30.82	29.46	28.71	28.24
4	21.20	18.00	16.69	15.98	15.52
5	16.26	13.27	12.06	11.39	10.97
6	13.75	10.92	9.78	9.15	8.75
7	12.25	9.55	8.45	7.85	7.46
8	11.26	8.65	7.59	7.01	6.63
9	10.56	8.02	6.99	6.42	6.06
10	10.04	7.56	6.55	5.99	5.64
11	9.65	7.21	6.22	5.67	5.32
12	9.33	6.93	5.95	5.41	5.06
13	9.07	6.70	5.74	5.21	4.86
14	8.86	6.51	5.56	5.04	4.69
15	8.68	6.36	5.42	4.89	4.56
16	8.53	6.23	5.29	4.77	4.44
17	8.40	6.11	5.18	4.67	4.34
18	8.29	6.01	5.09	4.58	4.25
19	8.18	5.93	5.01	4.50	4.17
20	8.10	5.85	4.94	4.43	4.10

APPENDIX F
Values of χ^2 (from Crocker 1969:123)

Degrees of freedom	$p < 0.05$	$p < 0.01$
1	3.84	6.63
2	5.99	9.21
3	7.81	11.34
4	9.49	13.28
5	11.07	15.09
6	12.59	16.81
7	14.07	18.48
8	15.50	10.09
9	16.90	21.67
10	18.31	23.21
11	19.68	24.72
12	21.03	26.22
13	22.36	27.69
14	23.68	29.14
15	25.00	30.58
16	26.30	32.00
17	27.59	33.41
18	28.87	34.81
19	30.14	36.19
20	31.41	37.57
21	32.67	38.93
22	33.92	40.29
23	35.17	41.64
24	36.42	42.98
25	37.65	44.31
26	38.89	45.64
27	40.11	46.96
28	41.34	48.28
29	42.56	49.59
30	43.77	50.89

APPENDIX G
Summary of Statistical Techniques

Technique	Formula/procedure	Use
Range	R = lowest score − highest score	To determine the spread of scores from the highest to the lowest
Mode	The observation in a set of data that occurs the most	A measure of central tendency
Median	The observation in a set of data that divides the set into halves of exactly equal numbers	A measure of central tendency
Mean	$\bar{x} = \dfrac{\Sigma x}{N}$	The most reliable measure of central tendency
Standard deviation	$s = \sqrt{\dfrac{\Sigma(x - \bar{x})^2}{N - 1}}$	A measure of dispersion
z-score	Relating scores in terms of the standard deviation	To deduce the proportion of cases above and below a given score
Standard error of the mean	$SEM = s/\sqrt{N}$	To determine the population mean from a sample mean
Standard error of the difference	$SED = \sqrt{SEM_1^2 + SEM_2^2}$	To determine if the difference between sample means is significant
t-test	$t = \dfrac{\bar{x}_1 - \bar{x}_2}{\sqrt{SEM_1^2 + SEM_2^2}}$	To determine if the difference between sample means is significant when samples are small
F-ratio	$F = \dfrac{\text{between variance}}{\text{within variance}}$	To determine if a significant difference exists among more than two samples

APPENDIX G continued

Technique	Formula/procedure	Use
χ^2 test	$\chi^2 = \Sigma \dfrac{(A - E)^2}{E}$	To determine if a result is significantly different from an expected result
Spearman's rank-order correlation	$\rho = 1 - \dfrac{6\Sigma d^2}{N(N^2 - 1)}$	A correlation coefficient
Pearson's product-moment correlation	$r = \dfrac{\Sigma xy - \dfrac{(\Sigma x)(\Sigma y)}{N}}{\sqrt{\left[\Sigma x^2 - \dfrac{(\Sigma x)^2}{N}\right]\left[\Sigma y^2 - \dfrac{(\Sigma y)^2}{N}\right]}}$	A correlation coefficient
Standard error measurement	$SEMeas. = s\sqrt{(1 - r)}$	To predict the 'true' score from a sample score

Glossary

acoustic phonetics The description of sounds in terms of the sound waves they generate.
affective-based methods Teaching methods based on the view that language teaching should be adapted to student needs, motivations, and learning styles.
affixes Morphemes which are adjoined to other morphemes. There are three types: prefixes, infixes, and suffixes.
affricates Consonants articulated in a combined fashion: they start as stops and end as fricatives (e.g., the *ch* in *church*).
allomorph The actual realization of a morpheme (e.g., *a* and *an* are allomorphs of the indefinite article morpheme in English).
allophone The realization of a phoneme. Allophones are the actual speech sounds of language as they are pronounced in their positions within words and phrases.
analysis by synthesis The perceptual strategy which allows us to reconstruct broken messages and to correct automatically in our minds the pronunciation errors that a foreign speaker makes.
aphasia Any speech impairment.
applied linguistics The application of the insights and findings of scientific linguistic to language teaching. Also called educational linguistics.
applied psycholinguistics As used in this book, it refers to the study of the pedagogical implications that can be derived from the research into the psychology of language learning.
articulatory phonetics The description and classification of speech sounds in terms of the organs involved in their production (mouth, teeth, etc.).
association The psychological ability to form a connection between stimuli or objects.
audio-lingual method An inductive teaching method based on behavioristic psychology. It uses pattern practice, imitation, repetition techniques together with aural and visual stimuli (tapes, slides, etc.).

babbling stage The stage during which infants from six to twelve months of age attempt to imitate adult speech patterns.
behaviorism The psychological theory which claims, in essence, that all learning results from conditioning.
bilingualism The mastery of two languages.
binits The units of measurement of information. Also known as bits.
brain plasticity The very flexible nature of the brain that allows it to recover functions lost through damage.
Broca's area An area in the left hemisphere of the brain where speech functions are contained.
central tendency The measurement of any overall trend in a set of data.
classical conditioning The view that a learning behavior occurs by associating a conditioned stimulus to an unconditioned one.
cloze test A test consisting of a passage which has been mutilated by the deletion of every *n*th word. The testee is required to supply the deleted words.
codifiability The grammatical coding and labeling a specific language assigns to the objects of reality.
cognition The ability to form thoughts and ideas. The various modes of knowing.
cognitive-code methods Teaching methods based on the principles of cognitive psychology and transformational linguistics. These methods stress rule-learning in meaningful contexts.
cognitive learning style The actual skills and abilities manifested by a learner.
cognitive theory The psychological theory that seeks to explain behavioral phenomena such as problem-solving, thinking, knowing, etc., which cannot be observed directly.
communicative competence The ability to use language in different communicative settings and to express different psychological states.
commutation The substitution of one unit by another in a specific slot (e.g., *pin–bin*). This linguistic procedure allows one to identify significant units of structure.
competence The overall knowledge of language structure. Also known as linguistic competence and langue.
complementary distribution A structural relationship by which units occur in mutually exclusive environments. For example, the two allomorphs *a* and *an* in English are in complementary distribution because *a* occurs before a consonant (a *boy*) and *an* before a vowel (an *apple*).
componential analysis The classification of words according to a limited and primitive set of features such as [animate], [human], [adult].
compound bilingualism The bilingual state of not being consciously aware of the differences between the two languages.
comprehension The process of understanding the speech stimuli in the learning environment.

concept formation The process of learning concepts; i.e., the ability to abstract a property and then generalize it.

constraint A rule describing a structural pattern or restriction in a language (e.g., /z/ cannot occur as the first consonant in word-initial clusters in English).

contextual generalization The ability on the part of children to induce specific units of constant grammatical value by analogic reasoning. Also called reasoning by analogy.

contiguity theory The behavioral theory that views learning as a consequence of repeated associations in close temporal contiguity. In other words, learning results from a chain of stimulus-response associations. Sometimes called higher-order conditioning.

contrastive analysis The technique of comparing the target language with the learner's native language in order to identify possible areas of interference.

controlled experiments Experiments designed in such a way that interfering variables are controlled in order to minimize or eliminate their influence on the outcome.

coordinate bilingualism The bilingual state of being consciously able to separate both languages.

correlation The statistical technique that allows one to establish the degree of relationship between any two sets of variables.

creativity The notion used by linguists to refer to the ability to produce and understand an infinite variety of stimulus-free utterances.

critical period The period of maximum brain plasticity during childhood when language is acquired effortlessly and relatively permanently.

deductive methods Teaching methods based on the view that rules must be used in some way to promote learning.

deep structure The underlying form of a sentence, i.e., the level at which it is interpreted.

derivational morpheme A morpheme which allows the formation of new words and parts of speech (e.g., teach*er*).

diachronic linguistics The description of how languages change over time.

dichotic listening technique A technique using auditory signals to explore how stimuli are processed by the individual hemispheres of the brain.

differentiation The ability to distinguish differences between stimuli or objects. Also known as cognitive discrimination.

diglossia The use in a society of more than one language.

direct methods Teaching methods which use the foreign language directly without any reference to the native language (e.g., the Berlitz Method).

discrete-point testing Tests on the units of linguistic structure.

egocentricity The view that learner's ego is largely responsible for success in language learning.

ego-dynamic level The level in glossodynamic theory that coordinates tactic and strategic functions (i.e., behavioristic and cognitive learning modes).

empiricist hypothesis The view of behavioral psychologists that the child starts *tabula* *rasa* in acquiring the native language and that the development of language depends on environmental conditioning.

entropy The average rate of information generated by a source.

entry behavior What is already known by an organism before a learning task.

error analysis The description and classification of errors produced during the learning process.

field-dependent style The ability to perceive the total field and to ignore particular items in the field.

field-independent style The learning style which refers to the ability to perceive a particular item in a field of distracting items.

foreign language Often used as a synonym for target language or second language in educational contexts.

fossilization The process by which second-language errors become relatively fixed or permanent.

four skills These are the basic language skills: listening, speaking, reading, and writing.

frequency distribution A chart of data arranged in logical numerical categories.

frequency polygon A smooth curve which represents a frequency distribution graphically.

fricatives Sounds produced by allowing the air to escape through a narrow constriction in the oral cavity (e.g., *f*in).

functional approaches Teaching methods based on language uses.

glossodynamic model A model which integrates various psychological schools of thought into one integrated view of the language-learning and -teaching processes.

grammar-translation method The teaching method based on the use of grammar rules and vocabulary lists and on their application to translation tasks.

grouping The cognitive ability to recognize pattern.

habit theory The behavioral view that a learned response is reinforced if it occurs regularly.

histogram A graph which displays a frequency distribution visually.

holophrases The typical one-word utterances produced by children around the first year of life.

humanistic psychology The school of psychology which focuses on affective and interpersonal learning parameters.

immediate constituent analysis The linguistic technique which analyzes syntactic relations in terms of the constituents (morphemes, phrases, etc.) of which given constructions are directly formed.

inductive methods Teaching methods based on the induction of pattern through exposure to language data.

infix The affix which is added to words in internal position.

inflectional morpheme The morpheme which expresses a grammatical category, e.g., clear*ly* (adverbialization).

information theory The theory stating that the information of a message has nothing to do with its content but is defined in terms of its predictability.

instrumental motivation The motivation to learn a language for utilitarian purposes.

integration The ability to group sounds into structural units.

integrative motivation The motivation to learn a language in order to become part of the culture.

integrative testing Testing techniques on the communicative aspects of language. Also known as global testing.

interlanguage The language that results from the learner's attempts to learn the target language. Also known as idiosyncratic dialect, approximative system, transitional competence.

interlinguistic errors Errors due to native-language interference.

intralinguistic errors Errors caused by specific learning strategies such as analogy, simplification.

language The unique human behavior which communicates emotions, ideas, etc., by means of arbitrary symbols that have become institutionalized within certain societies.

language acquisition The term used by Krashen to refer to the subconscious creative construction process used especially by children in developing the native language.

language-acquisition device The cognitive view that we are born with a device that allows us to construct the linguistic system of the native language from the data encountered.

language learning As used by Krashen, a conscious process by which explicit rules are assimilated and monitored.

langue Another term for linguistic competence.

lateralization The process by which language is localized into the brain.

lexical insertion rule A rule which inserts an item from the lexicon into the phrase structure rules.

linguistic relativity hypothesis The claim that one's perception of the world is shaped by the language one speaks. Also known as the Sapir-Whorf hypothesis.

linguistics The scientific study of language in all its dimensions.

liquid A category of sounds which are produced by allowing the air to escape laterally on both sides of the tongue. Laterals (*love*) and vibrants (*rare*) are examples of liquids.

long-term memory The final processing of incoming information by the memory system into indefinite storage where it is not always easily retrievable.

macrolinguistics The study of language diversity.

mean A statistical measure of central tendency based on the arithmetical average of a set of scores.

meaningful learning The process of relating new material to be learned to relevant areas of cognitive structure.

median A measure of central tendency based on the score which divides a set of data into two equal halves.

mediation theory The behavioral theory which attempts to account for processes of abstraction. It maintains that there exist implicit associative responses that mediate between an overt stimulus and an overt response.

memory The neuropsychological system which stores information for possible retrieval.

metalinguistic awareness What a child knows about language as a system.

microlinguistics The study of language proper.

mode A measure of central tendency based on the observation in a set of data that occurs the most frequently.

morpheme The minimal unit of language which has meaning (e.g., a word, an affix).

morphology The study of the morphemes in a language.

motivation The conscious or unconscious need that incites an individual to some action or behavior.

motor theory The theory which claims that for the perception of speech the learner actually reproduces silently the speech signal.

multilingualism The ability to speak more than one language.

nasals Sounds produced by allowing the air to flow through the nose.

native language The language developed in childhood. Also known as first language.

nativist hypothesis The view held by cognitive psychologists that the child has an innate predisposition towards the acquisition of language.

neurolinguistics The branch of linguistics which deals with the role of the brain in language processing, use, etc.

ogive An S-curve which shows a cumulative frequency distribution graphically.

open-endedness The ability to produce and understand an infinite variety of utterances. A synonym for creativity.

operant conditioning Skinner's theory that an organism maintains only a response that has been reinforced by a reward. Also known as instrumental learning.

overgeneralization The tendency to apply a rule analogically in those areas where it does not apply. Also known as analogy.

paradigm The structural linguistic concept which refers to the distinction, or opposition, of units on the same level.

parole Another word for performance.

perception The experience of objects and events in the environment upon stimulation of the sense organs.

perceptual integration The process of grouping sounds into structural units (words, phrases, etc.).

performance The actual use of language in speech acts.

personality The behavioral traits manifested by a particular individual.

phoneme The minimal unit of sound which signals a difference in meaning.

phonetic alphabet A conventionalized alphabet of symbols for transcribing speech sounds.
phonetic environment The position in which a sound occurs.
phonology The study of sounds and their structural relations.
phrase structure analysis The description of the basic phrases and clauses making up sentence structure in a language.
pivot grammar The type of grammatical structure exhibited by the two- and three-word utterances of children.
prefix The affix added to words at the beginning (e.g., *un*tidy).
production The ability to produce meaningful speech.
psychodynamic theories Theories of personality derived from clinical psychology.
psycholinguistics The interdisciplinary field (psychology and linguistics) that seeks to study the psychological aspects of language.
recognition The ability to recognize emic, or meaningful, cues in the flow of speech.
register A specific form speech takes on in specific social contexts.
reinforcement The behavioral view that claims that the probability of learning a response is increased by the repetition of the conditioning process.
reliability The accuracy with which a test measures whatever it is supposed to measure.
response The behavior elicited by a stimulus or set of stimuli.
retrieval The process of retrieving information from the memory storage system.
rote learning The mental storage of items without connecting them to existing cognitive structure.
second language A language learned after the first.
semantics The study and description of meaning.
sememe The basic unit of meaning. Some linguists prefer seme.
short-term memory The storing of information in chunks for early retrieval.
simplification The tendency to reduce complex target-language forms to simple linguistic models. Also known as pidginization.
sociolinguistics The study of the social manifestations of language.
source language The language already known by the learner.
spectograms Visual representations of speech sounds.
speech act A verbal performance behavior.
standard deviation The measure of the average deviation of scores from the mean.
stimulus A physical input from the environment that is capable of exciting one's sense organs.
stimulus generalization The process by which a learned behavior is generalized to similar stimuli which have not been encountered before.
stops Consonants produced by cutting off the flow of air completely (e.g., *p*in).
storage The process of storing away information by the memory system.
strategic level In glossodynamic theory, the level at which cognitive structuring occurs.

structuralism The school of linguistics which views language as a system composed of hierarchically structured units.
suffix The affix added on at the end of words (brave*ly*).
suggestopedia The method of language teaching which is based on subliminal techniques (e.g., meditation, relaxation). Also known as the Lozanov Method.
surface structure The actual spoken or written form of a sentence.
synchronic linguistics The description of language at a particular time, usually the present.
syntagm The structural concept that refers to the way units combine at all levels.
syntax The study of how words, phrases, and clauses are combined to form sentences.
syntaxeme The basic unit of syntax.
tactics The glossodynamic term for the level at which experiential learning occurs.
target language The language to be learned in an educational context.
telegraphic utterances The two- or three-word utterances which emerge in children around the age of 18 months.
test A method of measuring an individual's ability, skill, or knowledge in some area.
test battery A series of standardized tests designed to measure a specific area of knowledge administered within a certain period of time.
trait theories The identification of personality characteristics by means of traits or abilities (verbal, spatial, etc.).
transfer The unconscious transferal of native-language habits onto the learning of the target language.
transformationalism The school of linguistics originated by Chomsky which views language in terms of a deep and surface structure. Also known as transformational-generative grammar.
transformational rules Rules which convert deep structures to surface structures.
tree diagram A figure which represents the structure of sentences.
type theories Early theories of personality by which individuals were categorized according to physical constitution and temperament.
validity The extent to which a test measures what it is intended or expected to measure.
voiced sound A sound produced by vibrating the vocal cords (*z*ip).
voiceless sound A sound produced without vibrating the vocal cords (*s*ip).
Wernicke's area An area in the left hemisphere of the brain which is responsible for speech.

References

Akmajian, A., Demers, R.A., and Harnish, R.M. 1979. *Linguistics: An Introduction to Language and Communication.* Cambridge, Mass.: MIT Press

Allen, J.P.B. 1975. 'Some Basic Concepts in Linguistics.' In *The Edinburgh Course in Applied Linguistics*, vol. 2: *Papers in Applied Linguistics*, ed. by J.P.B. Allen and S. Pit Corder, pp. 16–44. Oxford: Oxford University Press

Allen, J.P.B., and Corder, S. Pit., eds. 1975. *The Edinburgh Course in Applied Linguistics*, vols. 1 and 2. Oxford: Oxford University Press

Allen, J.P.B., and Davies, A., eds. 1977. *The Edinburgh Course in Applied Linguistics*, vol. 3: *Testing and Experimental Methods.* Oxford: Oxford University Press

Allport, F.H. 1924. *Social Psychology.* Boston: Houghton Mifflin

Allport, G.W. 1965. *Pattern and Growth in Personality.* New York: Holt, Rinehart and Winston

Arcaini, E., Py, B., and Favretti, F.R. 1979. *Analyse contrastive et apprentissage des langues.* Bologna: Pàtron

Arkin, A., and Colton, R.R. 1970. *Statistical Methods*, 2nd ed. New York: Barnes and Noble

Asher, J.J. 1965. 'The Strategy of Total Physical Response: An Application to Learning Russian.' *International Review of Applied Linguistics* 3:292–9

– 1969. 'The Total Physical Approach to Second Language Learning.' *Modern Language Journal* 53:3–18

– 1972. 'Children's First Language as a Model for Second Language Learning.' *Modern Language Journal* 56:133–9

– 1977. *Learning Another Language through Actions: The Complete Teacher's Guide.* Los Gatos, Calif.: Sky Oaks Productions

Austin, J. 1962. *How to Do Things with Words.* Cambridge, Mass.: Harvard University Press

Ausubel, D.A. 1963. 'Cognitive Structure and the Facilitation of Meaningful Verbal Learning.' *Journal of Teacher Education* 14:217-21
- 1964. 'Adults vs. Children in Second Language Learning: Psychological Considerations.' *Modern Language Journal* 48:420-4
- 1968. *Educational Psychology: A Cognitive View.* New York: Holt, Rinehart and Winston
Bancroft, J. 1972. 'Foreign Language Teaching in Bulgaria.' *Canadian Modern Language Review* 28:9-13
- 1978. 'The Lozanov Method and Its American Adaptations.' *Modern Language Journal* 62:167-75
Bélanger-Popvassileva, M. 1979. 'La Méthode Lozanov et la formation des professeurs.' *Canadian Modern Language Review* 35:559-66
Bell, R. 1974. 'Error Analysis: A Recent Pseudoprocedure in Applied Linguistics.' *ITL: Review of Applied Linguistics* 25-6:35-49
Belyayev, B.V. 1963. *The Psychology of Teaching Foreign Languages.* London: Pergamon
Berko, J. 1958. 'The Child's Learning of English Morphology.' *Word* 14:150-77
Bialystock, E. 1979. 'An Analytical View of Second Language Competence: A Model and Some Evidence.' *Modern Language Journal* 63:257-62
Bloom, L., ed. 1978. *Readings in Language Development.* New York: John Wiley & Sons
Bloomfield, L. 1933. *Language.* New York: Holt, Rinehart and Winston
Boari, A. 1978. 'Rapporto su un anno di terapia di sviluppo del linguaggio svolta presso l'OASI Maria SS. di Troina.' *Quaderni OASI* 1:49-79
Bolinger, D.D. 1968. *Aspects of Language.* New York: Harcourt, Brace and World
Bowerman, M. 1977. 'The Acquisition of Word Meaning: An Investigation of Some Current Concepts.' In *Thinking: Readings in Cognitive Science*, ed. by P.N. Johnson-Laird and P.C. Wason, pp. 239-53. Cambridge: Cambridge University Press
Braine, M.D.S. 1963. 'The Ontogeny of English Phrase Structure.' *Language* 39:1-13
Brière, E.J. et al. 1978. 'A Look at Cloze Testing across Languages and Levels.' *Modern Language Journal* 62:23-6
Brodkey, D., and Shore, H. 1976. 'Student Personality and Success in an English Language Program.' *Language Learning* 26:153-9
Brooks, N. 1964. *Language and Language Learning.* New York: Harcourt, Brace and World
Brown, H. Douglas, ed. 1976. *Papers in Second Language Acquisition.* Special Issue no. 4 of *Language Learning*
- 1980. *Principles of Language Learning and Teaching.* Englewood Cliffs, NJ: Prentice-Hall
Brown, R. 1958. *Words and Things.* New York: Free Press
- 1970. *Psycholinguistics.* New York: Free Press
- 1973. *A First Language: The Early Stages.* Cambridge, Mass.: Harvard University Press

Brown, R., and Bellugi, U. 1964. 'Three Processes in the Acquisition of Syntax.' *Harvard Educational Review* 34:133-51
Bruner, J.S. 1956. *A Study of Thinking*. New York: John Wiley & Sons
- 1960. *The Process of Education*. Cambridge, Mass.: Harvard University Press
- 1964. 'The Course of Cognitive Growth.' *American Psychologist* 19:1-15
- 1966. *Studies in Cognitive Growth*. New York: John Wiley & Sons
Bühler, K. 1934. *Sprachtheorie*. Leipzig: Verlag
Burt, M.K., and Kiparsky, C. 1972. *The Gooficon: A Repair Manual for English*. Rowley, Mass.: Newbury House
Cairns, H.S., and Cairns, C.E. 1976. *Psycholinguistics: A Cognitive View of Language*. New York: Holt, Rinehart and Winston
Canale, M., Mougeon, R., and Beniak, E. 1978. 'Acquisition of Some Grammatical Elements in English and French by Monolingual and Bilingual Canadian Students.' *Canadian Modern Language Review* 34:505-24
Carroll, J.B. 1953. *The Study of Language*. Cambridge, Mass.: Harvard University Press
- 1958. 'Communication Theory, Linguistics, and Psycholinguistics.' *Review of Educational Research* 28:79-88
- 1959. *The Study of Language*, 2nd ed. Cambridge, Mass.: Harvard University Press
- 1961. 'The Prediction of Success in Intensive Language Training.' In *Training Research and Education*, ed. by R. Glaser. Pittsburgh: University of Pittsburgh Press
- 1964. *Language and Thought*. Englewood Cliffs, NJ: Prentice-Hall
- 1973. 'Linguistic Relativity and Language Learning.' In *The Edinburgh Course in Applied Linguistics*, vol. 1: *Readings for Applied Linguistics*, ed. by J.P.B. Allen and S. Pit Corder, pp. 103-13. Oxford: Oxford University Press
- 1981. 'Conscious and Automatic Processes in Language Learning.' *Canadian Modern Language Review* 37:464-74
Carroll, J.B., and Sapon, S.M. 1958. *Modern Language Aptitude Test*. New York: The Psychological Corp.
Catford, J.C. 1965. *A Linguistic Theory of Translation*. Oxford: Oxford University Press
Caulfield, J., and Smith, W.C. 1981. 'The Redundancy Test and the Cloze Procedure as Measures of Global Language Proficiency.' *Modern Language Journal* 65:54-8
Chastain, K. 1969. 'The Audio-lingual Habit Theory Versus the Cognitive-Code Learning Theory: Some Theoretical Considerations.' *International Review of Applied Linguistics* 7:97-106
- 1971. *The Development of Modern Language Skills: Theory to Practice*. Philadelphia: Center for Curriculum Development
- 1977. 'Evaluating Expressive Objectives.' *Canadian Modern Language Review* 34:62-70
Chomsky, C. 1969. *The Acquisition of Syntax in Children from 5 to 10*. Cambridge, Mass.: MIT Press
Chomsky, N. 1957. *Syntactic Structures*. The Hague: Mouton

- 1959. 'Review of *Verbal Behavior*.' *Language* 35:26–58
- 1965. *Aspects of the Theory of Syntax*. Cambridge, Mass.: MIT Press
- 1966. 'Linguistic Theory.' In *Northeast Conference on the Teaching of Foreign Languages*, ed. by R.G. Mead, pp. 43–9. Menasha, Wis.: Banta
- 1975. *Reflections on Language*. New York: Pantheon
- 1980. *Rules and Representations*. New York: Columbia University Press

Chomsky, N., and Halle, M. 1968. *The Sound Pattern of English*. New York: Harper and Row

Cipolla, F., Mosca, G., and Titone, R. 1978. 'Rendiconto parziale di un progetto sperimentale di ricupero linguistico per handicappati.' *Quaderni OASI* 1:83–130

Clark, E.V. 1973. 'Non-linguistic Strategies and the Acquisition of Word Meanings.' *Cognition* 2:161–82
- 1975. 'Knowledge, Context, and Strategy in the Acquisition of Meaning.' In *Developmental Psycholinguistics: Theory and Applications*, ed. by D.P. Dato, pp. 77–98. Washington, DC: Georgetown University Press
- 1977. 'First Language Acquisition.' In *Psycholinguistics: Developmental and Pathological*, ed. by J. Morton and J.C. Marshall, pp. 1–72. Ithaca: Cornell University Press

Clark, H.H., and Clark, E.V. 1977. *Psychology and Language: An Introduction to Psycholinguistics*. New York: Harcourt Brace Jovanovich

Clark, R. 1975. 'Adult Theories, Child Strategies, and Their Implications for the Language Teacher.' In *The Edinburgh Course in Applied Linguistics*, vol. 2: *Papers in Applied Linguistics*, ed. by J.P.B. Allen and S. Pit Corder, pp. 291–347. Oxford: Oxford University Press
- 1977a. 'Statistical Inference.' In *The Edinburgh Course in Applied Linguistics*, vol. 4: *Testing and Experimental Methods*, ed. by J.P.B. Allen and A. Davies, pp. 158–86. Oxford: Oxford University Press
- 1977b. 'The Design and Interpretation of Experiments.' In *The Edinburgh Course in Applied Linguistics*, vol. 4: *Testing and Experimental Methods*, ed. by J.P.B. Allen and A. Davies, pp. 105–45. Oxford: Oxford University Press
- 1977c. 'Procedures and Computations in the Analysis of Experiments.' In *The Edinburgh Course in Applied Linguistics*, vol. 4: *Testing and Experimental Methods*, ed. by J.P.B. Allen and A. Davies, pp. 146–57. Oxford: Oxford University Press

Corder, S. Pit. 1973. *Introducing Applied Linguistics*. Harmondsworth: Penguin
- 1974. 'Error Analysis.' In *The Edinburgh Course in Applied Linguistics*, vol. 3: *Techniques in Applied Linguistics*, ed. by J.P.B. Allen and S. Pit Corder, pp. 122–34. Oxford: Oxford University Press
- 1975. 'Applied Linguistics and Language Teaching.' In *The Edinburgh Course in Applied Linguistics*, vol. 2: *Papers in Applied Linguistics*, ed. by J.P.B. Allen and S. Pit Corder, pp. 1–15. Oxford: Oxford University Press

Crocker, A.C. 1969. *Statistics for the Teacher*. Harmondsworth: Penguin

Cronbach, L.J. 1961. *Essentials for Psychological Testing*. New York: Harper and Row
Cummins, J. 1978. 'Metalinguistic Development of Children in Bilingual Education Programs: Data from Irish and Canadian Ukrainian-English Programs.' In *The Fourth LACUS Forum*, ed. by M. Paradis, pp. 29–40. Columbia, SC: Hornbeam
Curran, C.A. 1961. 'Counseling Skills Adapted to the Learning of Foreign Languages.' *Bulletin of the Menninger Clinic* 25:79–83
– 1976. *Counseling-Learning in Second Languages*. Apple River, Ill.: Apple River Press
Danesi, M. 1979. 'Puzzles in Language Teaching.' *Canadian Modern Language Review* 35:269–77
– 1980a. 'Mathematical Games in Foreign Language Courses.' *Rassegna Italiana di Linguistica Applicata* 12:195–204
– 1980b. 'L'analisi contrastiva e l'analisi degli errori: Approcci eziologici all'insegnamento delle lingue seconde.' *Scuola Democratica* 15:18–21
– 1982. 'Idiolect, Dialect, Sociolect: What about "Psycholect"?' In *The Eighth LACUS Forum*, ed. by W. Gutwinski and G. Jolly, pp. 319–25. Columbia, SC: Hornbeam
Da Rocha, J. 1975. 'On the Reliability of Error Analysis.' *ITL: Review of Applied Linguistics* 29:53–61
Davies, A. 1974. 'Il *testing* linguistico: Aspetti teorici e pratici.' *Rassegna Italiana di Linguistica Applicata* 6:7–28
– 1977. 'The Construction of Language Tests.' In *The Edinburgh Course in Applied Linguistics*, vol. 4: *Testing and Experimental Research*, ed. by J.P.B. Allen and A. Davies, pp. 38–104. Oxford: Oxford University Press
Davies, N.F. 1980. 'Putting Receptive Skills First: An Experiment in Sequencing.' *Canadian Modern Language Review* 36:461–7
Davis, P.W. 1973. *Modern Theories of Language*. Englewood Cliffs, NJ: Prentice-Hall
Delacroix, H. 1930. *Le Langage et la pensée*. Paris: Alcan
Dennis, M., and Whitaker, H. 1976. 'Language Acquisition following Hemidecortication: Linguistic Superiority of the Left over the Right Hemisphere.' *Brain and Language* 3:404–33
De Saussure, F. 1916. *Cours de linguistique générale*. Paris: Pagot
De Vito, J.A. 1970. *The Psychology of Speech and Language: An Introduction to Psycholinguistics*. New York: Random House
Diebold, A.R. 1966. *The Consequences of Early Bilingualism in Cognitive Development and Personality Formation*. Arlington, Va.: ERIC
Dingwall, W.O. 1975. 'The Species-Specificity of Speech.' In *Developmental Psycholinguistics: Theory and Applications*, ed. by D.P. Dato, pp. 17–72. Washington, DC: Georgetown University Press
Di Pietro, R.J. 1972. *Language Structures in Contrast*. Rowley, Mass.: Newbury House
– 1976. 'Contrastive Patterns of Language Use: A Conversational Approach.' *Canadian Modern Language Review* 33:49–61

- 1978. 'Verbal Strategies, Script Theory, and Conversational Performances in ESL.' In *On TESOL*, ed. by C. Blatchford and J. Schachter, pp. 149–56. Washington, DC: TESOL
- 1979. 'Verbal Strategies in the Modern Language Classroom.' *The Bulletin* 57:3–10

Dulay, H.C., and Burt, M.K. 1976. 'Creative Construction in Second Language Learning and Teaching.' In *Papers in Second Language Acquisition*, ed. by H. Douglas Brown, pp. 65–79. Special Issue no. 4 of *Language Learning*

Dulay, H.C., Burt, M.K., and Hernández, C.E. 1975. *Bilingual Syntax Measure*. New York: Harcourt Brace Jovanovich

Dulay, H.C., Burt, M.K., and Krashen, S. 1982. *Language Two*. Oxford: Oxford University Press

Edwards, B. 1980. *The Readable Maths and Statistics Book*. London: Allen and Unwin

Eppert, F. 1977. 'Translation and Second-Language Teaching.' *Canadian Modern Language Review* 34:50–61

Ervin, S., and Osgood, C.E. 1954. 'Second Language Learning and Bilingualism.' *Journal of Abnormal and Social Psychology* 49:139–46

Ervin, S.E., Walker, D.E., and Osgood, C.E. 1965. 'Psychological Bases of Unit Formation.' In *Psycholinguistics: A Survey of Theory and Research Problems*, ed. by C.E. Osgood and T.A. Sebeok, pp. 50–60. Bloomington: Indiana University Press

Falk, J.S. 1978. *Linguistics and Language*, 2nd ed. New York: John Wiley & Sons

Farwell, C.B. 1973. 'The Language Spoken to Children.' *Papers and Reports on Child Language Development* 5:31–62

Ferguson, C.A. 1959. 'Diglossia.' *Word* 15:325–40

Fillmore, C.J. 1968. 'A Case for Case.' In *Universals in Linguistic Theory*, ed. by E. Bach and E.T. Harms. New York: Holt, Rinehart and Winston

Fillmore, C.J., Kempler, D., and Wang, W.S.-Y., eds. 1979. *Individual Differences in Language Ability and Language Behavior*. Berkeley: University of California Press

Fischer, R.A. 1979. 'The Inductive-Deductive Controversy Revisited.' *Modern Language Journal* 63:98–105

Fishman, J.A. 1970. *Sociolinguistics: A Brief Introduction*. Rowley, Mass.: Newbury House

- 1980. 'The Whorfian Hypothesis: Varieties of Valuation, Confirmation, and Disconfirmation.' *International Journal of the Sociology of Language* 26:25–40

Fodor, J.A., and Bever, T. 1965. 'The Psychological Reality of Linguistic Segments.' *Journal of Verbal Learning and Verbal Behavior* 4:414–20

Franzblau, A.N. 1958. *A Primer of Statistics for Non-statisticians*. New York: Harcourt, Brace and World

Gagné, R.M. 1965. *The Conditions of Learning*. New York: Holt, Rinehart and Winston

Gardner, R., and Gardner, B. 1969. 'Teaching Sign Language to a Chimpanzee.' *Science* 165:664–72

- 1975. 'Evidence for Sentence Constituents in Early Utterances of Child and Chimpanzee.' *Journal of Experimental Psychology* 104:244-67
Gardner, R.C., and Lambert, W.E. 1972. *Attitudes and Motivation in Second Language Learning.* Rowley, Mass.: Newbury House
Gardner, R.C., and Smythe, P.C. 1975. 'Motivation and Second-Language Acquisition.' *Canadian Modern Language Review* 31:218-33
Garrett, M., Bever, T., and Fodor, J.A. 1966. 'The Active Use of Grammar in Speech Perception.' *Perception and Psychophysics* 1:30-2
Gazzaniga, M. 1970. *The Bisected Brain.* New York: Appleton Century-Crofts
- 1973. *Fundamentals of Psychology.* New York: Academic
George, H.V. 1972. *Common Errors in Language Learning.* Rowley, Mass.: Newbury House
Ginneken, J. van. 1909. *Principes de psychologie linguistique.* Paris: Alcan
Gleason, H.A. 1961. *An Introduction to Descriptive Linguistics.* New York: Holt, Rinehart and Winston
Gleitman, L.R., Gleitman, H., and Shipley, E.F. 1972. 'The Emergence of the Child as Grammarian.' *Cognition* 1:137-64
Glucksberg, S., and Danks, J.H. 1975. *Experimental Psycholinguistics: An Introduction.* New York: John Wiley & Sons
Grabe, W. 1979. *Three Methods for Language Learning: Community Language Learning, the Silent Way, Suggestopedia.* Ohio University Working Paper in Applied Linguistics No. 5. Athens, Ohio: Ohio University Press
Greenberg, J.H., ed. 1966. *Universals of Language*, 2nd ed. Cambridge: Cambridge University Press
- 1977. *A New Invitation to Linguistics.* New York: Anchor
Greene, J. 1975. *Thinking and Language.* London: Methuen
Griffin, H. 1968. 'Language Development.' In *Developments in Applied Psycholinguistics*, ed. by S. Rosenberg and H. Koplin. New York: Macmillan
Grinder, J.T., and Elgin, S.H. 1973. *Guide to Transformational Grammar.* New York: Holt, Rinehart and Winston
Guiora, A.Z. et al. 1972. 'Empathy and Second Language Learning.' *Language Learning* 22:111-30
Haden Elgin, S. 1979. *What Is Linguistics?* Englewood Cliffs, NJ: Prentice-Hall
Hakuta, K. 1974. 'Prefabricated Patterns and the Emergence of Structure in Second Language Acquisition.' *Language Learning* 24:287-97
Halle, M., and Stevens, K.N. 1964. 'Speech Recognition: A Model and a Program for Research.' In *The Structure of Language: Readings in the Philosophy of Language*, ed. by J.A. Fodor and J.J. Katz. Englewood Cliffs, NJ: Prentice-Hall
Halliday, M.A.K. 1973. *Explorations in the Functions of Language.* London: Edward Arnold

- 1975. 'Learning How to Mean.' In *Foundations of Language Development: A Multidisciplinary Approach*, ed. by E.H. Lenneberg and E. Lenneberg. New York: Academic
Harris, Z.S. 1951. *Methods in Structural Linguistics.* Chicago: University of Chicago Press
Hatch, E.M. 1983. *Psycholinguistics: A Second Language Perspective.* Rowley, Mass.: Newbury House
Hendrickson, J.M. 1978. 'Error Correction in Foreign Language Teaching: Recent Theory, Research, and Practice.' *Modern Language Journal* 62:387-98
- 1979. 'Evaluating Spontaneous Conversation through Systematic Error Analysis.' *Foreign Language Annals* 12:357-64
Hockett, C.F. 1958. *A Course in Modern Linguistics.* New York: Macmillan
- 1961. 'Review of *Mathematical Theory of Communication*.' In *Psycholinguistics: A Book of Readings*, ed. by S. Saporta. New York: Holt, Rinehart and Winston
Howard, F. 1980. 'Testing Communicative Proficiency in French as a Second Language: A Search for Procedures.' *Canadian Modern Language Review* 36:272-89
Humboldt, W. von. 1935. *Gesammelte Schriften*, vol. 7. Ausgabe der Preussischen Akademie der Wissenschaften, Vienna
Ilyin, D. 1973. *Ilyin Oral Interview.* Rowley, Mass.: Newbury House
Ingram, E. 1974. 'Language Testing.' In *The Edinburgh Course in Applied Linguistics*, vol. 3: *Techniques in Applied Linguistics*, ed. by J.P.B. Allen and S. Pit Corder, pp. 313-43. Oxford: Oxford University Press
- 1977. 'Basic Concepts in Testing.' In *The Edinburgh Course in Applied Linguistics*, vol. 4: *Testing and Experimental Research*, ed. by J.P.B. Allen and A. Davies, pp. 11-37. Oxford: Oxford University Press
Jackendoff, R. 1972. *Semantic Interpretation in Generative Grammar.* Cambridge, Mass.: MIT Press
Jackson, H. 1976. 'Contrastive Linguistics: What Is It?' *ITL: Review of Applied Linguistics* 32:1-32
Jakobovits, L. 1968. 'Implications of Recent Psycholinguistic Developments for the Teaching of a Second Language.' *Language Learning* 19:89-109
Jakobovits, L.A., and Miron, M.S., eds. 1967. *Readings in the Psychology of Language.* Englewood Cliffs, NJ: Prentice-Hall
Jakobson, R. 1941. *Kindersprache, Aphasie und algemeine Lautgesetze.* Uppsala: Universitets Arsskrift
James, C. 1980. *Contrastive Analysis.* London: Longman
Johnson, F.S. 1967. 'Grammars: A Working Classification.' *Elementary English* 44:349-52
Joos, M. 1967. *The Five Clocks.* New York: Harcourt, Brace and World
Kainz, F. 1941. *Psychologie der Sprache.* Stuttgart: Encke
- 1946. *Einführung in die Sprachpsychologie.* Stuttgart: Encke

Kalton, G. 1966. *Introduction to Statistical Ideas for Social Scientists.* London: Chapman and Hall

Kantor, J.R. 1936. *An Objective Psychology of Grammar.* Bloomington: Indiana University Press

Kaplan, E.L., and Kaplan, G.A. 1970. 'The Prelinguistic Child.' In *Human Development and Cognitive Processes,* ed. by J. Eliot. New York: Holt, Rinehart and Winston

Kaplan, R.B., ed. 1980. *On the Scope of Applied Linguistics.* Rowley, Mass.: Newbury House

Kenyeres, E., and Kenyeres, A. 1938. 'Comment une petite Hongroise de sept ans apprend le français.' *Archives de Psychologie* 26:321–66

Koffka, K. 1935. *Principles of Gestalt Psychology.* New York: Harcourt, Brace and World

Köhler, W. 1947. *Gestalt Psychology,* 2nd ed. New York: Liveright

Kolers, P.A. 1963. 'Interlingual Word Association.' *Journal of Verbal Learning and Verbal Behavior* 5:314–19

Koplin, J.H. 1968. 'Applied Psycholinguistics: Aims and Current Status.' In *Developments in Applied Psycholinguistics Research,* ed. by S. Rosenberg and J.H. Koplin, pp. 3–16. New York: Macmillan

Krahnke, K.J., and Christison, A.C. 1983. 'Recent Language Research and Some Language Teaching Principles.' *TESOL Quarterly* 17:625–49

Krashen, S. 1973. 'Lateralization, Language Learning, and the Critical Period: Some New Evidence.' *Language Learning* 23:63–74

– 1975. 'The Development of Cerebral Dominance and Language Learning: More New Evidence.' In *Developmental Psycholinguistics: Theory and Applications,* ed. by P. Dato, pp. 79–192. Washington, DC: Georgetown University Press

– 1976. 'Formal and Informal Linguistic Environments in Language Acquisition and Language Learning.' *TESOL Quarterly* 10:157–68

– 1977. 'The Monitor Model for Adult Second Language Performances.' In *Viewpoints on English as a Second Language,* ed. by M. Burt, H. Dulay, and M. Finocchiaro. New York: Regents

– 1982. *Principles and Practice in Second Language Acquisition.* Oxford: Pergamon Press

Labov, W. 1966. 'The Linguistic Variable as a Structural Unit.' *Washington Linguistic Review* 3:4–22

– 1970. 'The Study of Language in Its Social Context.' *Studium Générale* 23:30–87

– 1975. *What Is a Linguistic Fact?* Lisse: Peter de Ridder

Lado, R. 1957. *Linguistics across Cultures.* Ann Arbor: University of Michigan Press

– 1961. *Language Testing.* London: Longman

Lamb, S.M. 1966. *Outline of Stratificational Grammar.* Washington, DC: Georgetown University Press

Lambert, W.E. 1956. 'Development Aspects of Second-Language Acquisition.' *Journal of Social Psychology* 43:83–98

- 1978. 'Cognitive and Socio-cultural Consequences of Bilingualism.' *Canadian Modern Language Review* 34:537–47
Lathrop, R.G. 1969. *Introduction to Psychological Research.* New York: Harper and Row
Lenneberg, E.H. 1962. 'Understanding Language without the Ability to Speak: A Case Report.' *Journal of Abnormal and Social Psychology* 65:419–25
- 1964. *New Directions in the Study of Language.* Cambridge, Mass.: MIT Press
- 1967. *The Biological Foundations of Language.* New York: John Wiley & Sons
Leopold, W.F. 1953-4. 'Patternings in Children's Language Learning.' *Language Learning* 5:1–14
Levelt, W.J.M. 1974. *Formal Grammars in Linguistics and Psycholinguistics*, vol. 3: *Psycholinguistic Applications.* The Hague: Mouton
Levy, J. 1979. 'Strategies of Linguistic Processing in Split-Brain Patients.' In *Individual Differences in Language Ability and Language Behavior*, ed. by C. Fillmore, D. Kempler, and W.S.-Y. Wang, pp. 289–302. Berkeley: University of California Press
Lieberman, P. 1972. *Speech Acoustics and Perception.* Indiaanapolis: Bobbs-Merrill
Liebert, R., Poulos, R., and Strauss, G. 1974. *Developmental Psychology.* Englewood Cliffs, NJ: Prentice-Hall
Lyons, J. 1968. *Introduction to Theoretical Linguistics.* Cambridge: Cambridge University Press
MacCorquodale, K. 1970. 'On Chomsky's Review of Skinner's *Verbal Behavior.*' *Journal of the Experimental Analysis of Behavior* 13:83–99
Mackey, W.F. 1976. *Bilinguisme et contact de langues.* Paris: Klincksieck
Magnan, S.S. 1979. 'Reduction and Error Correction for Communicative Language Use: The Focus Approach.' *Modern Language Journal* 63:342–9
Marrone, R.L., and Rasor, R.A. 1972. *Behavior Observation and Analysis.* San Francisco: Rinehart
Marshall, J.C. 1977. 'Disorders in the Expression of Language.' In *Psycholinguistics: Developmental and Pathological*, ed. by J. Morton and J.C. Marshall, pp. 125–60. Ithaca: Cornell University Press
Marx, M.H. 1964. *Theories in Contemporary Psychology.* New York: Macmillan
McCawley, J.D. 1968. 'The Role of Semantics in a Grammar.' In *Universals in Linguistic Theory*, ed. by E. Bach and E. Harms, pp. 124–69. New York: Holt, Rinehart and Winston
McDonough, S.H. 1981. *Psychology in Foreign Language Teaching.* London: Allen and Unwin
McKay, S.L. 1980. 'On Notional Syllabuses.' *Modern Language Journal* 64:179–86
McNeill, D. 1966. 'The Creation of Language.' *Discovery* 37:34–8
Mead, G.H. 1904. 'The Relation of Psychology and Philology.' *Psychological Bulletin* 1:375–91
Mednick, S.A., et al. 1973. *Learning,* 2nd ed. Englewood Cliffs, NJ: Prentice-Hall

Mehler, J., and Bertoncini, J. 1979. 'Infants' Perception of Speech and Other Acoustic Stimuli.' In *Psycholinguistics: Structures and Processes*, ed. by J. Morton and J.C. Marshall, pp. 67–105. Cambridge, Mass.: MIT Press
Menyuk, P. 1971. *The Acquisition and Development of Language*. Englewood Cliffs, NJ: Prentice-Hall
Mignault, L.B. 1978. 'Suggestopaedia: Is There a Better Way to Learn?' *Canadian Modern Language Review* 34:695–701
Miller, G.A. 1951. *Language and Communication*. New York: McGraw-Hill
– 1956. 'The Magical Number Seven, Plus or Minus Two: Some Limits on Our Capacity for Processing Information.' *Psychological Review* 63:81–97
– 1965. 'Some Preliminaries to Psycholinguistics.' *American Psychologist* 20:15–20
Miller, G.A., and Johnson-Laird, P.N. 1976. *Language and Perception*. Cambridge, Mass.: Harvard University Press
Miller, W.R. 1963. 'The Acquisition of Formal Features of Language.' *American Journal of Orthopsychiatry* 34:862–7
Miller, W., and Ervin, S. 1964. 'The Development of Grammar in Child Language.' In *The Acquisition of Language*, ed. by U. Bellugi and R. Brown, pp. 9–34. Chicago: University of Chicago Press
Mills, G. 1977. 'Contrastive Analysis and Translation.' *Canadian Modern Language Review* 33:732–45
Moffitt, A.R. 1971. 'Consonant Cue Perception by Twenty to Twenty-Four Week Old Infants.' *Child Development* 42:717–31
Mollica, A. 1976. 'Cartoons in the Language Classroom.' *Canadian Modern Language Review* 32:424–44
– 1978. 'The Film Advertisement: A Source for Language Activities.' *Canadian Modern Language Review* 34:221–43
– 1979a. 'Print and Non-print Materials: Adapting for Classroom Use.' In *Building on Experience – Building for Success*, ed. by J.K. Phillips, pp. 157–98. Skokie, Ill.: National Textbook
– 1979b. 'A Tiger in Your Tank: Advertisements in the Language Classroom.' *Canadian Modern Language Review* 35:691–743
– 1979c. 'Games and Language Activities in the Italian High School Classroom.' *Foreign Language Annals* 12:347–54
– 1981. 'Visual Puzzles in the Second-Language Classroom.' *Canadian Modern Language Review* 37:583–622
Mollica, A., Danesi, M., and Urbancic, A. 1983. *Cumulative Index of the Canadian Modern Language Review, Volumes 1–37*. Welland, Ont.: CMLR, Inc.
Morgan, C.T., and King, R.H. 1966. *Introduction to Psychology*, 3rd ed. New York: McGraw-Hill

Morse, P.A. 1972. 'The Discrimination of Speech and Nonspeech Stimuli in Early Infancy.' *Journal of Experimental Child Psychology* 14:477-92

Moulton, W.G. 1970. *A Linguistic Guide to Language Learning.* New York: Modern Language Association

Mowrer, O.H. 1954. 'A Psychologist Looks at Language.' *American Psychologist* 9:660-94

– ed. 1980. *Psychology of Language Learning.* New York: Plenum

Naiman, N., Fröhlich, M., and Stern, H.H. 1975. *The Good Language Learner.* Toronto: Ontario Institute for Studies in Education

Nelson, K. 1974. 'Concept, Word, and Sentence: Interrelations in Acquisition and Development.' *Psychological Review* 81:267-85

Noble, C.E. 1952a. 'An Analysis of Meaning.' *Psychological Review* 59:421-30

– 1952b. 'The Role of Stimulus Meaning *(m)* in Serial Verbal Learning.' *Journal of Experimental Psychology* 43:437-66

Nuttin, J. 1968. *La Structure de la personnalité.* Paris: Presses Universitaires de France

Ogden, C.K. 1942. *The General Basic English Dictionary.* New York: Norton

Oldfield, R.C., and Marshall, J.C., eds. 1968. *Language: Selected Readings.* Harmondsworth: Penguin

Oller, J.W. 1973. 'Cloze Tests of Second Language Proficiency and What They Measure.' *Language Learning* 23:105-18

– 1976. 'A Program for Language Testing Research.' In *Papers in Second Language Acquisition,* ed. by H. Douglas Brown. Special Issue no. 4 of *Language Learning*

Osgood, C.E. 1953. *Method and Theory in Experimental Psychology.* Oxford: Oxford University Press

– 1957. 'A Behavioristic Analysis of Perception and Language as Cognitive Phenomena.' In *Contemporary Approaches to Cognition.* Cambridge, Mass.: Harvard University Press

– 1963. 'On Understanding and Creating Sentences.' *American Psychologist* 18:735-51

Osgood, C.E., and Sebeok, T.A., eds. 1954. *Psycholinguistics: A Survey of Theory and Research Problems.* Bloomington: Indiana University Press

Paivio, A., and Begg, I. 1981. *Psychology of Language.* Englewood Cliffs, NJ: Prentice-Hall

Palmer, F. 1971. *Grammar.* Harmondsworth: Penguin

Papalia, A. 1975. 'Using Different Models of Second-Language Teaching.' *Canadian Modern Language Review* 31:212-16

– 1976. *Learner-Centered Language Teaching: Methods and Materials.* Rowley, Mass.: Newbury House

Pavlov, I. 1902. *The Work of Digestive Glands,* trans. by W.H. Thompson. London: Griffin

Pavlovitch, M. 1920. *Le Langage enfantin: Acquisition du serbe et du français par un enfant serbe.* Paris

Penfield, W. 1953. 'A Consideration of the Neurophysiological Mechanisms of Speech and Some Educational Consequences.' *Proceedings of the American Academy of Arts and Sciences* 82:201–14

– 1959. 'The Nature of Speech.' In *Memory, Learning, and Language*, ed. by W. Feindel, pp. 55–69. Toronto: University of Toronto Press

Perlmutter, D., and Postal, P. 1977. 'Towards a Universal Characterization of Passivization.' *Proceedings of the Annual Meeting of the Berkeley Linguistic Society* 3:394–417

Peterson, C., and McCabe, A. 1983. *Developmental Psycholinguistics.* New York: Plenum

Piaget, J. 1962. 'The Stages of the Intellectual Development of the Child.' *Bulletin of the Menninger Clinic* 26:120–45

– 1968. 'Language and Thought from the Genetic Point of View.' In *Six Psychological Studies*, pp. 73–6. London: University of London Press

Piattelli-Palmarini, M., ed. 1980. *Language and Learning: The Debate between Jean Piaget and Noam Chomsky.* Cambridge, Mass.: Harvard University Press

Pike, K.L. 1954. *Language in Relation to a Unified Theory of the Structure of Human Behavior.* The Hague: Mouton

Pilliner, A.E.G. 1974. '*Testing* soggettivo ed oggettivo.' *Rassegna Italiana di Linguistica Applicata* 6:29–48

Pimsleur, P. 1966. *Pimsleur Language Aptitude Battery.* New York: Harcourt, Brace and World

Plutchik, R. 1974. *Foundations of Experimental Research*, 2nd ed. New York: Harper and Row

Powell, P.B. 1975. *Error Analysis in the Classroom.* Arlington, Va.: ERIC

Pritchard, D.F.L. 1952. 'An Investigation into the Relationship between Personality Traits and Ability in Modern Languages.' *British Journal of Educational Psychology* 22:147–8

Pronko, N.H. 1946. 'Language and Psycholinguistics: A Review.' *Psychological Bulletin* 43:189–239

Reiss, S. 1959. *Language and Psychology.* New York: Philosophical Library

Richards, J.C. 1971. 'A Non-contrastive Approach to Error Analysis.' *English Language Teaching* 25:204–19

– ed. 1974. *Error Analysis: Perspectives on Second Language Acquisition.* London: Longman

Richards, J.C., and Sampson, G. 1974. 'The Study of Learner English.' In *Error Analysis: Perspectives on Second Language Acquisition*, ed. by J.C. Richards, pp. 3–18. London: Longman

Rivers, W. 1964. *The Psychologist and the Foreign Language Teacher.* Chicago: University of Chicago Press
Roback, A.A. 1955. 'Glossodynamics and the Present Status of Psycholinguistics.' In *Present-Day Psychology*, ed. by A.A. Roback, pp. 897–912. New York: Philosophical Library
Robins, R.H. 1971. *General Linguistics: An Introductory Survey*, 2nd ed. London: Longman.
Rogers, C. 1951. *Client Centered Therapy.* Boston: Houghton Mifflin
– 1961. *On Becoming a Person: A Therapist's View of Psychotherapy.* Boston: Houghton Mifflin
Ronjat, J. 1913. *Le Développement du langage observé chez un enfant bilingue.* Paris
Rosenberg, S., and Koplin, J.H., eds. 1968. *Developments in Applied Psycholinguistics Research.* New York: Macmillan
Sapir, E. 1921. *Language: An Introduction to the Study of Speech.* New York: Harcourt, Brace and World
Saporta, S., ed. 1961. *Psycholinguistics: A Book of Readings.* New York: Holt, Rinehart and Winston
Savignon, S. 1972. *Communicative Competence: An Experiment in Foreign Language Testing.* Philadelphia: Center for Curriculum Development
Scarcella, R.C., and Krashen, S., eds. 1980. *Research in Second Language Acquisition.* Rowley, Mass.: Newbury House
Schachter, J. 1974. 'An Error in Error Analysis.' *Language Learning* 24:205–14
Schnitzer, M.L. 1978. 'Cerebral Lateralization and Plasticity: Their Relevance to Language Acquisition.' In *The Fourth LACUS Forum*, ed. by M. Paradis, pp. 114–20. Columbia, SC: Hornbeam
Schumann, J.H. 1976a. 'Second Language Acquisition Research: Getting a More Global Look at the Learner.' In *Papers in Second Language Acquisition*, ed. by H. Douglas Brown, pp. 15–28. Special Issue no. 4 of *Language Learning*.
– 1976b. 'Second Language Acquisition: The Pidginization Hypothesis.' *Language Learning* 26:391–408
Scovel, T. 1969. 'Foreign Accents, Language Acquisition, and Cerebral Dominance.' *Language Learning* 19:245–54
Searle, J. 1969. *Speech Acts.* Cambridge: Cambridge University Press
Seliger, H.W. 1975. 'Inductive Method and Deductive Method in Language Teaching: A Re-examination.' *International Review of Applied Linguistics* 13:1–18
Selinker, L. 1972. 'Interlanguage.' *International Review of Applied Linguistics* 10:209–31
Shannon, C.E., and Weaver, W. 1949. *The Mathematical Theory of Communication.* Urbana: University of Illinois Press
Sheldon, W.H. et al. 1940. *The Varieties of the Human Physique: An Introduction to Constitutional Psychology.* New York: Harper and Row

- 1954. *Atlas of Men: A Guide for Somatyping the Adult Male at All Ages.* New York: Harper and Row
Skinner, B.F. 1938. *Behavior of Organisms: An Experimental Analysis.* New York: Appleton-Century-Crofts
- 1957. *Verbal Behavior.* New York: Appleton-Century-Crofts
Slobin, D.I. 1971. *Psycholinguistics.* Glenyiew, Ill.: Scott, Foresman and Co.
Smith, F., and Miller, G.A., eds. 1966. *The Genesis of Language: A Psycholinguistic Approach.* Cambridge, Mass.: MIT Press
Smith, M.E. 1926. *An Investigation of the Development of the Sentence and the Extent of Vocabulary in Young Children.* University of Iowa Studies in Child Welfare, 3 (No. 5)
Smith, N.V. 1979. 'Syntax for Psychologists.' In *Psycholinguistics: Structures and Processes,* ed. by J. Morton and J.C. Marshall, pp. 1–65. Cambridge, Mass.: MIT Press
Smith, P.D. 1970. *A Comparison of the Cognitive and Audiolingual Approaches to Language Instruction.* Philadelphia: Center for Curriculum Development
Spolsky, B. 1978. *Educational Linguistics.* Rowley, Mass.: Newbury House
- 1979. 'Contrastive Analysis, Error Analysis, Interlanguage, and Other Useful Fads.' *Modern Language Journal* 63:250–7
Stenson, N. 1974. 'Induced Errors.' In *New Frontiers of Second Language Teaching,* ed. by J. Schumann and N. Stenson. Rowley, Mass.: Newbury House
Stern, H.H. 1969. *Language and the Young School Child.* Oxford: Oxford University Press
- 1973. 'Bilingual Education: A Review of Recent North American Experience.' *Modern Languages* 54:57–62
- 1975. 'What Can We Learn from the Good Language Learner?' *Canadian Modern Language Review* 31:304–18
- 1976. 'Optimal Age: Myth or Reality?' *Canadian Modern Language Review* 34:680–7
- 1978. 'Language Research and the Classroom Practitioner.' *Canadian Modern Language Review* 34:680–7
- 1983. *Fundamental Concepts of Language Teaching.* Oxford: Oxford University Press
Stern, H.H., and Weinrib, A. 1978. 'Le lingue straniere ai bambini: Orientamenti e verifiche.' *Rassegna Italiana di Linguistica Applicata* 10:133–59
Stevick, E.W. 1976. *Memory, Meaning, and Method.* Rowley, Mass.: Newbury House
Stockwell, R.P., Bowen, J.D., and Martin, J.W. 1965. *The Grammatical Structures of English and Spanish.* Chicago: University of Chicago Press
Stones, E., ed 1970. *Readings in Educational Psychology.* London: Methuen
Strevens, P.D. 1964. 'Varieties of English.' *English Studies* 45:1–10
- 1978. 'The Nature of Language Teaching.' In *Understanding Second and Foreign Language Learning,* ed. by J.C. Richards. Rowley, Mass.: Newbury House
Studdert-Kennedy, M., ed. 1983. *Psychobiology of Language.* Cambridge, Mass.: MIT Press
Swain, M. 1980. 'French Immersion in Canada.' *Multiculturalism* 4:3–6

Swain, M., and Lapkin, S. 1977. 'Beginning French Immersion at Grade 8.' *Orbit* 39:10-13

Tanzarella, M. 1978. 'Le Modèle glottodynamique dans une approche psycholinguistique de l'aphasie.' *Rassegna italiana di Linguistica Applicata* 10:219-42

Tarone, E., Frauenfelder, U., and Selinker, L. 1976. 'Systemacity/Variability and Stability/Instability in Interlanguage Systems.' In *Papers in Second Language Acquisition*, ed. by H. Douglas Brown, pp. 93-134. Special Issue no. 4 of *Language Learning*

Tavakolian, S., ed. 1981. *Language Acquisition and Linguistic Theory.* Cambridge, Mass.: MIT Press

Taylor, I. 1978. 'Acquiring vs. Learning a Second Language.' *Canadian Modern Language Review* 34:455-72

Taylor, W.L. 1953. 'Cloze Procedure: A New Tool for Measuring Readability.' *Journalism Quarterly* 30:414-38

Terrell, T.D. 1977. 'A Natural Approach to Second Language Acquisition and Learning.' *Modern Language Journal* 61:325-37

– 1980. 'A Natural Approach to the Teaching of Verb Forms and Function in Spanish.' *Foreign Language Annals* 13:129-36

Titone, R. 1961. 'Difficulties on the Part of Italian Younger Adolescents in the Perception of Some Phonological Features of the English and French Languages.' *Orientamenti Pedagogici* 7:684-716

– 1964a. *Studies in the Psychology of Second Language Learning.* Zürich: PAS-Verlag

– 1964b. *La psicolinguistica oggi.* Zürich: PAS-Verlag

– 1966. *Le lingue estere.* Rome: PAS

– 1968. *Teaching Foreign Languages: An Historical Sketch.* Washington, DC: Georgetown University Press

– 'A Psycholinguistic Model of Grammar Learning and Foreign Language Teaching.' *Rassegna Italiana di Linguistica Applicata* 1:35-52

– 1971a. *Psicolinguistica applicata.* Rome: Armando

– 1971b. 'On Some Modalities of Syntactic Productivity and Choice.' In *The Psychology of Second Language Learning*, ed. by P. Pimsleur and T. Quinn, pp. 97-111. Cambridge: Cambridge University Press

– 1973. 'A Psycholinguistic Description of the Glossodynamic Model of Language Behavior and Language Learning.' *Rassegna Italiana di Linguistica Applicata* 5:1-18

– 1974a. 'Applied Psycholinguistics: Amphibian or Phantom?' *Rassegna Italiana di Linguistica Applicata* 3:91-4

– 1974b. *Modelli psicopedagogici dell'apprendimento.* Rome: Armando

– 1974c. *Bilinguisme précoce et éducation bilingue.* Brussels: Dessart

– 1975. *Foreign Language Teaching Today.* Florence: Valmartina

– 1976. 'Bilinguismo infantile e sviluppo della personalità,' *Rassegna italiana di Linguistica applicata* 8:49-61

- 1977a. 'A Humanistic Approach to Language Behavior and Language Learning.' *Canadian Modern Language Review* 33:309–17
- 1977b. *Insegnare le lingue oggi.* Turin: Società Editrice Internazionale
- 1977c. 'Psicolinguistica e psicolinguistiche.' *Rassegna Italiana di Linguistica Applicata* 9:187–92
- 1978. 'Some Psychological Aspects of Multilingual Education.' *International Review of Education* 24:283–94
- ed. 1979. *Bilingual Education: Educazione bilingue.* Milan-Rome: Oxford Institutes Italiani

Upshur, J.A. 1976. 'Discussion of a Program for Language Testing Research.' In *Papers in Second Language Acquisition*, ed. by H. Douglas Brown, pp. 167–74. Special Issue no. 4 of *Language Learning*

Valdman, A. 1975. 'Learner Systems and Error Analysis.' In *Perspectives: A New Freedom*, ed. by G.A. Jarvis, pp. 219–58. Skokie, Ill.: National Textbook

Valette, R.M. 1968. *Modern Language Testing: A Handbook.* New York: Harcourt, Brace and World

Velten, H.V. 1943. 'The Growth of Phonemic and Lexical Patterns in Infant Language.' *Language* 19:281–92

Wardhaugh, R. 1970. 'The Contrastive Analysis Hypothesis.' *TESOL Quarterly* 4:123–30
- 1974. *Topics in Applied Linguistics.* Rowley, Mass.: Newbury House
- 1977. *Introduction to Linguistics.* Rowley, Mass.: Newbury House

Wardhaugh, R., and Brown, H. Douglas, eds. 1976. *A Survey of Applied Linguistics.* Ann Arbor: University of Michigan Press

Waterson, N. 1971. 'Child Phonology: A Prosodic View.' *Journal of Linguistics* 7:179–211

Watson, J.B. 1913. 'Psychology as the Behaviorist Views It.' *Psychological Review* 20:158–77

Weinreich, U. 1953. *Languages in Contact.* New York: Linguistic Circle of New York

Weir, R.H. 1962. *Language in the Crib.* The Hague: Mouton

Weiss, A.P. 1925. 'Linguistics and Psychology.' *Language* 1:52–7

Wesche, M.B. 1981. 'Communicative Testing in a Second Language.' *Canadian Modern Language Review* 37:551–71

Whitaker, H.A. 1971. 'Neurolinguistics.' In *A Survey of Linguistic Science*, ed. by W.O. Dingwall, pp. 136–251. College Park: University of Maryland

Whitley, M.S. 1978. *Generative Phonology Workbook.* Madison: University of Wisconsin Press

Whitman, R., and Jackson, K. 1972. 'The Unpredictability of Contrastive Analysis.' *Language Learning* 22:29–41

Whorf, B. Lee. 1956. *Language, Thought, and Reality.* Cambridge, Mass.: MIT Press

Widdowson, H.G. 1972. 'The Teaching of English as Communication.' *English Language Teaching* 27:15–19

Wilkins, D.A. 1973. 'The Linguistic and Situational Content of the Common Core in a Unit/Credit System.' In *System Development in Adult Language Learning: A European Unit/Credit System for Modern Language Learning by Adults*. Strasbourg: Council of Europe
– 1976. *Notional Syllabuses*. Oxford: Oxford University Press
Willis, H. 1972. *Introductory Language Study*. Cambridge, Mass.: Schenkman
Wittwer, J. 1959. *Les Fonctions grammaticales chez l'enfant*. Neuchâtel: Delachaux et Niestlé
Woodford, P.E. 1980. 'Foreign Language Testing.' *Modern Language Journal* 64:97–102
Wright, H. 1976. *Visual Materials for the Language Teacher*. London: Longman
Wundt, W. 1901. *Sprachgeschichte und Sprachpsychologie*. Leipzig: Eugelmann
Yalden, J. 1981. *Communicative Language Teaching: Principles and Practice*. Toronto: Ontario Institute for Studies in Education
Yorio, C. 1976. 'Discussion of Explaining Sequence and Variation in Second Language Acquisition.' *Papers in Second Language Acquisition*, ed. by H. Douglas Brown, pp. 59–63. Special Issue no. 4 of *Language Learning*.
Zimmerman, B.J., and Whitehurst, G.T. 1979. 'Structure and Function: A Comparison of Two Views of the Development of Language and Cognition.' In *The Functions of Language and Cognition*, ed. by G.T. Whitehurst and B.J. Zimmerman, pp. 1–22. New York: Academic
Zipf, P. 1929. 'Relative Frequency as a Determinant of Phonetic Change.' *Harvard Studies in Classical Philology* 40:1–95

Index

affixes 14
affricates 12
allomorphs 13–14
allophones 9–10
analysis: by synthesis 47; componential 18; contrastive 94–6; error 94ff.; immediate constituent 15–16; phrase-structure 16ff.
aphasia 45ff.
Asher's total physical response 115, 117
association 49, 53ff., 78ff.
Austin, J. 30, 113

babbling stage 65
base component 21–3
behaviorism 52–7
Berko, J. 69–70
Berlitz method 108–9
Bilingual Syntax Measure 157
bilingualism 100–4; compound 101–2; coordinate 101–2
binits 39
Bloomfield, L. 8
brain 43–6, 85; plasticity of 46, 75, 84–5
Broca's area 44–5
Brown, R. 69, 71
Bruner, J.S. 57–8
Bühler, K. 37–9

Carroll, J.B. 31, 42, 89
case grammar 28
central tendency 133–7
Chi square test 147–8
Chomsky, N. 19, 22, 27, 34, 56
chunk formation 49
classical conditioning 52–4
cloze test 160–1
codifiability 41
cognition 49ff.
cognitive learning style 52, 89
cognitive theory 57–9
communication 28–33
commutation 9
competence 5–6, 90, 92; communicative 92, 113
complementary distribution 10
comprehension 50, 67, 71
concept formation 49, 72
confidence limit 143
constraint 5
contextualization 71
contiguity theory 53ff.
controlled experiments 162–4
correlation 51, 148–53; Pearson's product-moment 148–53; Spearman's rank-order 148–53
creativity 5–6

critical period 46, 84
critical ratio 143
Curran's community counseling 115, 117–18, 122
cyclical theory 25

decoding 33, 48
deep structure 20–3
degrees of freedom 144–5
De Saussure, F. 8
development 65–75; grammatical 67–71; lexical and semantic 72–5; phonological 65–7
dialect 30
dichotic listening technique 46
differentiation 49, 73
diglossia 101
discovery procedures 18
discrimination 48–9, 58, 66, 86
dispersion 137–41

egocentricity 51
ego-dynamic level 169ff.
emic relationship 10, 18
empiricist hypothesis 77
encoding 33, 48
English 4–5, 11, 14–15, 25–6, 29, 71, 94–5
entropy 39
entry behavior 42
errors 93ff.; interlinguistic 93–5; intralinguistic 93–6
etic relationship 10, 13, 18
experimenter bias 164

F-ratio 145–7
first-language acquisition 64ff; differences from second-language learning 89–90; theories of 77–81
fossilization 97
French 7, 95, 103

frequency distribution 129, 192
frequency polygon 130
Freud, S. 51
fricatives 12
functional approaches 112–15

Gazzaniga, M. 42, 44
German 103
Gleason, H.A. 40
glossodynamic model 168ff.
grammars 92ff.
Greek 98
grouping 49

Halliday, M.A.K. 27, 113
Hawthorne effect 164
histogram 129–30
Hockett, C.F. 8, 39
holophrases 65ff.
humanistic psychology 59–61
Humboldt, W. von 31
Hungarian 104

Ilyin Oral Interview 157
infix 14
information theory 33, 39, 41
integration 48, 86–7; perceptual 47
interlanguage 93
International Phonetic Alphabet 13
Italian 7, 94–5

Jakobson, R. 66
Joos, M. 29

Kainz, F. 40
kernels 20
Krashen, S. 43, 62, 75, 84, 112

Labov, W. 36
Lamb, S. 17

language 3ff.; acquisition 43; as
  pattern 4–5; universal characteristics 4
language-acquisition device 80–1
language learning 43
language teaching 108ff.; and applied
  psycholinguistics 118–23; and
  linguistics 33–4; glossodynamic view
  of 172–4; methods of 108–18; models
  of 123–4
lateralization 46, 75, 84–5
Latin 7, 98
Lenneberg, E.H. 65, 75, 80, 84
lexeme 14
lexical insertion rule 21
linguistic relativity hypothesis 41–2
linguistics 3ff.,; applied 34, 122ff.;
  diachronic 6–7; educational 34; and
  language teaching 33–4;
  stratificational 17; synchronic 6–8
liquids 12
Lozanov's suggestopedia 117–18

macrolinguistics 6
matrices, distinctive-feature 22–3, 25
mean 135
meaningful learning 58
median 134–5
mediation theory 55–6, 78–9
memory 49ff.; long-term 49; short-
  term 49
metalinguistic awareness 76, 86
methods 108ff.; affective-based 115–18;
  audio-lingual 109–10, 162; cognitive-
  code 110–12; direct 110–12; grammar-
  translation 110–11, 162;
  inductive 108–10
microlinguistics 6
Miller, G.A. 31, 57
mode 134
Modern Language Aptitude Test 157

monitoring 112
morpheme 13ff.; bound 14;
  derivational 14; free 14;
  inflectional 14; system 14
morphology 13ff.
motivation 87ff.; instrumental 88;
  integrative 87–8
motor theory 48
Mowrer, O.H. 55
multilingualism 101

nasals 12
nativist hypothesis 77, 79
neobehaviorism 54
neurolinguistics 42ff.
normal curve 130
notional-functional syllabus 112–13

ogive 131
open-endedness 5
operant conditioning 54
Osgood, C.E. 33, 56
overgeneralization 96

paradigmatic relationship 8ff.
Pavlov, I. 52–3
Pearson's product-moment
  correlation 148–53
Penfield, W. 101
Pennsylvania project 162
perception 46ff.
performance 5–6
personality 50ff., 89
phoneme 9ff.
phonetics 9ff.; acoustic 10;
  articulatory 10–13
phonology 9ff.
Piaget, J. 41, 57–8
Pike, K. 17
Pimsleur Language Aptitude Battery 157

pivot grammar 68ff.
prefix 14
production 50, 67, 71
psychodynamic theories 51
psycholinguistics 28, 31–3; applied 34, 122ff.; and language teaching 118–23

range 129
recognition 48, 86–7
register 29
reinforcement 54
relational grammar 28
reliability 154–5
response 52ff.
retrieval 49
Rivers, W. 34
Rogers, C. 59–60
rote learning 59
rules 19ff.

Sapir, E. 8, 41
Searle, J. 30
second-language learning 83ff.; differences from first-language acquisition 89–90; neurological aspects 84–6; pedagogical aspects 90–3; psychological aspects 86–90
semantics 17–18
sememe 17
simplification 96
skewed curve 130
Skinner, B.F. 54, 56, 78
sociolinguistics 28–31
sound: voiced 11; voiceless 11
Spanish 7, 95
Spearman's rank-order correlation 148–53
speech act 29, 40
standard deviation 137–41

standard error: of the difference 142–3; of the mean 141; of measurement 153
statistical population 138
statistical sample 138
statistical significance 142
Stern, H.H. 89, 123–4
stimulus 52ff.; generalization 53
stops 11
storage 48
strategic level 168ff.
structuralism 15ff.
suffix 14
surface structure 20ff.
syntagmatic relationship 8ff.
syntax 15
syntaxeme 15

t-test 143–5
tactics 168ff.
tagmemics 17
telegraphic utterances 68
Terrell's natural approach 115, 117, 122
test 154ff.; battery 157; discrete-point 159ff.; integrative 160ff.
trait theories 51
transfer 90ff.
transformationalism 19ff.
translation 98–100
tree diagram 15–16
type theories 50

validity 154–5
verbal behavior 37ff.

Watson, J.B. 53
Wernicke's area 44–5
Whorf, B.L. 41–2
words 14, 19

z-scores 141
Zipf, P. 40